Property and Conveyancing Library

LEASEHOLD ENFRANCHISEMENT

PROPERTY AND CONVEYANCING LIBRARY

HAGUE

ON

LEASEHOLD

ENFRANCHISEMENT

SECOND SUPPLEMENT TO THE FIFTH EDITION

by

ANTHONY RADEVSKY, LL.B.
of the Inner Temple, Barrister

and

DAMIAN GREENISH, B.A.
Solicitor
Chairman, Pemberton Greenish LLP

SWEET & MAXWELL  THOMSON REUTERS

Published in 2012 by Sweet & Maxwell,
100 Avenue Road, London NW3 3PF
Part of Thomson Reuters (Professional) UK Limited
(Registered in England & Wales, Company No 1679046.
Registered Office and address for service:
Aldgate House, 33 Aldgate High Street, London EC3N 1DL)

Typeset by Interactive Sciences Limited, Gloucester
Printed and bound in Great Britain by CPI Antony Rowe, Chippenham, Wiltshire

*For further information on our products and services, visit
www.sweetandmaxwell.co.uk

No natural forests were destroyed to make this product;
only farmed timber was used and replanted.

A CIP catalogue record for this book is available from the British Library

ISBN 978–0–41402–426–7

Crown copyright material is reproduced with the permission
of the Controller of HMSO and the Queen's Printer for Scotland.

HOW TO USE THIS SUPPLEMENT

This supplement generally follows the structure of the main work. Those chapters which have been updated are set out in the same order in which they appear in the main work, and are updated by reference to the relevant paragraph number. Appendix material which has been updated is set out in the same order in which it appears in the main work, and is updated by reference to the relevant page number. New Appendix material is referenced to the final page number of the main work and its lettered reference.

PREFACE

It is now over 18 months since the First Supplement was published and there has continued to be a stream of new material, which requires a Second Supplement to be produced. The Supreme Court's long-awaited decision in *Hosebay Ltd v Day* was determined in October 2012; there have been six other enfranchisement cases decided by the Court of Appeal and several in the Upper Tribunal Lands Chamber since the law was last stated. The Appendices have also been updated.

The law is stated as at 16 November 2012.

Anthony Radevsky
Falcon Chambers
London EC4Y 1AA

Damian Greenish
45 Cadogan Gardens
London SW3 2AQ

CONTENTS

Individual New Leases of Flats—Chapters 29–33

PRECEDENTS

APPENDICES

Statutes

Statutory Instruments

TABLE OF CASES

TABLE OF STATUTES

TABLE OF STATUTORY INSTRUMENTS

CHAPTER 1

INTRODUCTION

3.—SUBSEQUENT LEGISLATION

Housing and Regeneration Act 2008

Sections 300–302 were brought into force on September 7, 2009: The Housing   **1–33**
and Regeneration Act 2008 (Commencement No. 6 and Transitional and Savings
Provisions) Order 2009 (SI 2009/2096), set out at Appendix 2W.

6.—CRITICISMS

(3) Valuation

Footnote 302: The Court of Appeal has dismissed the appeal: [2010] EWCA Civ   **1–56**
1471; [2011] 1 E.G.L.R. 36, see para. 27–09. The nominee purchaser was
subsequently granted permission to appeal to the Supreme Court but the case was
settled before the appeal could be heard.

(6) Right to Enfranchise (RTE) company

In March 2010, the Department of Communities and Local Government pub-   **1–59**
lished the summary of responses to a Consultation on the RTE provisions. The
majority of respondents were of the view that the provisions should not be
brought into force. The conclusion was that, in light of the response, "there are
no current plans to proceed with implementation of these provisions." That
remains the position. In the circumstances it is considered that it would be helpful
if these provisions could be repealed.

Footnote 316: *Cadogan v Sportelli* is also reported at [2010] 1 A.C. 226.   **1–60**

7.—CONSTRUING THE LEGISLATION

Footnote 327: The court should also avoid so far as possible an interpretation   **1–62**
which confers rights going beyond those intended by Parliament. *Hosebay Ltd v
Day; Lexgorge Ltd v Howard de Walden Estates Ltd* [2012] UKSC 41, [2012] 1
W.L.R. 2884.

1–63 The Supreme Court also had regard to policy considerations when construing section 2(1) of the 1967 Act in light of the removal of the general residence test by the 2002 Act. *Hosebay Ltd v Day; Lexgorge Ltd v Howard de Walden Estates Ltd* [2012] UKSC 41, [2012] 1 W.L.R. 2884.

8.—Tax

Roll-over relief

1–66 Footnote 334: This relief is now contained in s. 80 of the Finance Act 2009, which has effect in relation to transactions with an effective date on or after April 22, 2009.

CHAPTER 2

ACQUIRING THE FREEHOLD—PREMISES QUALIFYING

1.—HOUSE

Definition

The definition has also been further considered by the Supreme Court in two   **2–02**
conjoined appeals; *Hosebay Ltd v Day; Lexgorge Ltd v Howard de Walden
Estates Ltd* [2012] UKSC 41, [2012] 1 W.L.R. 2884. The appeals were allowed
and the judgment[1] amounted to a radical departure from the previous authorities,
deciding that use rather than physical structure and appearance was in most cases
likely to be the determinative factor in deciding whether a building is a house
within the meaning of the Act. In the *Hosebay* case, three buildings, originally
designed as single houses, had been used since at least 1981 so as to provide
individual rooms with self-catering facilities—described by the judge at first
instance as a "self-catering hotel". In *Lexgorge*, the building, which had also
been originally designed as a single house, had been used wholly as offices since
1961. In both cases, the actual user did not accord with the user covenants in the
leases.

The court made it clear that the 1967 Act is a statute about houses and not
commercial buildings.[2] The primary definition of "house" needs to be read " . . .
*in the context of a statute which is about houses as places to live in, not about
houses as pieces of architecture, or features in a street scene, or names in an
address book*".[3]

Footnote 7: a proposition which was adopted by the Supreme Court in
Hosebay.[4]

"Designed or adapted for living in"

This part of the definition looks to the identity or function of the building based   **2–04**
on its physical characteristics.[5] The approach adopted in *Ashbridge*, was that the
identity or function of a building (not currently in use) is defined by reference to

---

[1] A single judgment given by Lord Carnwath with whom the other six Justices agreed.
[2] *Hosebay, supra* para. 1.
[3] *Hosebay supra* para. 9.
[4] Para. 35.
[5] *Hosebay, supra* para. 9.

the purpose of its construction or subsequent adaptation.[6] The word "adapted" simply means "made suitable" and does not imply any particular degree of structural change, although something more than just a change of furniture is required. It follows that, where a building is in active and settled use for a particular purpose, it is likely to have undergone a degree of physical adaptation to make it suitable for that purpose. Generally, that use can therefore be taken as conclusive evidence of the purpose of the adaptation.[7] This proposition can be extended to a property which is empty; in such cases it will be the purpose for which the building was designed or last adapted, derived from its last actual use, which is likely to be determinative. Although it was never a contested issue in *Lexgorge* whether the building in that case was "designed or adapted for living in" it seems likely that, on the basis of this test, it was not.[8]

In *Hosebay Ltd v Day; Lexgorge Ltd v Howard de Walden Estates Ltd* [2010] EWCA Civ 748; [2010] 1 W.L.R. 2317, Lord Neuberger MR had returned to the issue he had left open in *Boss*, referred to in the fifth paragraph of text in the main work, i.e. whether a building designed as a house always remained a house. He held that the point having been fully argued, he would now reject it (paragraph 31), although it was not necessary for the decision in that case. A building that had originally been designed for living in, but had been adapted away from residential use, could no longer be said to be "designed or adapted for living in". That "second thought" was approved by the Supreme Court.[9] However, the Supreme Court also considered that in light of that, the "literalist" approach that had been taken by the House of Lords in *Boss* to the construction of this element of the definition was "inappropriate". That did not mean that the decision in *Boss* was wrong; in that case, the upper floors of the building had been designed or last adapted for residential purposes and had not since been put to any other use. They had not therefore lost their identity merely by being disused and dilapidated at the date of the claim.[10]

The Court of Appeal had held in *Hosebay* that the physical adaptation of the buildings to their current use had amounted to adaptation into a different form of living accommodation. The Supreme Court held that "living in" means something more settled than "staying in" and that use as a self-catering hotel did not therefore qualify as "living in". However, because the appeal in *Hosebay* succeeded on the second part of the definition, the court left open the question whether on the facts of that case the evidence suggested that the original adaptation had contemplated the possibility of longer term occupation which would amount to "living in".[11]

"Reasonably so called"

2–05 This part of the definition is tied to the primary meaning of "house" as a single residence, as opposed to say a hostel or a block of flats. This has to be qualified however by the specific provision relating to houses divided horizontally.[12]

---

[6] *Hosebay supra*, para. 21.
[7] *Hosebay, supra* para. 35.
[8] The Supreme Court questioned the concession—para. 45.
[9] *Hosebay supra* para. 34.
[10] *Hosebay supra*, para. 36.
[11] *Hosebay supra*, para. 44.
[12] *Hosebay supra*, para. 9.

In *Hosebay Ltd v Day; Lexgorge Ltd v Howard de Walden Estates Ltd* [2010] EWCA Civ 748; [2010] 1 W.L.R. 2317, the Court of Appeal had held (doubting *Prospect Estates Ltd v Grosvenor Estates Belgravia*) that the user of the property by the lessee was immaterial to whether it was a house reasonably so called. The Court followed what it believed to be the approach in *Tandon* and observed that that appeared to present the landlords with a high hurdle to cross (paragraph 39). On that basis, the Court of Appeal held that the external and internal appearance of the properties were highly relevant factors on this issue. The Supreme Court reconsidered both *Lake v Bennett* [1970] 1 Q.B. 663 and *Tandon v Trustees of Spurgeons Homes* [1982] A.C. 755 and in particular Lord Roskill's three "propositions of law" referred to in the second paragraph of text in the main work. The court held that these "so-called" propositions needed to be viewed in the context of the facts in *Lake* and *Tandon* and doubted whether they were of wider application. As regards the first proposition (discussed in the third paragraph of text in the main work), this was directed at a building in mixed commercial and residential use. The fact that a building might be described as a house for other purposes is not enough to bring it within the definition.[13] As regards the second proposition (discussed in the fourth paragraph of the text of the main work), the court reviewed the various formulations of this in the judgments in *Lake* and *Tandon* but did not feel that they provided any assistances as to how the question should be answered in any particular case.[14] As regards the third proposition (discussed in the fifth and sixth paragraphs of the text of the main work), this did not mean that the fact that a building was "designed or adapted for living in" led to any presumption as to whether that building was a house "reasonably so called". The court decided that this proposition was "*more an expression of Lord Roskill's own view as to the correct policy approach to a building of the kind before him*".[15] This third proposition was also considered by the Court of Appeal in *Magnohard Ltd v Earl Cadogan and Cadogan Estates Ltd* [2012] EWCA Civ 594, [2012] H.L.R. 31, where Lord Neuberger MR suggested that it did not extend to a building comprising more than a single residence.

The Supreme Court approved the judgment of the Court of Appeal in *Prospect Estates Ltd v Grosvenor Estate Belgravia* [2009] 1 W.L.R. 1313 (referred to in the seventh paragraph of text in the main work) although doubted that lease terms should be treated as a major factor.

It is therefore use of the building, rather than its physical appearance that is determinative. The fact that a building might look like a house and might be referred to as a house for some purposes is not sufficient to displace the actual user. A building wholly used for commercial purposes, whatever its original design or current appearance, is not a house "reasonably so called".

In *Magnohard Ltd v Earl Cadogan and Cadogan Estates Ltd* [2012] EWCA Civ 594, [2012] H.L.R. 31, the Court of Appeal dismissed the appeal against the judgment of HH Judge Marshall QC who had held that a purpose-built block of flats cannot be a house "reasonably so called". The building in that case was a

---

[13] *Hosebay supra*, para. 25.
[14] *Hosebay supra*, para. 26.
[15] *Hosebay supra*, para. 27.

late Victorian mansion block over basement, ground and five upper floors. It comprised eight flats and three small shops. An application by the tenant to the Supreme Court for permission to appeal was refused after an oral hearing on the ground that there was no reasonable prospect of the appeal being successful.

It is now clear that buildings wholly (or very substantially) in settled commercial use are buildings that are neither "designed or adapted for living in" nor houses "reasonably so called". The position as regards mixed-use buildings however remains unclear and it is disappointing that the Supreme Court did not take the opportunity to deal with that issue. It is now said that the determinative factors in *Tandon* were (a) the proportions of residential use; and (b) the intention of Parliament that such buildings (small shops combined with living accommodation) should be within the Act. The determinative factors in *Prospect* were (a) the prescriptive terms of the lease; (b) the actual uses of the building and (c) the relative proportions of the mixed-use at the relevant date.

There is no doubt that mixed-use buildings and buildings "divided horizontally into flats and maisonettes" can be a house for the purpose of the Act. The uncertainty for mixed-use buildings is how the courts will now be prepared to extend the principles of *Lake* and *Tandon* and determine what was the intention of Parliament in relation to particular types of mixed-use buildings. How far will the courts be prepared to stretch the primary meaning of "house" as a single residence? When does a house divided into flats (which may be a house "reasonably so called") become a block of flats (which is not a house "reasonably so called")? All these are issues with which the court will no doubt need to grapple in the future.

Footnote 24: The word "So" should read "Co".

Footnote 32: See also the comments of Lord Neuberger MR in *Magnohard, supra* at para. 18 and also the comments of Lord Carnwath in *Hosebay* at para. 27

Footnote 45: In his judgment in *Hosebay* at para. 28, Lord Carnwath speculated that the only real difference between the majority and the minority in *Tandon* was a question of policy; i.e. whether or not Parliament had intended buildings of the kind in *Tandon* should come within the Act.

3.—Rateable Value

2–24   Section 300 of the Housing and Regeneration Act 2008 was brought into force on September 7, 2009: The Housing and Regeneration Act 2008 (Commencement No. 6 and Transitional and Savings Provisions) Order 2009 (SI 2009/2096), set out in Appendix 2W. There is a general saving provision for leases granted before 7 September 2009 in article 3(1).

CHAPTER 3

ACQUIRING THE FREEHOLD—TENANCIES QUALIFYING

1.—LONG TENANCY

Continuation tenancies

(1) *Statutory extensions*

Footnote 76: This case now reported as *Ackerman v The Portman Estate Nomi-*   **3–10**
nees (One) Ltd [2009] 1 W.L.R. 1556.

Concurrent tenancies

Footnote 101: replace para. 3–14 with para. 3–16.   **3–13**

Business tenancies

In *Hosebay Ltd v Day* [2009] P.L.S.C.S. 318 (CC), the company tenant underlet   **3–15**
the premises to an associated company, which carried on business in each of the
houses which were the subject of the claims. It was held (by HH Judge Marshall
Q.C.) that the tenant was not in business occupation for the purposes of Pt II of
the Landlord and Tenant Act 1954, and so was not precluded from claiming the
freehold by reason of not being able to fulfil the residence test. The sub-letting
arrangement was not a sham. Although permission to appeal was granted in
respect of the other issue in the case (i.e. whether the premises were each a
house) permission to appeal was not sought on this issue.

2.—LOW RENT

(a) *Background*

Section 300 of the 2008 Act was brought into force on September 7, 2009: article   **3–17**
2(2) of The Housing and Regeneration Act 2008 (Commencement No. 6 and
Transitional and Savings Provisions) Order 2009 (SI 2009/2096), set out in
Appendix 2W. The amendments do not apply to any long tenancy granted before
that date, or granted after that date but arising from a written agreement for the
grant of that tenancy made before that date: article 3(1).
   Footnote 125: should read SI 1997/618.

Excluded tenancy

3–18 Add to footnote 130: By art. 3(2) of the Housing and Regeneration Act 2008 (Commencement No. 6 and Transitional and Savings Provisions) Order 2009 (SI 2009/2096), the Housing (Right to Enfranchise) (Designated Protected Areas) (England) Order 2009 has effect for the purposes of s.1AA from September 7, 2009. It is set out at Appendix 2Y.

Add to (b): In *Lovat v Hertsmere Borough Council* [2011] EWCA Civ 1185, [2012] Q.B. 533, it was held that "adjoining land" meant neighbouring land which might or might not touch the house. Accordingly, where the tenant's house was surrounded by gardens and grounds, beyond which was non-residential land the freehold of which was owned by the same freeholder, the tenancy (which was not at a low rent) was an excluded tenancy. The tenant was therefore not entitled to acquire the freehold of her house. It will be a question of fact and degree in any future case as to whether the non-residential land is close enough to be regarded as adjoining the house.

(b) *1967 Act Test*

"The appropriate day"

3–21 In sub-paragraph (1) insert the word "a" before the word "hereditament".

(e) *Housing and Regeneration Act 2008*

3–50 Section 300 of the 2008 Act was brought into force on September 7, 2009: article 2(2) of The Housing and Regeneration Act 2008 (Commencement No. 6 and Transitional and Savings Provisions) Order 2009 (SI 2009/2096), set out in Appendix 2W. The amendments do not apply to any long tenancy granted before that date, or granted after that date but arising from a written agreement for the grant of that tenancy made before that date: article 3(1).

CHAPTER 4

ACQUIRING THE FREEHOLD—PERSONS QUALIFYING

1.—TENANT

Footnote 9: *The Wellcome Trust Ltd v Baulackey* is reported at [2010] 1 E.G.L.R. **4–01** 125.

CHAPTER 5

STATUTORY NOTICES AND THEIR EFFECT

1.—NOTICE OF TENANT'S CLAIM

Requirements of notice

Prescribed form

Footnote 3: The Government's response to the consultation paper was published **5–02** in August 2009. It said the Government aimed to review the forms following implementation of the regulations. Since these were brought into force on September 7, 2009, a review was needed before September 2011, when enfranchisement claims under leases granted since that date may be made. However, none has taken place to date.

Validity of the notice

The text of the second paragraph suggesting that the saving provision in para- **5–05** graph 6(3) applies only to those particulars expressly required by paragraph 6 and not to those additional particulars required by the prescribed form was approved in *Wishart v Birmingham City Council* (unreported, 2009, Birmingham County Court, HH Judge Worster).

Service of notice

In footnote 102, the reference to the Landlord and Tenant Act 1927, s. 22(5) **5–07** should be to the 1967 Act, s. 22(5).

In was held in *Calladine-Smith v Saveorder Ltd* [2011] EWHC 2501 (Ch), [2012] L. & T.R. 3, (where a landlord sent to the tenant a counter-notice under section 45 of the 1993 Act by ordinary post) that, under section 7 of the Interpretation Act 1978, where there is evidence to show that, on the balance of probabilities a properly addressed, pre-paid and posted letter was delivered late or not delivered at all, this will rebut the presumption of deemed service.

2.—EFFECT OF SERVICE OF TENANT'S NOTICE

Continuation of tenancy

Footnote 171: *Ackerman v Lay* is now reported as *Ackerman v The Portman* **5–13** *Estate Nominees (One) Ltd* [2009] 1 W.L.R. 1556.

Footnote 173: replace "1967 Act" with "1954 Act".

3.—OBLIGATIONS OF RECIPIENT OF TENANT'S NOTICE

Landlord's Notice in Reply

5–19   Footnote 240: The Government's response to the consultation paper was published in August 2009. It said the Government aimed to review the forms following implementation of the regulations. Since these were brought into force on September 7, 2009, a review was needed before September 2011, when enfranchisement claims under leases granted since that date may be made. However, none has taken place to date.

CHAPTER 6

ACQUIRING THE FREEHOLD—ACQUISITION TERMS

3.—CONTENTS OF CONVEYANCE

Easements and rights to be reserved

Specific rights

Footnote 133: In *Trustees of the Sloane Stanley Estate v Carey-Morgan &* **6–22**
another [2011] UKUT 415 (LC), the Lands Chamber decided that a provision in
a transfer stating that the transferee would not enjoy any rights of light or air over
the retained property of the transferor that would inhibit or prevent building did
not come within para. 3(2) of Sch. 7 to the 1993 Act. However, the wording of
para. 3(2)(b) of Sch. 7 to the 1993 Act is not the same as the wording of s.
10(2)(ii) of the 1967 Act.

Restrictive covenants

Generally

The landlord is not entitled to seek the imposition of positive covenants. Thus, in **6–26**
Ackerman v Mooney [2009] P.L.S.C.S. 266, the LVT refused to allow the
imposition of a covenant to erect and maintain walls and fences along the
boundaries of the property, and in *The Portman Estate Nominees (One) Ltd v
Great Peter Nominees Ltd* (unreported, 2010, LVT) a proposed covenant "not to
permit the property to fall into disrepair" was disallowed, since although
expressed in negative terms, it was in reality a positive one.

Footnote 148: see also *Kutchukian v John Lyon's Charity* [2012] UKUT 53
(LC), [2012] P.L.S.C.S. 73.

Restrictive covenants in tenant's lease

In order to be imposed, a restrictive covenant must enhance the value of other **6–28**
property belonging to the landlord. Thus it will not be imposed for the benefit of
property owned by a different set of trustees, albeit regarded by the landlord as
part of the same estate. Moreover, the other property must be sufficiently close
to the subject property to be affected by the covenant, and it was held to be
desirable to identify the benefited property clearly in the transfer: *Ackerman v*

Mooney [2009] P.L.S.C.S. 266. N.B. The President of the Lands Tribunal refused to grant permission to the landlord to appeal (decision dated January 25, 2010).

In *Kutchukian v John Lyon's Charity* [2012] UKUT 53 (LC), [2012] P.L.S.C.S. 73, the Lands Chamber held that there was no evidence that the restrictive covenants sought would materially enhance the value of the landlord's other property. Any benefits were theoretical. Material enhancement in value must be distinctly proved although not necessarily in monetary terms in respect of some identified property. In any event, the landlord had the protection of the covenants in an estate management scheme.

The word "require" in section 10(4) does not mean "demand", but rather "need": *Cadogan v Erkman* [2011] UKUT 90 (LC) paragraph 107, a decision on the equivalent wording in Paragraph 5(1) of Schedule 7 to the 1993 Act. This seems questionable in so far as it seeks to introduce a further qualifying condition on the imposition of a covenant.

4.—MERGER

6–36 The most recent edition of the Land Registry Practice Guide 27 is dated 20 July 2012. It can be found at Appendix 2U of this Supplement and the latest version can be viewed online at *www.landregistry.gov.uk/professional/guides/practice-guide-27*.

5.—WITHDRAWAL AND COSTS OF ENFRANCHISEMENT

Other costs

6–39 Add to (a): The landlord's valuation costs can, in an appropriate case, include Counsel's fees for advising as to the correct basis of valuation: *Holicater Ltd v Great Yarmouth Borough Council* [2012] UKUT 131 (LC).

CHAPTER 7

EXTENDING THE LEASE

Section 300 of the 2008 Act was brought into force on September 7, 2009: article **7–01** 2(2) of The Housing and Regeneration Act 2008 (Commencement No. 6 and Transitional and Savings Provisions) Order 2009 (SI 2009/2096), set out in Appendix 2W. The amendments do not apply to any long tenancy granted before that date, or granted after that date but arising from a written agreement for the grant of that tenancy made before that date: article 3(1). As anticipated by the main work, the low rent test in section 4(1) of the 1967 Act will continue to apply to a claim for an extended lease, even if the tenancy is granted on or after 7 September 2009.[1] Furthermore, it is necessary for the tenancy to have been at a low rent for a period of at least two years before the claim is made.[2]

2.—PREMISES QUALIFYING

The post-April, 1 1990 test
On June 14, 2011, the Department for Communities and Local Government **7–09** issued a Consultation Paper entitled "Leasehold Valuation Limits". One of the issues raised was whether the figure for R in the formula set out in the second paragraph of the main work should be increased from £25,000 to £100,000 and, if so, whether that increase should apply retrospectively. A summary of the responses to the Consultation was published by DCLG in February 2012. It is understood that the issue is still under consideration although, if there are to be any changes to R in the formula, they will not come into effect until April 2014 at the earliest.

Notional reduction in rateable value

Qualifying improvements
Footnote 54: Replace "1967 Act" with "1974 Act". **7–13**

---

[1] s. 1(1)(aa) of the 1967 Act as introduced by s. 300(1)(b) of the Housing and Regeneration Act 2008.
[2] s. 1(1)(b) of the 1967 Act as introduced by s. 300(1)(c) of the 2008 Act.

Maker of improvements

7–14   Footnote 56: Replace with "1974 Act Sch. 8 para. 1(1)."

Procedure

7–15   Footnote 62: Replace "947, col. 1" with "p. 86".

(1) *Schedule 8 notice*

7–16   Footnote 63: Replace "1967 Act" with "1974 Act".

3.—TENANCIES QUALIFYING

Low rent

7–26   Section 300 of the 2008 Act was brought into force on September 7, 2009: article 2(2) of The Housing and Regeneration Act 2008 (Commencement No. 6 and Transitional and Savings Provisions) Order 2009 (SI 2009/2096), sct out in Appendix 2W. The amendments do not apply to any long tenancy granted before that date, or granted after that date but arising from a written agreement for the grant of that tenancy made before that date: article 3(1). As anticipated by the main work, the low rent test in section 4(1) of the 1967 Act will continue to apply to a claim for an extended lease, even if the tenancy is granted on or after 7 September 2009.[3] Furthermore, it is necessary for the tenancy to have been at a low rent for a period of at least two years before the claim is made.[4]

9.—REGISTRATION OF TITLE

7–45   The most recent edition of the Land Registry Practice Guide 27 is dated 20 July 2012. It is at Appendix 2U of this Supplement and the latest version can be viewed online at *www.landregistry.gov.uk/professional/guides/practice-guide-27.*

11.—MISCELLANEOUS

Tenant's estate subject to a mortgage

Generally

7–50   Footnote 196: The most recent edition of the Land Registry Practice Guide 27 is dated 20 July 2012. It is at Appendix 2U of this Supplement and the latest version can be viewed online at *www.landregistry.gov.uk/professional/guides/practice-guide-27.*

---

[3]   s. 1(1)(aa) of the 1967 Act as introduced by s. 300(1)(b) of the Housing and Regeneration Act 2008.

[4]   s. 1(1)(b) of the 1967 Act as introduced by s. 300(1)(c) of the 2008 Act.

Registered land

The most recent edition of the Land Registry Practice Guide 27 is dated 20 July   **7–51**
2012. It is at Appendix 2U of this Supplement and the latest version can be
viewed online at *www.landregistry.gov.uk/professional/guides/practice-guide-
27.*

Chapter 8

EXTENDING THE LEASE—VALUATION

2.—Rent after Original Term Date

Site value

(2) The "standing-house" approach

Site value proportion
Footnote 79: [1977] instead of [1976].   **8–10**

CHAPTER 9

ACQUIRING THE FREEHOLD—VALUATION

Add to footnote 1: S. 300 of the 2008 Act was brought into force on September **9–01**
7, 2009: art. 2(2) of The Housing and Regeneration Act 2008 (Commencement
No. 6 and Transitional and Savings Provisions) Order 2009 (SI 2009/2096), set
out in Appendix 2W. The amendments do not apply to any long tenancy granted
before that date, or granted after that date but arising from a written agreement
for the grant of that tenancy made before that date: art. 3(1). However, the low
rent test will no longer be relevant in determining the basis for valuing the
freehold for leases granted on or after September 7, 2009. For an interesting
article, see "*Leasehold Enfranchisement and the Low Rent Test*" by P. Harrison
(2010) 14 L. & T. Rev. 147.

1.—VALUATION UNDER SECTION 9(1)

Qualification

In paragraph 4(ii) the figure of £16,233 should read £16,333. **9–02**

Add to footnote 9: On June 14, 2011, the Department for Communities and
Local Government issued a Consultation Paper entitled "Leasehold Valuation
Limits". One of the issues raised was whether the figure for R in the formula set
out in para. 7–09 of the main work should be increased from £16,333 to £66,666
and, if so, whether that increase should apply retrospectively. A summary of the
responses to the Consultation was published by DCLG in February 2012. It is
understood that the issue is still under consideration although, if there are to be
any changes to R in the formula, they will not come into effect until April 2014
at the earliest.

Marriage value

A helpful explanation of what is marriage value can be found in paragraphs 17 **9–04**
and 18 of the judgment of Mr Justice Morgan in *Carey-Morgan & another v The
Trustees of the Sloane Stanley Estate* [2012] EWCA Civ 1181.

Hope value

9–05 A helpful explanation of what is hope value can be found in paragraphs 19 to 21 of the judgment of Mr Justice Morgan in *Carey-Morgan & another v The Trustees of the Sloane Stanley Estate* [2012] EWCA Civ 1181.

(1) Capitalised value of the rent payable for the period of the unexpired term of the existing tenancy

Other evidence

9–12 In *31 Cadogan Square Freehold Ltd v Cadogan* [2010] UKUT 321 (LC) it was held that previous tribunal decisions may be relevant upon matters of fact or opinion evidence, as well as on questions of law or procedure (paragraph 79).

(2) Capitalised value of the Section 15 rent

Deferment

9–15 In *Freehold Properties Ltd's appeal* [2009] UKUT 172 (LC); [2010] P.L.S.C.S. 3, the Tribunal dismissed an appeal by the landlord against the LVT's use of a deferment rate of 5.5 per cent, in a West Midlands case. The Tribunal was of the view that, in order to apply the PCL rate of 4.75 per cent, a comparison should have been made between growth rates in the West Midlands and PCL, as indicated in *Re Mansal Securities Ltd's and others' application* [2009] 2 E.G.L.R. 87.

In *Re Clarise Properties Ltd's Appeal* [2012] UKUT 4 (LC) [2012] L. & T.R. 20, the Upper Tribunal held that the starting point for determining the deferment rate was the generic *Sportelli* rate of 4.75 per cent. To that was added 0.5 per cent to reflect the lesser prospects for capital growth in the West Midlands (as opposed to PCL) and 0.25 per cent to reflect the greater risk of physical deterioration in the property. The deferment rate applied was therefore 5.5 per cent to be consistent with the decision in *Zuckerman v The Trustees of the Calthorpe Estate* [2010] 1 E.G.L.R. 187—see paragraph 9–43 below. The same rate was used to capitalise and defer the modern ground rent. It was accepted that this was a departure from the approach adopted in *Re Mansal Securities Ltd's and others' application* [2009] 2 E.G.L.R. 87.

(3) Value of the landlord's ultimate reversion

The Haresign addition

9–16 The criticism of some LVT decisions in the penultimate paragraph was upheld in *Freehold Properties Ltd's appeal* [2009] UKUT 172 (LC); [2010] P.L.S.C.S. 3. It was confirmed that the enactment of section 143 of the Commonhold and Leasehold Reform Act 2002, giving a tenant who had an extended lease the right to acquire the freehold, did not preclude the valuation of the ultimate reversion in a section 9(1) case.

In *Re Clarise Properties Ltd's Appeal* [2012] UKUT 4 (LC); [2012] L. & T.R. 20, the Upper Tribunal held that the time has now come to move away from a two-stage valuation approach and to apply instead the three-stage approach i.e. to value the ultimate reversion in all cases. As a matter of good valuation practice, where a price has to be determined, every element of value should in general be separately assessed unless there is some good reason not to do so. It follows that the appropriate approach now is to capitalise the section 15 rent to the end of the 50-year extension and then to assess the value (if any) of the ultimate reversion.

A deduction of 20 per cent was made from the eventual reversion because of the risk of an assured tenancy arising under Schedule 10 to the Local Government and Housing Act 1989. That deduction is controversial, since there was no evidence adduced to support it, and it is substantially higher than the traditional ten per cent which was used to calculate the risk of a statutory tenancy arising under Part 1 of the Landlord and Tenant Act 1954, and the much lower discount to reflect 1989 Act rights: see paragraph 9–42 of the main work.

Long term unexpired
Footnote 127: Such an approach is also consistent with the approach of the Upper **9–21** Tribunal (Lands Chamber) in *Re Clarise Properties Ltd's Appeal* [2012] UKUT 4 (LC) [2012] L. & T.R. 20 where it was said that in general every element of value should be separately assessed.

2.—Valuation of Freehold Under Section 9(1A)

Marriage value
A helpful explanation of what is marriage value can be found in paragraphs 17 **9–29** and 18 of the judgment of Mr Justice Morgan in *Carey-Morgan & another v The Trustees of the Sloane Stanley Estate* [2012] EWCA Civ 1181.

Hope value
A helpful explanation of what is hope value can be found in paragraphs 19 to 21 **9–30** of the judgment of Mr Justice Morgan in *Carey-Morgan & another v The Trustees of the Sloane Stanley Estate* [2012] EWCA Civ 1181.

Cadogan v Pitts/Sportelli is now reported at [2010] 1 A.C. 226.

In *Grosvenor Estate Belgravia v Klaasmeyer* [2010] UKUT 69 (LC); [2010] 16 E.G. 107 (CS), the Tribunal had to consider a valuation of the freehold and intermediate leasehold interests, where the lease was of the whole of the Belgravia Estate. Under that lease, the lessee (GEB) had to pay the freeholder a rising proportion of receipts after 2026; hence it is known as the 'escalator' lease. The effects of the escalator could be avoided by postulating a number of transactions, described as Options 1–5 (paragraph 16). Three of these which involved future deals with the occupational tenant were ruled out by virtue of the ban on taking into account hope value.

Valuation assumptions

(a) *Estate sold*
In *Sillvote Ltd v Liverpool City Council* [2010] UKUT 192 (LC), the Tribunal **9–31** was concerned with a house in mixed use. It adopted a rental value method of

valuation, and for the commercial element took account of market rates, rather than the actual rent roll; otherwise the tenant would be profiting from its own inertia: paragraph 41.

(b) *Part I of the Landlord and Tenant Act 1954/ Schedule 10 to the Local Government and Housing Act 1989*

9–34 Footnote 198: In *Sillvote Ltd v Liverpool City Council* [2010] UKUT 192 (LC), where there were eleven years unexpired on the lease, a ten per cent deduction was not made where there was no evidence to justify a deduction.

(c) *Repairs*

9–35 The interrelation between a claim for dilapidations and the assumption in section 9(1A)(c) was considered by HH Judge Hazel Marshall QC in *Anstruther v Vidas Ltd* (unreported, 2010, Central London CC), although primarily in the context of the effect of a potential claim under the 1967 Act on the dilapidations claim rather than the effect of an outstanding dilapidations claim on the enfranchisement price. See in particular the discussion in paragraphs 167–183.

Footnote 202: In *Sillvote Ltd v Liverpool City Council* [2010] UKUT 192 (LC), an allowance of £100,000 was made from the value because of disrepair resulting from the tenant's own breach of covenant. "*Whilst it was perfectly understandable for the council [the landlord] to argue that it would be totally iniquitous if the tenant were to be able to profit (by paying a lower price) as a result of its failure to adhere to the terms of the lease, and to refer [to] the passage in Vignaud, the fact remains that, under s. 9(1A)(c) that is precisely what the Tribunal must do.*" Mr P. Francis FRICS at para. 32.

(d) *Improvements*

9–36 Footnote 211: replace "62F" with "para. 31".

The last paragraph of text was relied on by the appellant in *Sillvote Ltd v Liverpool City Council* [2010] UKUT 192 (LC). The Tribunal made a deduction for the value of the tenant's improvements, even though these had been carried out in breach of a covenant requiring the landlord's consent to be obtained. Any right of the landlord to take action for breach of covenant had expired. In any event, there was no justification for giving the value of the improvements to the landlord: paragraph 33.

(2) Value of landlord's reversion after original term date, on the assumptions as to Part I of the Landlord and Tenant Act 1954 and Schedule 10 to the Local Government and Housing Act 1989 and as to repairs and improvements mentioned above

(a) *Statutory rights*

9–42 Footnote 240: The rent limit for an assured tenancy in England was increased to £100,000 with effect from October 1, 2010: The Assured Tenancies (Amendment) (England) Order 2010 (SI 2010/908). On June 14, 2011, the Department for Communities and Local Government issued a Consultation Paper entitled "Leasehold Valuation Limits". One of the issues raised was whether the value limits for long leaseholder security of tenure rights under the Local Government and Housing Act 1989 should be increased to £100,000 (or some other figure) and, if so, whether that increase should apply retrospectively. A summary of the responses to the Consultation was published by DCLG in February 2012. It is understood that the issue is still under consideration although, if there are to be any changes to the limits, they will not come into effect until April 2014 at the earliest.

(b) *Deferment rate*

A helpful explanation of what is a deferment rate can be found in paragraphs 11 **9–43** to 16 of the judgment of Mr Justice Morgan in *Carey-Morgan & another v The Trustees of the Sloane Stanley Estate* [2012] EWCA Civ 1181.

In *Sherwood Hall (East End Road) Management Co Ltd v Magnolia Tree Ltd* [2009] UKUT 158 (LC); [2010] 1 E.G.L.R. 181, a case under the 1993 Act, the Tribunal declined to adjust the five per cent guideline rate in *Cadogan v Sportelli* on the ground that the unexpired term of the flat leases was long, namely 88 years.

In *Culley v Daejan Properties Ltd* [2009] UKUT 168 (LC); [2009] 3 E.G.L.R. 165, a case under the 1993 Act, the Tribunal applied the five per cent rate in the case of a block of flats in outer London, there being no evidence of higher growth rates in Prime Central London to support a higher deferment rate.

In *Zuckerman v Trustees of the Calthorpe Estates* [2009] UKUT 235 (LC); [2010] 1 E.G.L.R. 187, a case under the 1993 Act, a deferment rate of six per cent was applied in a number of new lease claims concerning flats in a block in Edgbaston, West Midlands. The additional one per cent was made up of three elements: (i) 0.25 per cent for the greater risk of deterioration and obsolescence of these flats compared to that in the high value period properties in Prime Central London; (ii) 0.5 per cent for the greater risk that the assumed two per cent growth rate would not be achieved when comparing these flats with those in PCL: the Tribunal was presented with detailed comparative evidence of historic growth rates, showing that those in PCL rose considerably more than those in the West Midlands; (iii) 0.25 per cent to reflect the fact that there were greater management risks in relation to flats in the light of increasingly burdensome service charge regulation, in particular the introduction of the Service Charges (Consultation Requirements) (England) Regulations 2003. Had the original head-lease been in place, the Tribunal would not have adjusted for this factor. Element (iii) would not apply to single houses.

The same 0.25 per cent adjustment for obsolescence/deterioration was made in *Re Lethaby and Regis's appeal* [2010] UKUT 86 (LC), a missing landlord case under the 1993 Act concerning two flats in East London. The Tribunal followed *Zuckerman* (above). In the absence of evidence of differing growth rates between East London and PCL, the 0.5 per cent adjustment was not made. The 0.25 per cent flats adjustment was not made, because the repairing obligations for the building were divided between the lessees of the two flats.

In *Ashdown Hove Ltd v Remstar Properties Ltd* [2010] 37 E.G. 138, the LVT determined a deferment rate of six per cent in respect of a 1970s block of flats in Brighton. The *Zuckerman* case was followed. Even though there was a headlease of the common parts the additional 0.25 per cent for management difficulties was applied. The lessee was a leaseholder-owned management company, and there was evidence that it might fold, due to a history of management problems, leaving the freeholder having to step in.

In *Re Midland Freeholds Ltd's appeal* [2011] UKUT 173 (LC), a case under the 1993 Act, the Upper Tribunal allowed the landlord's appeal in circumstances where the Leasehold Valuation Tribunal had adjusted the deferment rate to reflect inferior location where neither party had adduced evidence on the issue.

In *City & Country Properties Ltd v Yeats* [2012] UKUT 227 (LC), a case under the 1993 Act, the Lands Chamber was concerned with a new lease claim for a very modest flat in Horsham, West Sussex. Although not relevant to single houses, the 0.25 per cent adjustment made in *Zuckerman* (above) for the additional risks resulting from service charge regulation was applied. However, the 0.5 per cent addition for the difference in assumed growth rate with PCL was not allowed, because the comparative evidence relating to that location was inadequate. The adopted deferment rate was, therefore, 5.5 per cent.

In *Polydorou v Management Nominees (Reversions) Ltd* [2010] UKUT 236 (LC), [2010] P.L.S.C.S. 239, the Lands Chamber determined a deferment rate of 5.5 per cent in respect of a house in London which was converted into flats and used as bedsits. The 4.75 per cent rate used in *Sportelli* was increased by 0.25 per cent because the property was divided into flats, and 0.25 per cent reflected the greater management problems attributable to flats. A further 0.5 per cent was justified for the lesser prospect of capital growth for houses in multiple occupation.

Footnotes 268 and 269: The cases where the unexpired term is between 10 and 20 years were considered by the Upper Tribunal (Lands Chamber) in five conjoined appeals in collective enfranchisement claims, *Cadogan Square Properties Ltd v Cadogan* [2010] UKUT 427 (LC); [2011] 1 E.G.L.R. 155. In each case the net rental yield and formula based methods was rejected. The starting point was the *Sportelli* rate of five per cent for flats. This was adjusted upwards to 5.25 per cent for 2005 (for terms between 17.3 and 17.8 years) and to 5.5 per cent for 2007 (for terms of 15.6 and 16.1 years). This reflected an adjustment in the real growth rate which would be negotiated between willing seller and willing purchaser. For terms of less than ten years, which were not before the Lands Chamber, different questions could arise, and using a net rental yield would have to be examined in such a case. In the case of a building divided into flats, but with the prospect of reconverting it back into a house, it was appropriate to use the deferment rate for flats rather than houses. The Tribunal stated that this case should have the same effect in future cases as the guidelines in *Sportelli* itself.

The deferment rate to be applied in the case of a lease with an unexpired term of less than five years was considered by the Upper Tribunal (Lands Chamber) in *Trustees of the Sloane Stanley Estate v Carey-Morgan & another* [2011] UKUT 415 (LC), a 1993 Act case. In the case of such short reversions, the *Sportelli* formula is not applicable. Such interests contain the guarantee of the early enjoyment of possession at which time the purchaser can look forward to being able to let, occupy, keep vacant or redevelop the property as he chooses. The correct approach is therefore to start with the value of the freehold interest and then make explicit adjustments to reflect the fact that the right to possession is deferred. There are three such adjustments. First, there is the value of possession that is lost during the currency of the lease. This is allowed for by discounting at the net rental yield, the best evidence of which will likely be found within the subject premises. Secondly, there is the owner's lack of control during the unexpired term. This is reflected in an end allowance. Thirdly, there is the element of real growth. This will be reflected in the freehold vacant possession value. On the facts of this case, the first element produced a rate of 3.25 per cent and the second a 5 per cent discount to the capital value, producing an "equivalent" deferment rate of 4.37 per cent. This is a further guidance case with the Lands Chamber stating that " . . . *the deferment rate for reversions of less than five years should be the net rental yield that the evidence shows to be appropriate for the property in question; and that in addition there should be an end allowance, which in the absence of evidence establishing some other percentage, should be 5%"*.

In *Carey-Morgan & another v Trustees of the Sloane Stanley Estate* [2012] EWCA Civ 1181, the Court of Appeal dismissed the appeal of the nominee purchaser against the decision of the Lands Chamber. However, the guidance set out above was qualified in a case where the Rent Act 1977, Housing Act 1988 or Local Government and Housing Act 1989 might apply. In such a case the relevant tribunal would have to consider how that should be dealt with because this case does not provide any guidance on that.

(3) Share of marriage value of freehold and leasehold interests

(a) *Calculation of marriage value*

Footnotes 289 and 292: *Nailrile Ltd v Cadogan* is now fully reported at [2009] 2 E.G.L.R. 151.   **9–46**

Footnote 290: In October 2009, the RICS published its report on Graphs of Relativity, in response to the suggestion in *Arrowdell*. The Leasehold Relativities Group, chaired by Jonathan Gaunt QC, and comprising eight surveyors, considered all the published graphs, but were unable to agree upon definitive graphs to be used as evidence by LVTs, as had been proposed by the Lands Tribunal. The report reproduced all the published graphs together with details of the data that lies behind each.

In *Re Coolrace Limited and others' appeal* [2012] UKUT 69 (LC); [2012] 24 EG 84 (a case under the 1993 Act where the LEASE graph of relativities was adopted when there was no reliable transactional evidence available) the member P R Francis FRICS reflected that the RICS report did however represent the broadest study on relativity presently available. He suggested that a single line graph derived from the evidence in that report might prove a useful guide for valuers in circumstances where reliance on such information was the only available option.

4.—V<small>ALUATION UNDER</small> S<small>ECTION</small> 9(1c)

The heading *"Notice given after the original term date—section 1(1AA)(b)"* should read *"Notice given after the original term date—section 9(1AA)(b)"*   **9–58**

5.—COMPENSATION

9–59   Add to Footnote 338: Other cases in which compensation for other loss has been considered are as follows. In *Howard de Walden Estates Ltd v Zur* (unreported, 2003, LVT) compensation of £23,256 (£30,000 deferred for the unexpired term of the lease) was awarded upon the enfranchisement of a large house, there being a loss in "dividing" the property from the mews. In *Grosvenor Estate Belgravia v Mizouko Investment Ltd* (unreported, LVT, 2004) compensation of £48,100 was awarded upon the enfranchisement of a mews representing the loss of additional value of the freeholder being able to combine it with a large house. This represented a loss of £100,000 deferred for the remainder of the lease. The freeholder had claimed the loss was £500,000, but provided no proper evidence of the value of the main house. The Tribunal rejected an argument by the tenant that the deferment rate should be higher than that adopted in the main valuation because it was a riskier proposition. In *Grosvenor Estate Belgravia v Mehta* (unreported, LVT, 2009), the Tribunal would have awarded compensation of £707,350, i.e. £1,000,000 deferred for the unexpired term of the lease, for loss of the ability to combine a mews with a large house, but for the fact that it was common ground that the tenants of the mews were very likely indeed to enfranchise. Accordingly, and because s. 9A compensation had to be assessed in an "Act world", the house and mews would realistically never come into the freeholder's hands with vacant possession: the mews would already have been enfranchised.

In *Cadogan Estates Ltd v Panagopoulos* (unreported, 2008, LRA/97 & 108/2006), in the course of a collective enfranchisement hearing, the Lands Tribunal accepted evidence from the tenant that the value of a large London house was enhanced by ten per cent if it had an adjacent mews (the landlord having argued for five per cent).

Example valuations—freehold price under section 9(1C)

Example 2—Medium term unexpired: rent review, improvements to be disregarded; compensation under section 9A

9–63   There is an omission in the calculation of the Freeholder's interest. The capitalised ground rent (£6,500 × 0.4820), namely £3,133, should be shown as the first figure in the right hand column.

CHAPTER 11

SUB-TENANTS

2.—ACQUISTION OF FREEHOLD

Purchase price

In *Grosvenor Estate Belgravia v Klaasmeyer* [2010] UKUT 69 (LC); [2010] 16 **11–14**
E.G. 107 (CS), the Upper Tribunal, Lands Chamber considered a complex
valuation dispute involving a house in Belgravia. The house was demised as part
of the Grosvenor Belgravia Estate headlease, which included an "escalator"
clause, entitling the freeholders to an increasing proportion of the rents and
premiums payable in respect of the demised estate. The headlessee had its rental
income capitalised at the same rate as the freeholder (i.e. 4.75 per cent) until the
escalator became operative, and thereafter a 0.75 per cent increase was applied.
An increase in the *Sportelli* deferment rate of 4.75 per cent, to 5.5 per cent, was
appropriate when assessing the basic value that a purchaser was certain to enjoy
until 2040. The rest of the value of the headlease was valued using a 4.75 per cent
deferment rate.

"Minor superior tenancy"

Footnotes 79, 80, 81 and 88: *Nailrile Ltd v Cadogan* is now fully reported at **11–17**
[2009] 2 E.G.L.R. 151.

CHAPTER 12

RENTCHARGES

The most recent edition of the Land Registry Practice Guide 27 is dated 20 July **12–01**
2012. It is at Appendix 2U of this Supplement and the latest version can be
viewed online at *www.landregistry.gov.uk/professional/guides/practice-guide-27.*

Chapter 13

MORTGAGES

1.—Acquisition of Freehold—Mortgage of Landlord's Estate

Consequences of payment to mortgagee

Registered land
The most recent edition of the Land Registry Practice Guide 27 is dated 20 July **13–05**
2012. It is at Appendix 2U of this Supplement and the latest version can be
viewed online at *www.landregistry.gov.uk/professional/guides/practice-guide-27*.

CHAPTER 14

SPECIAL CLASSES OF LANDLORD

1.—PUBLIC BODIES

Right of Possession

Public bodies qualifying

In (1), add any economic prosperity board and any combined authority estab- **14–02**
lished under the Local Democracy, Economic Development and Construction
Act 2009, and joint waste authorities (established by an order under section 207
of the Local Government and Public Involvement in Health Act 2007).

Also, delete "any police authority . . . ." to the end of the paragraph and add
"any police and crime commissioner and the Mayor's Office for policing and
crime".

In (4), replace the words "New Town authorities, namely the Commission for
the New Towns" with "the new towns residuary body": substituted by the
Housing and Regeneration Act 2008, section 56, Schedule 8, paragraph 6.

In (6) delete "any Strategic Health Authority" and "any Primary Care Trust"
and add "the National Health Service Commissioning Board, any clinical commissioning group".

In (8) delete "the National Rivers Authority" and add "the Environment
Agency".

Any reference in section 28(5) to a county council shall as regards Wales,
include a county borough council.

Minister's certificate

In (i)(a) replace "Town and Country Planning Act 1990" with "Planning and **14–03**
Compulsory Purchase Act 2004".

In (iv), replace "Health Authority" with "Local Health Board": substituted by
the References to Health Authorities Order 2007, SI 2007/961, article 3, paragraph 5.

Also, delete "any Strategic Health Authority" and "any Primary Care Trust"
and add "the National Health Service Commissioning Board, any clinical commissioning group" and delete "National Health Services Act 1977" and substitute "National Health Service Act 2006 and National Health Service (Wales)
Act 2006".

Any reference in section 28(6) to a county council shall as regards Wales, include a county borough council.

Shared ownership leases granted after the coming into force of section 33A and Schedule 4A

Bodies qualifying

14–10   Footnote 60: Delete "Sch. 4" and substitute therefor "Sch. 4A"
Footnote 61: Delete "Sch. 4" and substitute therefor "Sch. 4A"
Footnote 62: Delete "Sch. 4" and substitute therefor "Sch. 4A"

3.—New Town Authorities

Right to possession

14–21   Delete "the Commission for the New Towns and any development corporation within the New Towns Act 1965" and substitute therefor "the new towns residuary body and any development corporation within the meaning of the New Towns Act 1981".

Reservation of development rights

14–23   The power of compulsory purchase is now given only to a Welsh new towns residuary body.

3A.—Housing Action Trust

Reservation of development rights

14–24A   A housing action trust also has the same powers as a local authority to impose in any conveyance or extended lease granted by it, a covenant restricting the development or clearing of land—section 29(6C) of the 1967 Act as inserted by the Housing Act 1988 section 140 Schedule 17 Part 1. However, a housing action trust is not given a power of compulsory purchase.

4.—University Bodies

Reservation of development rights

14–26   Footnote 127: Add "and s. 29(7)".
Footnote 128: Delete "which were based on . . . ." to the end of the footnote and substitute therefor "as amended by the Education and Inspections Act 2006, s. 177(1), (3).

8.—Other Landlords and Shared Ownership Leases

14–39   Sections 301 and 302 of the 2008 Act were brought into force on September 7, 2009: article 2(2) of The Housing and Regeneration Act 2008 (Commencement

No. 6 and Transitional and Savings Provisions) Order 2009 (SI 2009/2096) (set out at Appendix 2W). The amendments do not apply to any long tenancy granted before that date, or granted after that date but arising from a written agreement for the grant of that tenancy made before that date: article 3(1).

Shared ownership leases granted after the coming into force of section 301 of the Housing and Regeneration Act 2008

The Housing (Shared Ownership Leases)(Exclusion from Leasehold Reform Act **14–40** 1967) (England) Regulations 2009 (SI 2009/2097) (which are set out in Appendix 2X) prescribe the matters referred to in paragraph 3A(2).

For the condition in paragraph 3A(1)(b), see regulation 4. The condition is that the lease must set out the amount of any rent payable and the basis for calculating or determining any increase in the rent payable.

For the detailed requirements prescribed in paragraph 3A(2)(c) see regulation 5, to which reference should be made.

For the detailed circumstances prescribed in paragraph 3A(2)(e) see regulation 6, to which reference should be made.

For the detailed requirements prescribed in paragraph 3A(2)(f) see regulation 7, to which reference should be made.

Shared ownership leases granted after the coming into force of section 302 of the Housing and Regeneration Act 2008

The Housing (Shared Ownership Leases) (Exclusion from Leasehold Reform Act **14–41** 1967) (England) Regulations 2009 (SI 2009/2097) (which are set out in Appendix 2X) prescribe the matters referred to in paragraph 4A(2).

For the detailed conditions prescribed in paragraph 4A(1)(c) see regulation 8, to which reference should be made.

For the detailed requirements prescribed in paragraph 4A(2)(c) see regulation. 9, to which reference should be made.

For the detailed circumstances prescribed in paragraph 4A(2)(e) see regulation 10, to which reference should be made.

Footnote 179: The Housing (Right to Enfranchise) (Designated Protected Areas) (England) Order 2009 (SI 2009/2098) (set out in Appendix 2Y) designates the protected areas.

10.—PROPERTY TRANSFERRED FOR PUBLIC BENEFIT

Qualifying property

The HMRC website lists all land designated as being of outstanding scenic, **14–47** historic or scientific interest for inheritance tax purposes, and provides various details and maps that may help identify whether property is part of the designated land: see *http://www.hmrc.gov.uk/heritage/lbsearch.htm.*

CHAPTER 16

COURT AND TRIBUNAL PROCEEDINGS

3.—LEASEHOLD VALUATION TRIBUNALS

Procedure

A consultation process is taking place in relation to rules to be brought in when **16–11**
the LVT becomes incorporated into the Tribunal system, expected to be in
2013.

In *Crosspite Ltd v Sachdev & others* [2012] UKUT 321 (LC) HH Judge Gerald
noted that there had been a number of recent cases where a Leasehold Valuation
Tribunal, of its own motion, had decided to take a point or issue not raised by the
parties and had then decided the case on the basis of that point or issue. It was
stressed that the Leasehold Valuation Tribunal had no power to do this. However,
if a Leasehold Valuation Tribunal felt compelled to introduce a novel point or
issue, it must first invite comments from the parties as to whether it is appropriate
or relevant to do so and certainly before making any decision.

Footnote 124. Add: The decision in *Re Clarise Properties Ltd's Appeal* [2012]
UKUT 4 (LC); [2012] L. & T.R. 20 includes a useful discussion on the extent and
limits of the LVT's power to issue a correction certificate.

Appeal

The Lands Tribunal has been replaced by the Lands Chamber of the Upper **16–12**
Tribunal.

4.—LANDS TRIBUNAL

Appeal from leasehold valuation tribunal

Footnote 138: *Grosvenor Belgravia Estate v Adams* is fully reported at [2008] **16–13**
R.V.R. 173.

Procedure

Footnote 163: the reference to nn. 131–134 should be to nn. 159–162. **16–14**

On November 29, 2010, new procedural rules came into force concerning the **16–13—**
Lands Chamber of the Upper Tribunal. These are The Tribunal Procedure (Upper **16–17**

Tribunal) (Lands Chamber) Rules 2010, which are set out in Appendix 2Z of this Supplement. On the same date, a new set of Practice Directions for the Lands Chamber came into force, and these are set out in Appendix 2ZA. The substantive rules are similar to the previous rules. There are three important differences, which should be highlighted. First, a respondent to an application for permission to appeal may seek permission to cross-appeal if the applicant is granted permission to appeal: rule 22(1)(b). This is the case even if the respondent has not himself applied to the LVT for permission to appeal. This is an improvement on the previous position where the position of a respondent who was prepared to accept the LVT's decision, but who would wish to cross-appeal only in the event of the other party appealing, was unclear. The 2010 Rules do not provide for a respondent to apply for permission to cross-appeal where the LVT has granted permission to appeal.

Secondly, the requirement that an application for permission to appeal to the Court of Appeal must first be made to the Lands Chamber (which was introduced into the old Rules in 2009—see paragraph 16-19 of the main work) has been continued in the new rules: see rule 55.

Thirdly, the costs rules have been amended (see now rule 10 of the 2010 Rules). The Upper Tribunal (Lands Chamber) may not make an order for costs except: (a) under section 29(4) of the Tribunals, Courts and Enforcement Act 2007; this allows a wasted costs order to be made against a party's legal or other representative as a result of any improper, unreasonable or negligent act or omission; (b) it may order a party to pay the whole or any part of any fee paid; (c) if the Tribunal considers that a party has acted unreasonably in bringing, defending or continuing the proceedings, it can order it to pay costs not exceeding £500. It should be noted that the Rules are inconsistent with paragraph 12.6 of the Practice Directions which states that only the £500 referred to in (c) applies to an appeal from the LVT. The authors understand that a correction will be made to the Practice Directions in due course. For an example where the Respondent was ordered to pay a successful Appellant's fee of £450, see *Holicater Ltd v Great Yarmouth Borough Council* [2012] UKUT 131 (LC).

The Tribunal Procedure Committee is currently conducting a consultation exercise seeking views on consequential amendments proposed to the Upper Tribunal Lands Chamber Rules due to the planned introduction of a new Property Chamber in the First-tier Tribunal in 2013. It is also seeking views on some costs issues in the Upper Tribunal Lands Chamber following recommendations made in the 'Costs in Tribunals' report published by the Senior President of Tribunals in December 2011.

Footnote 188: The position is not affected by the fact that the Lands Tribunal is now the Upper Tribunal (Lands Chamber); *The Wellcome Trust Limited v 19–22 Onslow Gardens Freehold* [2012] EWCA Civ 1024.

Footnote 193: There have been a number of other such appeals since 2008.

Fees

16–17A   The fees payable in respect of an appeal are set out in the Upper Tribunal (Lands Chamber) Fees Order 2009, as amended, which is set out in Appendix 2ZB of this Supplement.

CHAPTER 17

MISCELLANEOUS

1.—CONTRACTING OUT

Add:

Localism Act 2011

Schedule 11 to the Localism Act 2011 adds a new Schedule 4C to the Town and **17–02A**
Country Planning Act 1990. Paragraph 11 of that Schedule provides for regulations to make provision for securing that, in prescribed circumstances (a) an enfranchisement right (which includes the right of enfranchisement under Part 1 of the 1967 Act) is not exercisable in relation to land the development of which is authorised by a community right to build order, or (b) the exercise of an enfranchisement right in relation to that land is subject to modifications provided for by the regulations. A community right to build order is defined in paragraph 2 of Schedule 4C.

The relevant regulations have been made under Part 7 of The Neighbourhood Planning (General) Regulations 2012 (SI 2012 No. 637).

Regulation 28 provides

"(1) Subject to paragraph (2), for the purposes of paragraph 11 of Schedule 4C to the 1990 Act, a community organisation may only provide that an enfranchisement right is not exercisable in relation to a property which is not an existing residential property.

(2) An enfranchisement right is not exercisable in relation to land the development of which is authorised by a community right to build order if the community organisation specified in the order proposal—

    (a) the enfranchisement rights which are not exercisable; and

    (b) the properties, or types of properties, in relation to which those rights are not exercisable.

(3) In this regulation—

"existing residential property" means a property (including part of a building)—

(a) which exists on the date the order proposal was submitted by the community organisation to the local planning authority under regulation 22; and

(b) in relation to which, on that date, any tenant of the property has an enfranchisement right in respect of the property."

4.—MISSING LANDLORD

Sub-tenant

17–17 The missing landlord procedure under section 50 of the 1993 Act cannot be used where the landlord is dead, simply because probate of his will has not been granted. In such a case, section 18 of the Law of Property (Miscellaneous Provisions) Act 1994 applies, which is referred to in paragraph 34–17 below: *Power v Stanton* [2010] 3 E.G.L.R. 71, Central London County Court, Judge Dight. Where the deceased leaves a will, the property of the deceased vests in the executor from the moment of the testator's death: *Whitmore v Lambert* [1955] 2 All E.R. 147 applied. This decision would apply equally to section 27 of the 1967 Act.

Procedure

(3) *Advertisement, valuation and conveyance*

17–20 (b) *Ascertainment of sum to be paid into court*

(i) *Purchase price*

17–21 In *Re Ballinger Hill House, Great Missenden,* [2012] UKUT 226 (LC) a case under section 27(5) of the 1967 Act, it was decided that it was necessary for the Tribunal to determine, for the purpose of calculating the enfranchisement price, whether or not the property enjoyed a right of way (in circumstances where the facts were inconclusive) rather than just examine how the hypothetical purchaser might assess the value in light of the uncertainty.

CHAPTER 18

ENLARGEMENT OF LONG TERMS

Add to footnote 1: *Panagopoulos v Cadogan* was reversed by the High Court on **18–01** this point: *Earl Cadogan v Panagopoulos* [2010] EWHC 422 (Ch); [2011] Ch. 177. Roth J. held that s. 153 did not apply to a lease where the lessee covenanted to pay an insurance rent and a service charge recoverable as rent. These items were rent within the meaning of s. 153(1)(b). This argument had not been advanced below. The Court of Appeal dismissed the landlord's appeal on a different issue, which did not involve this point: [2010] EWCA Civ 1259; [2011] Ch. 177.

Chapter 20

THE RIGHT TO COLLECTIVE ENFRANCHISEMENT

In March 2010 the Department of Communities and Local Government pub-   **20–01**
lished the summary of responses to its Consultation on the RTE provisions. The
majority of respondents were of the view that the provisions should not be
brought into force. The conclusion was that, in light of the response, "there are
no current plans to proceed with implementation of these provisions." That
remains the position. In the circumstances it is considered that it would be helpful
if these provisions were repealed.

1.—Pros and Cons of Collective Enfranchisement

Footnote 14: *Nailrile Ltd v Cadogan* is now fully reported at [2009] 2 E.G.L.R.   **20–03**
151.

2.—Property Included in the Claim

Add to footnote 28: In *Hemphurst Ltd v Durrels House Ltd* (unreported, LVT,   **20–05**
December 10, 2008) the tribunal was satisfied that the proposals set out in the
landlord's counter-notice as regards permanent rights gave the tenants as nearly
as may be the same rights as they enjoyed under their leases notwithstanding that
the proposals were (in part) drawn in general terms. In consequence, the tribunal
had no discretion. The Upper Tribunal (Lands Chamber) refused leave to appeal,
stating that any objection to the exact scope of the rights under s. 1(4) would be
decided at the contract stage and if necessary determined under s. 24 of the 1993
Act (see para. 28–14 for the subsequent determination under s. 24).

In *Fluss v Queensbridge Terrace Residents Ltd* [2011] UKUT 285 (LC), it was
held that the rights actually enjoyed at the relevant date must be considered under
s. 1(4) of the 1993 Act. Thus, if the leases allowed the landlord to restrict rights
in the future, or to impose regulations, but that right had not been exercised at the
relevant date, the landlord could not reserve the right to restrict the rights in the
future in the freehold transfer. If the lessor seeks to impose a liability to
contribute a service charge for maintaining the retained land, the lessees' rights

under the Landlord and Tenant Act 1985 would be sufficiently replicated by requiring them to pay "a reasonable proportion of the reasonable costs of maintaining" the land. The rights enjoyed by the qualifying tenants on the relevant date are not just the rights set out in the flat leases; they are the rights set out in the flat leases as affected by the laws of England.

Acquisition of leasehold interests

20–09   Footnote 47: In *Earl Cadogan v Panagopoulos* [2010] EWHC 422 (Ch); [2011] Ch. 177, the appeal was dismissed in relation to the caretaker's flat issue (although Roth J. found for the landlord on some of the other grounds). It was held that a flat housing a caretaker who services the building at the relevant date constitutes a common part irrespective of whether the obligation under the leases to provide a caretaker requires the caretaker to be resident. The Court of Appeal dismissed the landlord's appeal: [2010] EWCA Civ 1259; [2011] Ch. 177. It was not necessary to decide the issue as to whether the provision of a resident caretaker in the flat was required by the flat leases, although Carnwath L.J. saw the force of Roth J.'s approach: paras 21–22.

Footnote 48: In *Hemphurst Ltd v Durrels House Ltd* [2011] UKUT 6 (LC) [2011] L. & T.R. 16, the Upper Tribunal (Lands Chamber) allowed the nominee purchaser's appeal, and held that the participating tenants could elect to acquire only part of a lease which demised common parts, under s. 2(3). The nominee purchaser was not obliged to acquire parts of a lease that it did not wish to acquire, namely that part of a roof over the building that was intended for redevelopment; this was consistent with the statutory aim. It did not matter that the result was a severance of the lease in question. The landlord's cross-appeal was also allowed; the valuation of those parts of the lease which were to be acquired was remitted to the leasehold valuation tribunal. The landlord was granted permission to appeal to the Court of Appeal but the appeal was withdrawn before the hearing.

CHAPTER 21

PREMISES QUALIFYING

1.—"SELF-CONTAINED BUILDING"

In *Gala Unity Ltd v Ariadne Road RTM Company Ltd* [2012] EWCA Civ 1372 **21–02**
a case concerned with the right to manage provisions in the 2002 Act, a
proposition that a structurally detached building must be able to function inde-
pendently, without the need to make use of any shared facilities, in order to be
a "self-contained building" was rejected.

"Part of a building"
In *41–60 Albert Palace Mansions (Freehold) Ltd v Craftrule Ltd* [2010] EWHC **21–03**
1230 (Ch); [2010] 1 W.L.R. 2046, it was held by Henderson J. that premises
could qualify as part of a building even though they could be sub-divided into
smaller parts each of which satisfied the test of being a self-contained part of a
building. Thus, the tenants of 41–60, part of a terrace known as Albert Palace
Mansions, were able to claim the freehold of that part, even though Nos. 41–50
and 51–60 each comprised a self-contained part. There was no reason of policy,
nor construction of the words of the Act, nor consideration of decisions on other
statutes, which required the court to come to a different conclusion. The Court of
Appeal dismissed the landlord's appeal: [2011] EWCA Civ 185; [2011] 1 W.L.R.
2425. On the natural meaning of the words, the expression "self-contained part
of a building" included a self-contained part of a building that was itself capable
of being divided into smaller self-contained units.

2.—TWO OR MORE FLATS HELD BY QUALIFYING TENANTS

Footnote 13: It is not clear whether the cases under s. 2 of the 1967 Act on **21–04**
"designed or adapted for living in"—discussed in para. 2–04—may be of
assistance in construing the words "constructed or adapted for use for the
purposes of a dwelling". It is difficult to discern a policy reason for adopting a
different definition. On the other hand, different words were presumably chosen
deliberately.

In *Farndale Court Freehold Ltd v G & O Rents* (unreported, 2011, Central London County Court) HH Judge Cowell held that "flat" included premises comprising six rooms each with en suite WC, basin and shower, and a shared kitchen. A building comprising a number of such flats was susceptible to a collective enfranchisement claim.

Footnote 17: In *Howard de Walden Estates Ltd v Broome* [2012] L. & T.R. 16, *Cadogan v Gwynne* was followed in a new lease claim, where the flat was held under two separate leases, and the tenant had held one lease for less than two years at the date when the s. 42 notice was served.

4.—EXCLUDED PREMISES

(1) Part non-residential use

21–08 Footnote 36: In *Earl Cadogan v Panagopoulos* [2010] EWHC 422 (Ch); [2011] Ch. 177, the appeal was dismissed in relation to the caretaker's flat issue (although Roth J. found for the landlord on some of the other grounds). It was held that a flat housing a caretaker who services the building at the relevant date constitutes a common part irrespective of whether the obligation under the leases to provide a caretaker requires the caretaker to be resident. The Court of Appeal dismissed the landlord's appeal: [2010] EWCA Civ 1259; [2011] Ch. 177. It was held that common parts constituted areas of a building that were available for shared use or benefit. The common benefit from the caretaker's flat consisted primarily in the services of the caretaker as a person, rather than the use of the flat itself. However, since s. 101(1) defined common parts as including any common facilities within them, the provision of a resident caretaker and a flat for that caretaker's use could reasonably be regarded as a facility within that definition. Although there was force in the contention that a legal entitlement to the facility was not necessary for it to be a common part, that was not an issue in the instant case because there was a specific legal entitlement by two of the tenants. It was also necessary for the tenants to acquire those common parts for their proper management or maintenance. If they did not acquire the leasehold interest in the caretaker's flat, they would be unable to use that flat to accommodate a caretaker and it would not be maintained as a common part.

21–10 Footnote 47: the word "mange" should read "manage".

(2) Resident landlord

21–12 Footnote 50: the reference should be to n. 59 below.

CHAPTER 22

TENANCIES QUALIFYING

1.—LONG LEASES

Exceptions

(1) *Business lease*

In *Farndale Court Freehold Ltd v G & O Rents* (unreported, 2011, Central **22–05** London County Court) HH Judge Cowell held that the lease of a flat (comprising six rooms with washing facilities and a shared kitchen) where the lessee had a "so-called business" of letting the rooms in the flat was not a business lease (*Graysim Holdings Ltd v P&O Properties Holdings Ltd* [1996] 1 AC 329 applied).

Chapter 23

QUALIFYING TENANTS AND LANDLORDS

1.—Multiple Tenancies

In *Smith v Jafton Properties Ltd* [2011] EWCA Civ 1251, [2012] Ch. 519, the **23–02** Court of Appeal was concerned with the partial assignment of a lease of a building containing four flats to different lessees. Two flats were assigned to one tenant, and two to another. It was held, considering *Lester v Ridd* [1990] 2 Q.B. 430, discussed in paragraph 4–02 of the main work, that the holder of each severed part of the lease held only that property. Accordingly, each tenant was the lessee of only two flats, and they were each the qualifying tenants of those two flats only. Consequently, they were not prevented by section 5(5) of the 1993 Act from joining together to make a collective enfranchisement claim.

4.—Landlords

Footnote 32: The fact that "may" was held to be equivalent to "must" in **23–08** *Willingale v Globalgrange Ltd* [2000] 2 E.G.L.R. 55 does not mean that the same construction has to be applied wherever the 1993 Act uses the word "may": *Majorstake Ltd v Curtis* [2008] UKHL 10; [2008] A.C. 787, per Lord Scott at para. 14.

Chapter 24

PARTICIPATING TENANTS AND NOMINEE PURCHASER (THE RTE COMPANY AND PARTICIPATION IN A CLAIM)

1.—Participating Tenants

Footnote 2: *The Wellcome Trust Ltd v Baulackey* is now reported at [2010] 1 **24-01** E.G.L.R. 125.

Footnote 3: On the appeal, the parties agreed that, for the purpose of the marriage value calculation under Sch. 6 to the 1993 Act, there was no participating tenant of the flat in consequence of the assignee from the original participating tenant having decided not to participate. *Earl Cadogan v Erkman* [2011] UKUT 90 (LC). The principle of the issue was however argued and decided in *Earl Cadogan v Cadogan Square Ltd* [2011] UKUT 154 (LC), [2011] 3 E.G.L.R. 127—see para. 27–09.

3.—RTE Companies

In March 2010, the Department of Communities and Local Government pub- **24-15** lished the summary of responses to the Consultation on the RTE provisions. The majority of respondents were of the view that the provisions should not be brought into force. The conclusion was that, in light of the response, "there are no current plans to proceed with implementation of these provisions." That remains the position although the relevant sections have not been repealed.

CHAPTER 25

PROCEDURE—PRELIMINARY INQUIRIES AND INITIAL NOTICE

2.—INITIAL NOTICE

Signature

Add to footnote 99: The Court of Appeal has upheld the decision of the county **25–13**
court in *City & Country Properties Ltd v Plowden Investments Ltd: Hilmi &*
Associates Ltd v 20 Pembridge Villas Freehold Ltd [2010] EWCA Civ 314;
[2010] 1 W.L.R. 2750. In the case of a company participating tenant, it must sign
the initial notice by executing it in accordance with s. 36A of the Companies Act
1985, the provision in force at the relevant date in that case. The signature of a
single director who said he was authorised to sign the notice was insufficient.
Since April 6, 2008, execution of documents by a company is governed by s. 44
of the Companies Act 2006. A document is validly executed by the affixing of the
company's common seal or if it is signed by two authorised signatories, or by a
director of the company in the presence of a witness who attests the signature: s.
44(1), (2). Authorised signatories are every director of the company, or in the
case of a private company with a secretary or a public company, the secretary (or
any joint secretary) of the company: s. 44(3). S. 44 does not require express
words spelling out that the signatures are "by or on behalf of" the company if it
was clear that they were so signing: *Redcard Ltd v Williams* [2011] EWCA Civ
466, [2011] 2 E.G.L.R. 67.

In the case of an overseas company, reg.4 of the Overseas Companies (Execution of Documents and Registration of Charges) Regulations 2009 (SI
2009/1917) modifies s. 44 of the Companies Act 2006. A document is executed
by affixing its common seal, or if it is executed in any manner permitted by the
laws of the territory in which the company is incorporated for the execution of
documents by such a company. A document which is signed by a person who, in
accordance with the laws of the territory in which the overseas company is
incorporated, is acting under the authority (express or implied) of the company,
and is expressed (in whatever form of words) to be executed by the company, has
the same effect as if executed by an English company under its common seal.

The last paragraph of text will not apply, given that the Government has
announced that it will not be bringing the RTE provisions into force (see para.
24–15).

Effect of service of initial notice

25–15   Add after the end of the second paragraph: Accordingly once a contract is entered into, this should be registered separately.

Freehold

(1) *Dealings prohibited*

Footnote 120: The county court decision was appealed and heard by Roth J.: *Cadogan v Panagopoulos* [2010] EWHC 422 (Ch); [2011] Ch. 177. It was held that the grant of the lease was not a severance of the freehold by reason of s. 153 of the Law of Property Act 1925. The appeal was dismissed on other grounds.

Footnote 121: In *Cadogan v Panagopoulos* [2010] EWHC 422 (Ch); [2011] Ch. 177, Roth J. upheld the county court Judge's decision that the caretaker's flat was a common part. It was held that a flat housing a caretaker who services the building at the relevant date constitutes a common part irrespective of whether the obligation under the leases to provide a caretaker requires the caretaker to be resident. The Court of Appeal dismissed the landlord's appeal: [2010] EWCA Civ 1259; [2011] Ch. 177. It was not necessary to decide the issue as to whether the provision of a resident caretaker in the flat was required by the flat leases, although Carnwath L.J. saw the force of Roth J.'s approach: paras 21–22.

The freeholder is not prevented from altering the premises once an initial notice has been served. Thus, in *Barrie House Freehold Ltd v Merie Binmahfouz Co (UK) Ltd* [2012] EWHC 353 (Ch); [2012] P.L.S.C.S. 15, Roth J refused to grant an injunction to the nominee purchaser to restrain the freeholder from constructing two lightwells for which planning permission was granted after service of the initial notice. It was held that the 1993 Act provides a detailed and comprehensive code and, in particular, s. 19 contains an express anti-avoidance provision. There was no implied duty on the freeholder not to alter the premises.

The reference to *Cawthorne v Hamdan* should be to para. 29 of Lloyd L.J.'s judgment, rather than to para. 30.

(2) *Effect on other dealings*

Footnote 128: In *Cadogan v Panagopoulos* [2010] EWHC 422 (Ch); [2011] Ch. 177, Roth J. reversed the county court judge's decision on this point. The grant of a lease was not the disposal of the landlord's interest. The landlord's appeal was dismissed on other grounds.

(3) *Suspension of contract*

25–16   Footnote 130: It is considered that a prior Notice of Tenant's Claim under the Leasehold Reform Act 1967 given by a headlessee, which gives rise to a form of statutory contract (see para. 5–09 of the main work), would probably be suspended by s. 19(4). If so, this would meet the practical difficulty of there being concurrent claims to acquire the freehold under the 1967 and 1993 Acts. See the detailed discussion of this issue in *A Piece of the Puzzle* by Kester Lees [2011] 75 Conv. 454.

Leasehold

Footnote 143: *Ackerman v Lay* is now reported as *Ackerman v The Portman* **25–17**
Estate Nominees (One) Ltd [2009] 1 W.L.R. 1556.

Restriction on giving notice

Where proceedings under section 22(1) are discontinued before trial, and the **25–19**
initial notice is thereby deemed withdrawn, the right of the qualifying tenants to
serve a further section 13 notice after twelve months have elapsed (section 13(9))
carries with it the right to start fresh proceedings under section 22(1). The
nominee purchaser is not required to seek the permission of the court under CPR
38.7, even though the underlying facts are substantially the same as those which
were in issue in the first proceedings: *Westbrook Dolphin Square Ltd v Friends
Life Ltd* [2012] EWCA Civ 666, [2012] 1 W.L.R. 2752.

CHAPTER 26

PROCEDURE FOLLOWING INITIAL NOTICE

2.—New Agreements by Nominee Purchasers

Footnote 34: *Cadogan v Sportelli* is now reported at [2010] 1 A.C. 226.   **26–04**

Counter-notice admitting the right

(b)   **26–06**
Add to footnote 66: In *Hemphurst Ltd v Durrels House Ltd* (unreported, LVT, December 10, 2008) the tribunal was satisfied that the proposals set out in the landlord's counter-notice as regards permanent rights gave the tenants as nearly as may be the same rights as they enjoyed under their leases notwithstanding that the proposals were (in part) drawn in general terms. In consequence, the tribunal had no discretion. The Upper Tribunal (Lands Chamber) refused leave to appeal, stating that any objection to the exact scope of the rights under s. 1(4) would be decided at the contract stage and if necessary determined under s. 24 of the 1993 Act (see para. 28–14 for the subsequent determination under s. 24).

3.—The Counter-notice

Applications where terms are in dispute or no contract is entered into

"Agreed"
In *Lord Mayor and Citizens of the City of Westminster v CH 2006 Ltd* [2009]   **26–11**
UKUT 174 (LC); [2010] P.L.S.C.S. 13, it was held that there may be a binding agreement as to part of the price. The earlier decision of the Lands Tribunal in *Ellis & Dines v Logothetis* (LRA/3/2000) was followed, where the President had said in a new lease case: *"It has to be a complete agreement in the sense that each party commits itself unconditionally to such terms as are agreed."* In this case, the agreement was not conditional upon agreement or determination of other terms. In *Pledream Properties Ltd v 5 Felix Avenue London Ltd* [2010] EWHC 3048 (Ch); [2011] 12 E.G. 116, Lewison J. held that there must be an actual agreement, and that is a question of fact. The Act does not deem a term to

have been agreed when in fact it has not been agreed. A dispute may arise in fact even if the outcome of a dispute is a foregone conclusion. Even if terms are proposed which are consistent with Schedule 7 to the 1993 Act, it is open to the parties to agree a departure from the default provisions. Silence will not be taken to be a positive agreement. Terms which are not agreed remain in dispute for the purposes of section 24.

Footnote 131: *Goldeagle Properties Ltd v Thornbury Court Ltd* is reported at [2008] 3 E.G.L.R. 69.

Applications where no counter-notice

26–12   Footnote 144. Add: It was held in *Calladine-Smith v Saveorder Ltd* [2011] EWHC 2501 (Ch), [2012] L. & T.R. 3, (where a landlord sent to the tenant a counter-notice under s. 45 of the 1993 Act by ordinary post) that, under s. 7 of the Interpretation Act 1978, where there is evidence to show that, on the balance of probabilities a properly addressed, pre-paid and posted letter was delivered late or not delivered at all, this will rebut the presumption of deemed service.

CHAPTER 27

PURCHASE PRICE AND TERMS

2.—THE PRICE

Freehold owned by same person
Footnote 14: *Nailrile Ltd v Cadogan* is now fully reported at [2009] 2 E.G.L.R.   **27–03**
151.
   Footnote 21: *Cadogan v Sportelli* is now reported at [2010] 1 A.C. 226.

Four main assumptions
Footnote 24: *Cadogan v Sportelli* is now reported at [2010] 1 A.C. 226   **27–04**
   Add to (b): In *Cadogan v Sportelli* [2010] 1 A.C. 226, there was a difference
of opinion as to the effect of the words in brackets in paragraph 3(1)(b) of
Schedule 6, namely that a section 42 notice served by a non-participating tenant
may be taken into account. Lord Neuberger considered that one could take into
account service of a section 42 notice as evidence that the non-participating
tenant is interested in acquiring a new lease of his flat by negotiation, but not that
he has the right to a new lease (paragraph 107), whereas Lord Walker indicated
that the non-participating tenant's statutory right to a new lease could be taken
account of (paragraph 45). The other Law Lords did not express a view on that
issue. The difference between the two approaches was referred to in a Note of
qualification in *Cadogan v Erkman* [2011] UKUT 90 (LC), paragraph 116. It was
not necessary to resolve it in that case, but it was pointed out that it may need to
be decided in a future case.
   In *Earl Cadogan v Cadogan Square Ltd* [2011] UKUT 154 (LC), [2011] 3
E.G.L.R. 127, a section 42 notice was served by a predecessor in title of a
participating tenant who then assigned the benefit of the notice with the lease of
Flat 1 to a participating tenant. It was held that the section 42 notice could be
taken into account. However, since the lessee of flat 1 was now participating in
the acquisition of the freehold, there was no hope value arising from the section
42 notice. In those circumstances, it was not necessary to resolve the difference
of view in *Cadogan v Sportelli,* and referred to in *Cadogan v Erkman:* paragraphs 101–116.

Other assumptions

27–06 In a number of cases, development value has been allowed by the Lands Tribunal: e.g. *Arrowdell Ltd v Coniston Court (North) Hove Ltd* [2007] R.V.R. 39, *Sherwood Hall (East End Road) Management Co Ltd v Magnolia Tree Ltd* [2009] UKUT 158 (LC); [2010] 1 E.G.L.R. 181. The amount of development value depends on how a purchaser of the interest in the market would view the opportunity, and would include consideration of whether there is, or is likely to be, planning permission. In the latter case, the development value was limited to £10,000, being no more than the existing use value of a garage on the suggested development site. In *Trustees of Sloane Stanley Estate v Carey-Morgan* [2011] UKUT 415 (LC), [2012] R.V.R. 92, the Lands Chamber accepted the LVT's assessment of a nominal £10,000 "gambling chip" development value for the prospect of building an extra storey on a block of flats, the freeholder having argued for £664,000. At the valuation date, there was no planning permission for such a development. It was likely that planning permission would be refused, and there was no evidence as to what would be the likely decision on appeal.

In several recent cases, the Lands Tribunal has considered the issue as to whether there is additional value in the freehold as a result of the potential to redevelop the building into a single house: *Cadogan Estates Ltd v Panagopoulos* (unreported, 2008, LRA/97 & 108/2006), *Cadogan v 2 Herbert Crescent Freehold Ltd* [2009] P.L.S.C.S. 168, *31 Cadogan Square Freehold Ltd v Cadogan* [2010] UKUT 321 (LC). The latter two decisions considered in significant detail the risk factors associated with obtaining possession of flats let on long leases under the 1993 Act, subject to redevelopment rights under section 61 and Schedule 14. It was held that a bottom up, rather than a top down approach should be adopted. This involves assessing the value of the building in its existing state as flats, and then making an appropriate addition to reflect the development value: *31 Cadogan Square Freehold Ltd v Cadogan* [2010] UKUT 321 (LC), at paragraphs 157 et seq. In that case, only 15 per cent of the development value was allowed, there being an 85 per cent discount for risk. In *Kutchukian v John Lyon's Charity* [2012] UKUT 53 (LC) where a similar point arose, the Upper Tribunal determined that the correct approach in such a case is to assess the price by analysing the hypothetical purchaser's bid on the basis of (i) the likely strengths and weaknesses of his position at the date of the reversion (in that case 2046) both in the context of legal difficulties (the construction and application of section 61 and Schedule 14) and other uncertainties such as planning and value movements. This would involve identifying the potential gains and the potential difficulties and uncertainties of obtaining these gains and reaching an informed business decision as to how much this chance of a successful redevelopment at the reversion date was worth at the valuation date. On the facts of that case, the Upper Tribunal decided a 5 per cent deduction for the risk of adverse changes in planning policy, a 35 per cent deduction for the risk of future changes in the market and in the economics of conversion and a 30 per cent deduction for the uncertainty over the construction and application of section 61 and Schedule 14. The risk of a delay in obtaining vacant possession at the date of the reversion was reflected by adding one year to the deferment period. The landlord has obtained permission to appeal to the Court of Appeal on the issue of the 30 per cent deduction for section 61 and Schedule 14 uncertainties.

Statutory rights

The rent limit for an assured tenancy in England was increased to £100,000 with effect from October 1, 2010: The Assured Tenancies (Amendment) (England) Order 2010 (SI 2010/908).

In *Re Clarise Properties Ltd's Appeal* [2012] UKUT 4 (LC) [2012] L. & T.R. 20, a case under section 9 of the 1967 Act, the Upper Tribunal held that a deduction of 20 per cent should be made from the eventual reversion because of the risk of an assured tenancy arising under Schedule 10 to the Local Government and Housing Act 1989. That deduction is controversial, not only because it is inconsistent with the deductions made in earlier cases but also because there was no evidence adduced to support it.

Hope value

A helpful explanation of what is hope value can be found in paragraphs 19 to 21 of the judgment of Mr Justice Morgan in *Carey-Morgan & another v The Trustees of the Sloane Stanley Estate* [2012] EWCA Civ 1181.

As pointed out in *Earl Cadogan v Erkman* [2011] UKUT 90 (LC) the basis for assessing hope value remains unclear in circumstances where a flat is held by a non-participating tenant but a section 42 notice has been given prior to the valuation date; see paragraph 27–04.

Cadogan v Sportelli is now reported at [2010] 1 A.C. 226.

In *Culley v Daejan Properties Ltd* [2009] UKUT 168 (LC); [2009] 3 E.G.L.R. 165, hope value was assessed at ten per cent of marriage value in respect of the two non-participating tenants' flats. There were four flats in all, and the Tribunal took account of the fact that 50 per cent of the tenants were not participating and that the unexpired terms were 65 years. It was held (at paragraph 63) that the amount of hope value would be greater if the proportion of non-participating flats is relatively large; it will be lower if the unexpired terms are particularly long.

In *Earl Cadogan v Erkman* [2011] UKUT 90 (LC) an "end allowance" was made to reflect limited hope value on a single flat with an unexpired term of 17.33 years. " ... *a purchaser would be cautious about attributing any significant value to the prospect of a single tenant, holding a short lease and who has given no indication to date that he wants to extend his lease, making an early approach to negotiate a new lease and to share the (diminishing) marriage value*".

In *Earl Cadogan v Cadogan Square Ltd* [2011] UKUT 154 (LC) no hope value was attributed to a flat with an unexpired term of nearly 108 years and hope value of five per cent of marriage value was assessed for a flat with an unexpired term of 17.75 years.

In *Trustees of Sloane Stanley Estate v Carey-Morgan* [2011] UKUT 415 (LC), [2012] R.V.R. 92, the Lands Chamber assessed hope value in respect of non-participating tenants as 20 per cent of marriage value in the case of four flats with 4.74 years unexpired, and 10 per cent in the case of one flat with 70.25 years unexpired. The appeal of the nominee purchaser was dismissed by the Court of

Appeal: [2012] EWCA Civ. 1181; the decision on hope value disclosed no error of law.

Yield

27–08   A helpful explanation of what is a deferment rate can be found in paragraphs 11 to 16 of the judgment of Mr Justice Morgan in *Carey-Morgan & another v The Trustees of the Sloane Stanley Estate* [2012] EWCA Civ 1181.

In *Sherwood Hall (East End Road) Management Co Ltd v Magnolia Tree Ltd* [2009] UKUT 158 (LC); [2010] 1 E.G.L.R. 181, the Tribunal declined to adjust the five per cent guideline rate in *Cadogan v Sportelli* on the ground that the unexpired term of the flat leases was long, namely 88 years.

In *Culley v Daejan Properties Ltd* [2009] UKUT 168 (LC); [2009] 3 E.G.L.R. 165, the Tribunal applied the five per cent rate in the case of a block of flats in outer London, there being no evidence of higher growth rates in Prime Central London to support a higher deferment rate.

In *Zuckerman v Trustees of the Calthorpe Estates* [2009] UKUT 235 (LC); [2010] 1 E.G.L.R. 187, a deferment rate of six per cent was applied in a number of new lease claims concerning flats in a block in Edgbaston, West Midlands. The additional one per cent was made up of three elements: (i) 0.25 per cent for the greater risk of deterioration and obsolescence of these flats compared to that in the high value period properties in Prime Central London; (ii) 0.5 per cent for the greater risk that the assumed two per cent growth rate would not be achieved when comparing these flats with those in PCL: the Tribunal was presented with detailed comparative evidence of historic growth rates, showing that those in PCL rose considerably more than those in the West Midlands; (iii) 0.25 per cent to reflect the fact that there were greater management risks in relation to flats in the light of increasingly burdensome service charge regulation, in particular the introduction of the Service Charges (Consultation Requirements) (England) Regulations 2003. Had the original headlease been in place, the Tribunal would not have adjusted for this factor.

The same 0.25 per cent adjustment for obsolescence/deterioration was made in *Re Lethaby and Regis's appeal* [2010] UKUT 86 (LT), a missing landlord case concerning two flats in East London. The Tribunal followed *Zuckerman* (above). In the absence of evidence of differing growth rates between East London and PCL, the 0.5 per cent adjustment was not made. The 0.25 per cent flats adjustment was not made, because the repairing obligations for the building were divided between the lessees of the two flats.

In *Ashdown Hove Ltd v Remstar Properties Ltd* [2010] 3 E.G.L.R. 61, the LVT determined a deferment rate of six per cent in respect of a 1970s block of flats in Brighton. The *Zuckerman* case was followed. Even though there was a headlease of the common parts the additional 0.25 per cent for management difficulties was applied. The lessee was a leaseholder-owned management company, and there was evidence that it might fold, due to a history of management problems, leaving the freeholder having to step in.

In *Re Midland Freeholds Ltd's appeal* [2011] UKUT 173 (LC), the Upper Tribunal allowed the landlord's appeal in circumstances where the Leasehold

Valuation Tribunal had adjusted the deferment rate to reflect inferior location where neither party had adduced evidence on the issue.

In *City & Country Properties Ltd v Yeats* [2012] UKUT 227 (LC), the Lands Chamber was concerned with a new lease claim for a very modest flat in Horsham, West Sussex. The 0.25 per cent adjustment made in *Zuckerman* (above) for the additional risks resulting from service charge regulation was applied. However, the 0.5 per cent addition for the difference in assumed growth rate with PCL was not allowed, because the comparative evidence relating to that location was inadequate. The adopted deferment rate was, therefore, 5.5 per cent.

The Upper Tribunal went on to suggest that the distinction made in *Zuckerman* between a building subject to a headlease and a building in direct management is not so clear cut. The mere existence of a headlease will not in itself be sufficient to justify the conclusion that the extra 0.25 per cent should be omitted from the deferment rate. In effect, the burden of proof has shifted, so that the landlord will need to produce "clear evidence" showing that the purchaser of the freehold reversion would realise, upon the facts of a particular case, that it was extremely improbable that as freeholder it would ever become burdened with any responsibility for management. The existence of the headlease and the nature of such headlease and of the headlessee will be relevant to this. A landlord will now need to show, if he wishes to avoid the *Zuckerman* uplift of 0.25 per cent (in addition to the *Sportelli* uplift of 0.25 per cent), that there is a suitably worded headlease and a suitably solid headlessee coupled with evidence showing that there is no reason to believe that the headlessee would ever fail in its obligations. Even then, that "may" only be sufficient to justify the conclusion that the extra 0.25 per cent should not be added.

In *Tamworth Gardens Properties Ltd v Charles Gallagher Ltd* (unreported, LVT, August 30, 2010) the LVT considered that a deferment rate of 4.75 per cent was correct for four blocks of 30 flats in Farnborough, Hampshire, on the ground that the reversion was without management liability and problems (there being a headlease in place) and was no different to that of a house.

Footnote 75: The cases where the unexpired term is less than 20 years were determined by the Upper Tribunal (Lands Chamber) in five conjoined appeals in collective enfranchisement claims, *Cadogan Square Properties Ltd v Cadogan* [2010] UKUT 427 (LC); [2011] 1 E.G.L.R. 155. In each case the net rental yield and formula based methods was rejected. The starting point was the *Sportelli* rate of five per cent for flats. This was adjusted upwards to 5.25 per cent for 2005 (for terms between 17.3 and 17.8 years) and to 5.5 per cent for 2007 (for terms of 15.6 and 16.1 years). This reflected an adjustment in the real growth rate which would be negotiated between willing seller and willing purchaser. For terms of less than ten years, which were not before the Lands Chamber, different questions could arise, and using a net rental yield would have to be examined in such a case. In the case of a building divided into flats, but with the prospect of reconverting it back into a house, it was appropriate to use the deferment rate for flats rather than houses. This is a guideline case (as was *Sportelli*): see para. 195.

In *Trustees of Sloane Stanley Estate v Carey-Morgan* [2011] UKUT 415 (LC); [2012] R.V.R. 92, the building contained 25 flats, of which six had unexpired terms of 4.74 years. The Lands Chamber held that in a case where the unexpired term was less than five years, the net rental yield method should be used to assess the deferment rate (coming to 3.25 per cent), with an end allowance of five per cent. This was said to be the method that should be used in all such cases in the future (para. 143). On appeal by the nominee purchaser, the Court of Appeal dismissed the appeal: [2012] EWCA Civ. 1181. The nominee purchaser had sought to argue that the lessees had rights to remain as assured tenants under Sch. 10 of the Local Government and Housing Act 1989. Since this was a new argument, not raised in the Upper Tribunal, and unsupported by evidence, the nominee purchaser was not permitted to run it. The Court of Appeal indicated, however, that in a future case it could be taken into account if the evidence warranted it.

Marriage value

27–09 A helpful explanation of what is marriage value can be found in paragraphs 17 and 18 of the judgment of Mr Justice Morgan in *Carey-Morgan & another v The Trustees of the Sloane Stanley Estate* [2012] EWCA Civ 1181.

In the second paragraph of the main work (definition of marriage value in the 1993 Act), in the fourth line of that definition delete the words "participating tenants" and insert in their place "persons who are participating tenants immediately before a binding contract is entered into in pursuance of the initial notice" and in sub-paragraph (a) delete the words "participating tenants" and insert in their place "persons who are participating tenants immediately before a binding contract is entered into in pursuance of the initial notice".[1]

Footnote 95: The appeal in *McHale v Cadogan (Erkman intervening)* has been dismissed [2010] EWCA Civ 1471; [2011] 1 E.G.L.R. 36. This paragraph of text has been approved. As a matter of statutory interpretation, it is necessary to apply the same assumptions throughout the marriage value calculation as in valuing the freehold under para. 3 of Sch. 6 i.e. including when valuing the participating tenants' existing leases. This produces a consistent valuation; to do otherwise would be to thwart Parliament's obvious purpose of identifying marriage value on a principled basis: per Arden L.J. at para. 32. The presence of artificial assumptions necessarily displaces the presumption that the valuation is to be conducted on the basis of reality. Permission to appeal to the Supreme Court was granted, but the appeal was not pursued.

Footnote 98: The tenants' appeal in *Forty-five Holdings Ltd v Grosvenor (Mayfair) Estate* was dismissed by the Upper Tribunal (Lands Chamber): [2009] UKUT 234 (LC); [2010] L. & T.R. 21. The ability of the tenants to vary their existing leases and to extend the premises could be taken into account in assessing the value of the freehold when held by the nominee purchaser.

In *Earl Cadogan v Cadogan Square Ltd* [2011] UKUT 154 (LC), [2011] 3 E.G.L.R. 127, one of the participating tenants at the date of the claim subsequently assigned her lease of the flat in circumstances where the assignee did not

[1] Art. 4(1) The Commonhold and Leasehold Reform Act 2002 (Commencement No 5 and Saving and Transitional Provision) Order 2004 SI 2004/3056. On the basis that ss 121–124 of the 2002 Act are never likely to be brought into force these amendments can be considered as permanent.

choose to become a participating tenant. It was held that that flat could not be included in the marriage value calculation because there was no-one who was a participating tenant immediately before the contract. On those facts, the landlord was also unable to claim hope value on that flat because there was a participating tenant at the valuation date. The Upper Tribunal doubted that this was the intention of the legislators.

In *Themeline Ltd v Vowden Investments Ltd* [2011] UKUT 168 (LC), it was held that the marriage value arises only by virtue of the participating tenants being able to be granted by the nominee purchaser new leases of their flats. The definition therefore excludes marriage value arising from the grant to the participating tenants of a lease of the whole building.

By contrast, in *Cravecrest Ltd v Duke of Wesmtinster Trustees* [2012] UKUT 68 (LC); [2012] P.L.S.C.S. 171, it was held that in valuing a long leasehold interest in a flat in a building which was ripe for development back to a house, it was permissible to take account of the development value inherent in a capital value of that lease. It was not precluded by the exclusion of "hope value" as discussed in *Cadogan v Sportelli* [2010] 1 AC 226, which was dealing with a different issue, namely the prospect of unlocking marriage value. The Court of Appeal has granted the nominee purchaser permission to appeal.

Relativity

Footnotes 108 and 109: *Nailrile Ltd v Cadogan* is now fully reported at [2009] **27–10** 2 E.G.L.R. 151. Evidence of graphs was also used in *Dependable Homes Ltd v Mann* [2009] UKUT 171 (LC); [2009] P.L.S.C.S. 326. There was no evidence in that case to support the suggestion that relativity depended on location, and the Tribunal relied on the graph of graphs (compiled by Beckett & Kay): para. 40.

In October 2009, the RICS published its report on Graphs of Relativity, in response to the suggestion in *Arrowdell*. The Leasehold Relativities Group, chaired by Jonathan Gaunt QC and comprising eight surveyors, considered all the published graphs but were unable to agree upon definitive graphs to be used as evidence by LVTs, as had been proposed by the Lands Tribunal. The report reproduced all the published graphs together with details of the data that lies behind each.

In *Re Coolrace Ltd* [2012] UKUT 69 (LC); [2012] 24 E.G. 84, the Lands Chamber adopted the Lease graph of relativities, based on Tribunal decisions across the country, in preference to a local West Midlands graph, which had been applied by the LVT. A plea for a further attempt to agree a graph was made.

In *Trustees of Sloane Stanley Estate v Carey-Morgan* [2011] UKUT 415 (LC); [2012] R.V.R. 92, the Lands Chamber assessed the value of short leases with 4.74 years unexpired by capitalising the unimproved rental value to the end of the term. This was appropriate for such a short lease, instead of using graphs of relativity.

In *Earl Cadogan v Cadogan Square Ltd* [2011] UKUT 154 (LC); [2011] 3 E.G.L.R. 127, the Upper Tribunal was faced with the difficulty of conflicting evidence as between evidence of adjusted transactions (producing a relativity of 53 to 56 per cent) and evidence from graphs (producing a relativity of 38 per cent). An analysis of the evidence from the Savills 2002 enfranchisable graph as against the Gerald Eve non-enfranchisable graph suggested that the adjustment of ten per cent made by the nominee purchaser to adjust the transactional evidence to reflect 1993 Act rights was too low and the Tribunal decided that a deduction of 25 per cent was appropriate. The unexpired terms in that case were 17.75 years.

Additional compensation

27–13   In *Hemphurst Ltd and Grovehurst Ltd v Durrels House Ltd* (unreported, LVT, November 7, 2012) it was decided, on a "finely balanced" argument that compensation is assessed at the date of the initial notice rather than the date of acquisition.

Example 3

On page 488 there are three corrections:

Under the heading *"Value of freeholder's present interest in 5 flats for which leases extended"* the PV should be 132 years, not 32 years.

Under the heading *"Value of intermediate leaseholder's present interest in 75 flats for which leases not been extended"*, *"leasholder"* should read *"leaseholder"*

Term 2 Profit rent, the word "and" should be inserted between "9.00%" and "2.25%"

Freehold owned by different persons

Intermediate leasehold interest

27–15   Footnote 137: *Nailrile Ltd v Cadogan* is now fully reported at [2009] 2 E.G.L.R. 151.

(i) *Value of intermediate lease*

27–16   In *McHale v Cadogan* [2010] EWCA Civ 14; [2010] 1 E.G.L.R. 51, the Court of Appeal allowed the nominee purchaser's appeal from the Lands Tribunal on this issue. The loss of rack rent on the caretaker's flat fell within the definition of "the cost of outgoings for such accommodation" in the underlease. This was of value to the intermediate landlord, even though the flat was required to be licensed to the caretaker rent-free. The headlease should be valued on the assumption that the head lessee was entitled to be compensated in the service charge for the loss of rack-rent on the caretaker's flat.

In *Earl Cadogan v Cadogan Square Ltd* [2011] UKUT 154 (LC); [2011] 3 E.G.L.R. 127, the Lands Chamber held that the market rent for the caretaker's flat should be reduced by 50 per cent to take account of the restriction in the Headlease, namely that it should be used by a full-time caretaker who is to reside in a service basis (see paragraphs 93–100).

Footnotes 147 and 148: *Nailrile Ltd v Cadogan* is now fully reported at [2009] 2 E.G.L.R. 151.

Interest with negative value

27–19   Footnote 179: *Nailrile Ltd v Cadogan* is now fully reported at [2009] 2 E.G.L.R. 151.

CHAPTER 28

TERMINATION OR COMPLETION OF CLAIM

2.—DEEMED WITHDRAWAL

Add to (2): Where proceedings under section 22(1) are discontinued before trial, **28–04** and the initial notice is thereby deemed withdrawn, the right of the qualifying tenants to serve a further section 13 notice after 12 months have elapsed (section 13(9)) carries with it the right to start fresh proceedings under section 22(1). The nominee purchaser is not required to seek the permission of the court under CPR 38.7, even though the underlying facts are substantially the same as those which were in issue in the first proceedings: *Westbrook Dolphin Square Ltd v Friends Life Ltd* [2012] EWCA Civ 666; [2012] 1 W.L.R. 2752.

4.—INHERITANCE TAX

The HMRC website lists all land designated as being of outstanding scenic, **28–07** historic or scientific interest for inheritance tax purposes, and provides various details and maps that may help identify whether property is part of the designated land: see *http://www.hmrc.gov.uk/heritage/lbsearch.htm*

6.—COMPLETION AND CONVEYANCE

Preparation of contract

Footnote 66: It would have been preferable if this time limit had been expressed **28–11** to run from the date when any determination by the LVT becomes final, as to which see s. 101(9) of the 1993 Act. If there is an outstanding appeal or application for permission to appeal, it would be sensible to wait until that is disposed of before starting the process of entering into a contract.

Terms of conveyance

In *Hemphurst Ltd v Durrels House Ltd* (unreported, LVT, February 14, 2011), the **28–14** tribunal had to consider the detailed terms of the transfer in a collective enfranchisement claim, both in the context of section 1(4) and in the context of section 34 and Schedule 7. The landlord decided to retain the grounds surrounding the block of flats and to offer the nominee purchaser under section 1(4) of the Act rights equivalent to those enjoyed by the lessees under their leases. The tribunal held that the rights falling within section 1(4) included the benefit of covenants (including positive covenants) and there was no reason in principle why implied rights and obligations would not also fall within section 1(4). However, "rights" under section 1(4) did not extend to statutory rights. The landlord covenanted under the leases to maintain the gardens, and the tenants covenanted to contribute to the cost by way of service charge. All those provisions had to be replicated in the transfer, in order to ensure that the rights were indeed equivalent. The covenant by the landlord only had to be given to the nominee purchaser, not to the lessees as well. Because this was a freehold transfer, the service charge protection given to lessees by the Landlord and Tenant Act 1985 was no longer available. Consequently, the tribunal ordered that the nominee purchaser must pay a fair and reasonable proportion of the reasonable costs of performing the landlord's obligations in relation to the retained property. Any dispute would have to be decided by the county court, as the LVT would have no jurisdiction. Given that the nominee purchaser would not have the benefit of the right to statutory consultation in advance of major expenditure, the tribunal considered that equivalence could best be achieved by requiring payment only in arrears.

In *Hemphurst Ltd and Grovehurst Ltd v Durrels House Ltd* (unreported, LVT, November 7, 2012), it was decided that the tribunal's jurisdiction to determine the terms of the transfer on acquisition of part of a leasehold interest extended beyond the terms identified in section 34 and Schedule 7. The LVT had power to insert in a transfer of part of a leasehold interest such terms made necessary by the severance of the interest. That power did not extend to introducing any terms which are in conflict with the lease.

(b) *Rights of supports etc.*
In *Trustees of Sloane Stanley Estate v Carey-Morgan* [2011] UKUT 415 (LC); [2012] R.V.R. 92, the Lands Chamber refused to include a clause that the property shall not enjoy any rights of light or air over the landlord's estate which will inhibit or prevent the free use of the estate for building or other purposes (paragraph 148). The proposed clause did not fall within paragraph 3 of Schedule 7 to the 1993 Act.

(d) *Restrictive covenants*
In *Trustees of Sloane Stanley Estate v Carey-Morgan* [2011] UKUT 415 (LC); [2012] R.V.R. 92, the Lands Chamber refused to include a covenant restricting alterations in the transfer where there was no evidence that this would materially enhance the value of the landlord's other property, merely assertion by the freeholder's counsel (paragraph 152). See also *Cadogan v Erkman* [2011] UKUT 90 (LC), paragraph 105, as to the sort of evidence required.

The word "require" in section 10(4) does not mean "demand", but rather "need": *Cadogan v Erkman* [2011] UKUT 90 (LC) paragraph 107.

Leases back

Terms of lease back

In *Lord Mayor and Citizens of the City of Westminster v CH 2006 Ltd* [2009] **28–16**
UKUT 174 (LC); [2010] P.L.S.C.S. 13, the Council failed to have included in six
lease backs to it (of flats subject to secure tenancies) a provision indemnifying it
against unexpected increases in service charge which could not be recovered
from the tenants exercising the right to buy. This would unfairly devolve the
Council's responsibility under section 125 of the Housing Act 1985 to the
nominee purchaser.

CHAPTER 29

THE INDIVIDUAL RIGHT TO A NEW LEASE

2.—OWNERSHIP CONDITION

Footnote 17: In *Howard de Walden Estates Ltd v Broome* [2102] L. & T.R. 16, **29–04** it was held that, where the flat is held under two separate leases, the tenant must have held both leases for at least two years before being in a position to serve a s. 42 notice.

Footnote 19: *The Wellcome Trust Ltd v Baulackey* is now reported at [2010] 1 E.G.L.R. 125.

4.—THE LANDLORD

Add: **29–06**

Split reversions
Unlike Chapter 1 (as to which see section 9(2A), Schedule 1, Part 1A), Chapter 2 contains no provision dealing with the situation where there is a split reversion i.e. where the tenant has more than one landlord. This problem has arisen where the flat itself is in a building with a landlord, but appurtenant property such as a garden forming part of the extended definition of "flat" by virtue of section 62(2) (see paragraph 29–05 of the main work) has a different landlord. This may occur where, for example, the landlord sells off to another person the reversion to the land outside the building containing the flats. If the garden is let under a different lease, it appears that in such a case the tenant will not be entitled to claim a new lease which includes the garden, since it will not be regarded as let to the tenant with the flat: see the discussion of "Let to the tenant with the flat" under paragraph 29–05. One factual situation which has arisen is where the landlord sold the freehold of appurtenant land, but took a lease back of it. He remained the tenant's immediate landlord of both the flat and the garden. In those circumstances, it is considered that the tenant could probably claim a new lease of all the property demised by his lease, even though the landlord is not the competent landlord of the garden. Where the tenant has a single lease of both the flat and the garden, the fact that there are different landlords does not prevent section

62(2) from applying. It is considered that, in those circumstances both landlords together would be regarded as "the landlord". There is a useful and detailed discussion about the same problem in the context of Part 2 of the Landlord and Tenant Act 1954 in *Renewal of Business Tenancies* by Reynolds & Clark 3rd edition, paragraphs 3–186—3–195.

CHAPTER 30

NEW LEASE—PROCEDURE

2.—NOTICE OF CLAIM

Contents of notice
Footnote 36: The reference should be to [1996] 4 All E.R. 643, not [1994].   **30–07**

Signature
Add to Footnote 66: The Court of Appeal has upheld the decision of the county   **30–08**
court in *City & Country Properties Ltd v Plowden Investments Ltd: Hilmi &
Associates Ltd v 20 Pembridge Villas Freehold Ltd* [2010] EWCA Civ 314;
[2010] 1 W.L.R. 2750. In the case of a company qualifying tenant, it must sign
the initial notice by executing it in accordance with s. 36A of the Companies Act
1985, the provision in force at the relevant date in that case. The signature of a
single director who said he was authorised to sign the notice was insufficient.
Since April 6, 2008, execution of documents by a company is governed by s. 44
of the Companies Act 2006. A document is validly executed by the affixing of the
company's common seal or if it is signed by two authorised signatories, or by a
director of the company in the presence of a witness who attests the signature: s.
44(1), (2). Authorised signatories are every director of the company, or in the
case of a private company with a secretary or a public company, the secretary (or
any joint secretary) of the company: s. 44(3). S. 44 does not require express
words spelling out that the signatures are "by or on behalf of" the company if it
was clear that they were so signing: *Redcard Ltd v Williams* [2011] EWCA Civ
466, [2011] 2 E.G.L.R. 67.

In the case of an overseas company, reg. 4 of the Overseas Companies
(Execution of Documents and Registration of Charges) Regulations 2009 (SI
2009/1917) modifies s. 44 of the Companies Act 2006. A document is executed
by affixing its common seal, or if it is executed in any manner permitted by the
laws of the territory in which the company is incorporated for the execution of
documents by such a company. A document which is signed by a person who, in
accordance with the laws of the territory in which the overseas company is
incorporated, is acting under the authority (express or implied) of the company,
and is expressed (in whatever form of words) to be executed by the company, has
the same effect as if executed by an English company under its common seal.

The effect of serving a notice

Restriction on termination

30–11   Footnote 98: *Ackerman v Lay* is now reported as *Ackerman v The Portman Estate Nominees (One) Ltd* [2009] 1 W.L.R. 1556.

3.—Post-Notice Procedure

Rights of landlord

Counter-notice

30–15   Add to Footnote 121: It was held in *Calladine-Smith v Saveorder Ltd* [2011] EWHC 2501 (Ch), [2012] L. & T.R. 3, (where a landlord sent to the tenant a counter-notice under section 45 of the 1993 Act by ordinary post) that, under s. 7 of the Interpretation Act 1978, where there is evidence to show that, on the balance of probabilities a properly addressed, pre-paid and posted letter was delivered late or not delivered at all, this will rebut the presumption of deemed service.

Add to Footnote 124: See also *The Wellcome Trust Ltd v Baulackey* [2010] 1 E.G.L.R. 125, referred to at para. 24–01.

Counter-notice not admitting the claim

30–16   Add to footnote 143: However, it appears that the corresponding date rule does not apply in these circumstances: *R (Zaporozhchenko) v City of Westminster Magistrates Court* [2011] 1 W.L.R. 994. Accordingly, in the example given, the application must be issued by June 3, not June 4.

Counter-notice admitting the claim

30–21   Footnote 180: There is now a one month period for providing a notice of appeal to the Upper Tribunal (Lands Chamber) after permission to appeal has been given: r. 24(2) of The Tribunal Procedure (Upper Tribunal) (Lands Chamber) Rules 2010 permission now being required in appeals from the LVT.

In *Ellis and Dines v Logothetis* (unreported, 2000, Lands Tribunal LRA/3/2000), there was a dispute as to whether terms of acquisition had been agreed for the purposes of s. 48(3) of the 1993 Act. It was held by the President that an agreement has to be a complete agreement in the sense that each party commits itself unconditionally to such of the terms as are agreed (para. 10).

In *Panagopoulos v Cadogan* (unreported, 2010, Central London County Court) it was held by HH Judge Cowell that an application can be issued before the second period of two months begins, as well as during the second period of two months. The court can only make an order under s. 48(3) if all the terms of acquisition have been agreed or determined and a new lease has not been entered into. That decision is controversial, since there is no completed cause of action for an order under s. 48(3) until the first period of two months has expired.

Completion

Add to Footnote 195: Service of a notice to complete merely fixes the completion **30–22** date for the purpose of the procedure under the Regulations. The 1993 Act does not provide any consequence for the failure to comply with a notice to complete, for which time is not of the essence. The landlord is not, therefore entitled to treat the tenant's notice as withdrawn upon failure to comply with its notice to complete: *Ayres v Roberts* [2012] L. & T.R. 1.

Failure to serve a counter-notice

See also paragraph 26–11 for the meaning and requirements of "agreed" in this **30–23** context.

In *Tuebner & another v Howard de Walden Estates Ltd* (unreported, Central London County Court, June 2011) it was held that since the flat and the garage in that case were defined in the lease by reference to a plan, the plan was an integral part of the lease and therefore of the terms of acquisition.

Chapter 31

TERMINATION AND SUSPENSION OF NEW LEASE CLAIM

3.—Collective Enfranchisement Claim

Add to footnote 23: Under s. 54(11)(b)(ii) of the 1993 Act, the contract remains **31–03** in force until it is completed by registration or is discharged.

CHAPTER 32

THE GRANT OF THE NEW LEASE

1.—TERMS OF NEW LEASE

Changes to existing lease

Footnote 44: The appeal in *Cadogan v Chelsea Properties Ltd (No. 2)* was not **32–05**
pursued.

New lease to sub-tenant

Footnote 63: *Nailrile Ltd v Cadogan* is now fully reported at [2009] 2 E.G.L.R. **32–09**
151.

2.—MORTGAGES

Mortgage of landlord's interest

The most recent edition of the Land Registry Practice Guide 27 is dated 20 July **32–10**
2012. It can be found at Appendix 2U of this Supplement and the latest version
can be viewed online at *www.landregistry.gov.uk/professional/guides/practice-guide-27*.

Mortgage of tenant's interest

The most recent edition of the Land Registry Practice Guide 27 is dated 20 July **32–12**
2012. It can be found at Appendix 2U of this Supplement and the latest version
can be viewed online at *www.landregistry.gov.uk/professional/guides/practice-guide-27*.

Costs

In *Fitzgerald v Safflane Ltd* [2010] UKUT 37 (LC); [2010] P.L.S.C.S. 109, it was **32–17**
reaffirmed that the recoverable valuation costs should be based on an hourly rate
and time spent, rather than on a fixed fee agreed with the landlord. *Blendcrown
Ltd v The Church Commissioners for England* [2004] 1 E.G.L.R. 143 was
applied.

In *Dashwood Properties Ltd v Chrisostom-Gooch* [2012] UKUT 215 (LC) it
was held that (i) the value of a dispute and the amount to be gained or lost by a

party is always a matter to be borne in mind in considering whether to incur costs and the level of those costs and (ii) it is not unreasonable for an intermediate landlord to carry out an independent investigation of the tenant's right to a new lease.

Termination of new lease—redevelopment

32–19 Footnote 112: *Cadogan v 2 Herbert Crescent Freehold Ltd* is reported at [2009] P.L.S.C.S. 168. See also *31 Cadogan Square Freehold Limited v Cadogan* [2010] UKUT 321 (LC), where a further argument for reducing the compensation payable was advanced (para. 125), but the same approach was followed (paras 150–151). In *Kutchukian v John Lyon's Charity* [2012] UKUT 53 (LC) where a similar point arose, the Upper Tribunal determined that the landlord for the purposes of s. 61 is the competent landlord. However, it went on to include a 30 per cent deduction for the risk of litigation over that issue. The landlord has obtained permission to appeal to the Court of Appeal on the issue of that deduction.

The amount of compensation

32–22 In *Cadogan v 2 Herbert Crescent Freehold Ltd* [2009] P.L.S.C.S. 168, the proposition in the fourth sentence was argued, but not decided. The risk that the landlord would be regarded as a special purchaser and that the tenant could demand a ransom value was taken into account in assessing the value of the lease of a flat in a collective enfranchisement claim. See also *31 Cadogan Square Freehold Limited v Cadogan* [2010] UKUT 321 (LC), where a further argument for reducing the compensation payable was advanced (paragraph 125), but the same approach was followed (paragraphs 150–151). See also *Kutchukian v John Lyon's Charity* [2012] UKUT 53 (LC) where the Upper Tribunal expressed the view that an underlessee would not be entitled under Schedule 14 to any share of development value.

Footnote 152: *Cadogan v Sportelli* is reported at [2010] 1 A.C. 226.

CHAPTER 33

NEW LEASE—PREMIUM

1.—CALCULATION OF PREMIUM

Diminution in the value of the landlord's interest—assumptions

Footnotes 7, 17 and 18: *Cadogan v Sportelli* is reported at [2010] 1 A.C. 226.   **33–03**
    Footnote 18: "Caldogan" should read "Cadogan"

(i) *Statutory right to remain*

Footnote 21: There is no outstanding appeal relating to 17 Devonshire St.   **33–04**

The rent limit for an assured tenancy in England was increased to £100,000 with effect from October 1, 2010: The Assured Tenancies (Amendment) (England) Order 2010 (SI 2010/908).

On June 14, 2011, the Department for Communities and Local Government issued a Consultation Paper entitled "Leasehold Valuation Limits". One of the issues raised was whether the value limits for long leaseholder security of tenure rights under the Local Government and Housing Act 1989 should be increased to £100,000 (or some other figure) and, if so, whether that increase should apply retrospectively. A summary of the responses to the Consultation was published by DCLG in February 2012. It is understood that the issue is still under consideration although, if there are to be any changes to the limits, they will not come into effect until April 2014 at the earliest.

In *Re Clarise Properties Ltd's Appeal* [2012] UKUT 4 (LC); [2012] L. & T.R. 20, a case under s. 9 of the 1967 Act, the Upper Tribunal held that a deduction of 20 per cent should be made from the eventual reversion because of the risk of an assured tenancy arising under Sch. 10 to the Local Government and Housing Act 1989. That deduction is controversial, not only because it is inconsistent with the deductions made in earlier cases but also because there was no evidence adduced to support it.

Yield rates

A helpful explanation of what is a deferment rate can be found in paragraphs 11   **33–05**
to 16 of the judgment of Mr Justice Morgan in *Carey-Morgan & another v The Trustees of the Sloane Stanley Estate* [2012] EWCA Civ 1181.

In *Sherwood Hall (East End Road) Management Co Ltd v Magnolia Tree Ltd* [2009] UKUT 158 (LC); [2010] 1 E.G.L.R. 181, the Tribunal declined to adjust the five per cent guideline rate in *Cadogan v Sportelli* on the ground that the unexpired term of the flat leases was long, namely 88 years.

In *Culley v Daejan Properties Ltd* [2009] UKUT 168 (LC); [2009] 3 E.G.L.R. 165, the Tribunal applied the five per cent rate in the case of a block of flats in outer London, there being no evidence of higher growth rates in Prime Central London to support a higher deferment rate.

In *Zuckerman v Trustees of the Calthorpe Estates* [2009] UKUT 235 (LC); [2010] 1 E.G.L.R. 187, a deferment rate of six per cent was applied in a number of new lease claims concerning flats in a block in Edgbaston, West Midlands. The additional one per cent was made up of three elements: (i) 0.25 per cent for the greater risk of deterioration and obsolescence of these flats compared to that in the high value period properties in Prime Central London; (ii) 0.5 per cent for the greater risk that the assumed two per cent growth rate would not be achieved when comparing these flats with those in PCL: the Tribunal was presented with detailed comparative evidence of historic growth rates, showing that those in PCL rose considerably more than those in the West Midlands; (iii) 0.25 per cent to reflect the fact that there were greater management risks in relation to flats in the light of increasingly burdensome service charge regulation, in particular the introduction of the Service Charges (Consultation Requirements) (England) Regulations 2003. Had the original headlease been in place, the Tribunal would not have adjusted for this factor.

The same 0.25 per cent adjustment for obsolescence/deterioration was made in *Re Lethaby and Regis's appeal* [2010] UKUT 86 (LC), a missing landlord case concerning two flats in East London. The Tribunal followed *Zuckerman* (above). In the absence of evidence of differing growth rates between East London and PCL, the 0.5 per cent adjustment was not made. The 0.25 per cent flats adjustment was not made, because the repairing obligations for the building were divided between the lessees of the two flats.

In *Ashdown Hove Ltd v Remstar Properties Ltd* [2010] 3 E.G.L.R. 61, the LVT determined a deferment rate of six per cent in respect of a 1970s block of flats in Brighton. The *Zuckerman* case was followed. Even though there was a headlease of the common parts the additional 0.25 per cent for management difficulties was applied. The lessee was a leaseholder-owned management company, and there was evidence that it might fold, due to a history of management problems, leaving the freeholder having to step in.

In *Re Midland Freeholds Ltd's appeal* [2011] UKUT 173 (LC), the Upper Tribunal allowed the landlord's appeal in circumstances where the Leasehold Valuation Tribunal had adjusted the deferment rate to reflect inferior location where neither party had adduced evidence on the issue.

In *City & Country Properties Ltd v Yeats* [2012] UKUT 227 (LC), the Lands Chamber was concerned with a very modest flat in Horsham, West Sussex. The 0.25 per cent adjustment made in *Zuckerman* (above) for the additional risks resulting from service charge regulation was applied. However, the 0.5 per cent addition for the difference in assumed growth rate with PCL was not allowed, because the comparative evidence relating to that location was inadequate. The adopted deferment rate was, therefore, 5.5 per cent.

The Upper Tribunal went on to suggest that the distinction made in *Zuckerman* between a building subject to a headlease and a building in direct management is not so clear cut. The mere existence of a headlease will not in itself be sufficient to justify the conclusion that the extra 0.25 per cent should be omitted from the deferment rate. In effect, the burden of proof has shifted, so that the landlord will need to produce "clear evidence" showing that the purchaser of the freehold reversion would realise, upon the facts of a particular case, that it was extremely improbable that as freeholder it would ever become burdened with any responsibility for management. The existence of the headlease and the nature of such headlease and of the headlessee will be relevant to this. A landlord will now need to show, if he wishes to avoid the *Zuckerman* uplift of 0.25 per cent (in addition to the *Sportelli* uplift of 0.25 per cent), that there is a suitably worded headlease and a suitably solid headlessee coupled with evidence showing that there is no reason to believe that the headlessee would ever fail in its obligations. Even then, that "may" only be sufficient to justify the conclusion that the extra 0.25 per cent should not be added.

In *Tamworth Gardens Properties Ltd v Charles Gallagher Ltd* (unreported, LVT, August 30, 2010) the LVT considered that a deferment rate of 4.75 per cent was correct for four blocks of 30 flats in Farnborough, Hampshire, on the ground that the reversion was without management liability and problems (there being a headlease in place) and was no different to that of a house.

A number of cases where the unexpired term is less than 20 years were determined by the Upper Tribunal (Lands Chamber) in five conjoined appeals in collective enfranchisement claims, *Cadogan Square Properties Ltd v Cadogan* [2010] UKUT 427 (LC); [2011] 1 E.G.L.R. 155. In each case the net rental yield and formula based methods were rejected. The starting point was the *Sportelli* rate of 5 per cent for flats. This was adjusted upwards to 5.25 per cent for 2005 (for terms between 17.3 and 17.8 years) and to 5.5 per cent for 2007 (for terms of 15.6 and 16.1 years). This reflected an adjustment in the real growth rate which would be negotiated between willing seller and willing purchaser. For terms of less than ten years, which were not before the Lands Chamber, different questions could arise, and using a net rental yield would have to be examined in such a case. In the case of a building divided into flats, but with the prospect of reconverting it back into a house, it was appropriate to use the deferment rate for flats rather than houses. This is a guideline case (as was *Sportelli*): see paragraph 195.

In *Trustees of Sloane Stanley Estate v Carey-Morgan* [2011] UKUT 415 (LC), [2012] R.V.R. 92, the building contained 25 flats, of which six had unexpired terms of 4.74 years. The Lands Chamber held that in a case where the unexpired term was less than five years, the net rental yield method should be used to assess the deferment rate (coming to 3.25 per cent), with an end allowance of five per cent. This was said to be the method that should be used in all such cases in the future (paragraph 143). On appeal by the nominee purchaser, the Court of Appeal dismissed the appeal: [2012] EWCA Civ. 1181. The nominee purchaser had sought to argue that the lessees had rights to remain as assured tenants under Schedule 10 of the Local Government and Housing Act 1989. Since this was a new argument, not raised below, and unsupported by evidence, the nominee purchaser was not permitted to run it. The Court of Appeal indicated, however, that in a future case it could be taken account if the evidence warranted it.

Footnote 35: *Cadogan v Sportelli* is reported at [2010] 1 A.C. 226.

Marriage value

33–06 A helpful explanation of what is marriage value can be found in paragraphs 17 and 18 of the judgment of Mr Justice Morgan in *Carey-Morgan & another v The Trustees of the Sloane Stanley Estate* [2012] EWCA Civ 1181.

Footnote 42: *Cadogan v Sportelli* is reported at [2010] 1 A.C. 226.

Relativity

Footnotes 49 and 50: *Nailrile Ltd v Cadogan* is fully reported at [2009] 2 E.G.L.R. 151; [2009] R.V.R. 95.

Footnote 50: Evidence of graphs was also used in *Dependable Homes Ltd v Mann* [2009] UKUT 171 (LC); [2009] P.L.S.C.S. 326. There was no evidence in that case to support the suggestion that relativity depended on location, and the Tribunal relied on the graph of graphs (compiled by Beckett & Kay): para. 40.

In October 2009, the RICS published its report on Graphs of Relativity, in response to the suggestion in *Arrowdell*. The Leasehold Relativities Group, chaired by Jonathan Gaunt QC and comprising eight surveyors, considered all the published graphs but were unable to agree upon definitive graphs to be used as evidence by LVTs, as had been proposed by the Lands Tribunal. The report reproduced all the published graphs together with details of the data that lies behind each.

In *Re Coolrace Ltd* [2012] UKUT 69 (LC); [2012] 24 E.G. 84, the Lands Chamber adopted the Lease graph of relativities, based on Tribunal decisions across the country, in preference to a local West Midlands graph, which had been applied by the LVT. A plea for a further attempt to agree a graph was made.

In *Trustees of Sloane Stanley Estate v Carey-Morgan* [2011] UKUT 415 (LC), [2012] R.V.R. 92, the Lands Chamber assessed the value of short leases with 4.74 years unexpired by capitalising the unimproved rental value to the end of the term. This was appropriate for such a short lease, instead of using graphs of relativity.

In *Earl Cadogan v Cadogan Square Ltd* [2011] UKUT 154 (LC); [2011] 3 E.G.L.R. 127, the Upper Tribunal was faced with the difficulty of conflicting evidence as between evidence of adjusted transactions (producing a relativity of 53 to 56 per cent) and evidence from graphs (producing a relativity of 38 per cent). An analysis of the evidence from the Savills 2002 enfranchisable graph as against the Gerald Eve non-enfranchisable graph suggested that the adjustment of 10 per cent made by the nominee purchaser to adjust the transactional evidence to reflect 1993 Act rights was too low and the Tribunal decided that a deduction of 25 per cent was appropriate. The unexpired terms in that case were 17.75 years.

Additional compensation
Footnotes 64 and 65: *Nailrile Ltd v Cadogan* is fully reported at [2009] 2 **33–09**
E.G.L.R. 151; [2009] R.V.R. 95. The case was resolved by agreement before a
decision was given in respect of the additional compensation claim.

Intermediate leases
Footnotes 77, 79 and 85: *Nailrile Ltd v Cadogan* is fully reported at [2009] 2 **33–10**
E.G.L.R. 151; [2009] R.V.R. 95. It is a final decision.
    Paragraph (a)—the word "required" is misspelt
    Paragraph (b)—the word "component" is misspelt
    Paragraph (j)—the word "Neither" is misspelt
    Paragraph (n)—the word "bit" should read "but"

Example 1
At the bottom of p. 590, the *Total* should be 10,893, *Say* 10,900, not 16,297, *Say* **33–11**
16,300.

CHAPTER 34

MISCELLANEOUS

1.—MISSING LANDLORD—COLLECTIVE ENFRANCHISEMENT

See 34–08 below.   **34–01**

2.—MISSING LANDLORD—NEW LEASE

The missing landlord procedure under section 50 of the 1993 Act cannot be used   **34–08**
where the landlord is dead, simply because probate of his will has not been
granted. In such a case, section 18 of the Law of Property (Miscellaneous
Provisions) Act 1994 applies, which is referred to in paragraph 34–17 below:
Power v Stanton [2010] 3 E.G.L.R. 71, Central London County Court, Judge
Dight. Where the deceased leaves a will, the property of the deceased vests in the
executor from the moment of the testator's death: *Whitmore v Lambert* [1955] 2
All E.R. 147 applied.

4.—OTHER MATTERS

Notices
Add to end of first paragraph: In *Calladine-Smith v Saveorder Ltd* [2011] EWHC   **34–16**
2501 (Ch), [2012] L. & T.R. 3, a landlord sent a counter-notice under section 45
of the 1993 Act by post. It was placed in an envelope, correctly addressed,
prepaid and posted. However, it was not received by the tenant. It was held that
the tenant had established that the "contrary" had been provided, under section
7 of the Interpretation Act 1978, and the counter-notice had not, therefore, been
deemed served. The consequence was that the tenant was entitled to a new lease
on the terms proposed in the section 42 notice. The decision is a cautionary tale
for landlords who use ordinary post for serving counter-notices, particularly if
they are served at the last minute, whereby there is no opportunity to confirm
receipt before the deadline arrives.

Localism Act 2011

34–19   Schedule 11 to the Localism Act 2011 adds a new Schedule 4C to the Town and Country Planning Act 1990. Paragraph 11 of that Schedule provides for regulations to make provision for securing that in prescribed circumstances (a) an enfranchisement right (which includes the right of collective enfranchisement under Chapter 1 of Part 1 of the 1993 Act) is not exercisable in relation to land the development of which is authorised by a community right to build order; or (b) the exercise of an enfranchisement right in relation to that land is subject to modifications provided for by the regulations. A community right to build order is defined in paragraph 2 of Schedule 4C.

The relevant regulations have been made under Part 7 of The Neighbourhood Planning (General) Regulations 2012. (SI 2012 No. 637).

Regulation 28 provides

"(1) Subject to paragraph (2), for the purposes of paragraph 11 of Schedule 4C to the 1990 Act, a community organisation may only provide that an enfranchisement right is not exercisable in relation to a property which is not an existing residential property.

(2) An enfranchisement right is not exercisable in relation to land the development of which is authorised by a community right to build order if the community organisation specified in the order proposal—

    (a)   the enfranchisement rights which are not exercisable; and

    (b)   the properties, or types of properties, in relation to which those rights are not exercisable.

(3) In this regulation—

    "existing residential property" means a property (including part of a building)—

        (a)   which exists on the date the order proposal was submitted by the community organisation to the local planning authority under regulation 22; and

        (b)   in relation to which, on that date, any tenant of the property has an enfranchisement right in respect of the property."

CHAPTER 35

MANAGEMENT SCHEMES

3.—1993 ACT SCHEMES

Obligatory contents of a scheme

(3) Transfer of powers of landlord
There is no jurisdiction to impose on the landlord an obligation to enforce the **35–22**
scheme by taking action against owners who might be in breach of obligations
under it: *Donath v Trustees of 2nd Duke of Westminster Will Trust* [2010] 2
E.G.L.R. 89, LVT.

Variation of existing schemes

There is no jurisdiction to impose on the landlord an obligation to enforce the **35–42**
scheme by taking action against owners who might be in breach of obligations
under it. An application by the owner of an enfranchised house to vary the
Grosvenor Belgravia Scheme to include such an obligation was dismissed:
Donath v Trustees of 2nd Duke of Westminster Will Trust [2010] 2 E.G.L.R. 89,
LVT.

PRECEDENTS

PRECEDENT E16

Leasehold Reform, Housing and Urban Development Act 1993 Section 21

Counter-notice admitting claim

Add after 7 (and re-number 8 and 9):   **698**

8. The reversioner [or any other relevant landlord] considers that the following provisions should be included in the transfer to the nominee purchaser in accordance with section 34 and Schedule 7: [set out]

PRECEDENT F15E

Declaration as to redevelopment

Replace (a) with "at any time during the period of twelve months ending on   **719** [term date of original lease]".

APPENDICES

Contents

Add the following listings:

Statutory Instruments

Update:

STATUTES

APPENDIX 1A

Leasehold Reform Act 1967

Tenants entitled to enfranchisement or extension.

Replace section 1(1) with the following text: **725–729**

(1) This Part of this Act shall have effect to confer on a tenant of a leasehold house [. . .]¹ a right to acquire on fair terms the freehold or an extended lease of the house and premises where—

[(a) his tenancy is a long tenancy [...]¹ᴬ and,—

  (i) if the tenancy was entered into before 1st April 1990 [, or on or after 1st April 1990 in pursuance of a contract made before that date, and the house and premises had a rateable value at the date of commencement of the tenancy or else at any time before 1st April 1990,]² subject to subsections (5) and (6) below, the rateable value of the house and premises on the appropriate day was not more than £200 or, if it is in Greater London, than £400; and

  (ii) if the tenancy [does not fall within sub-paragraph (i) above,]³ on the date the contract for the grant of the tenancy was made or, if there was no such contract, on the date the tenancy was entered into R did not exceed £25,000 under the formula—

$$R = \frac{P \times I}{1 - (1 + I)^{-T}}$$

where—

P is the premium payable as a condition of the grant of the tenancy (and includes a payment of money's worth) or, where no premium is so payable, zero,

I is 0.06, and

T is the term, expressed in years, granted by the tenancy (disregarding any right to terminate the tenancy before the end of the term or to extend the tenancy);]⁴ and

[(aa) in the case of a right to acquire an extended lease, his long tenancy is a tenancy at a low rent;]⁴ᴬ and

(b) at the relevant time (that is to say, at the time when he gives notice in accordance with this Act of his desire to have the freehold or to have an extended lease, as the case may be) he has

  [(i) in the case of a right to acquire the freehold, been tenant of the house under a long tenancy for the last two years; and

  (ii) in the case of a right to acquire an extended lease,] been tenant of the house under a long tenancy at a low rent for the last [two years];⁵

and to confer the like right in the other cases for which provision is made in this Part of this Act.

Add new Footnote 1A: Words in s. 1(1)(a) were omitted by the Housing and Regeneration Act 2008 c. 17, s. 300 as from September 7, 2009.
Add new Footnote 4A: S. 1(1)(aa) was inserted by the Housing and Regeneration Act 2008 c. 17, s. 300 as from September 7, 2009.
Add to the end of Footnote 5: S. 1(1)(b) was amended by the Housing and Regeneration Act 2008 c. 17, s. 300 as from September 7, 2009.

Replace section 1(1A) with the following:

  [(1A) The references in subsection (1)[...]⁸ᴬ to a long tenancy [...]⁸ᴬ do not include a tenancy excluded from the operation of this Part by section 33A of and Schedule 4A to this Act]

Add new Footnote 8A: words omitted by the Housing and Regeneration Act 2008 c. 17, s.300(2)(a) for leases granted since September 7, 2009.

Replace section 1(3A) with the following:

(3A) For the purposes of subsection (3) above this subsection applies as follows—

(a) where the tenancy was created after the commencement of Chapter III of Part I of the Leasehold Reform, Housing and Urban Development Act 1993, this subsection applies to any right to acquire the freehold of the house and premises; but

(b) where the tenancy was created before that commencement, this subsection applies only to any such right exercisable by virtue of any one or more of the provisions of sections 1A, 1AA and 1B below;

and in that subsection "charitable housing trust" means a housing trust within the meaning of the Housing Act 1985 which is a charity [...][11A].

Add new Footnote 8A: words omitted by SI 2011/1396, Sch. as from March 14, 2012.

Add at the end of Section 1: In the case of a lease granted since September 7, 2009, s. 1 of the Leasehold Reform Act is as follows:

1.—Tenants entitled to enfranchisement or extension.

(1) This Part of this Act shall have effect to confer on a tenant of a leasehold house a right to acquire on fair terms the freehold or an extended lease of the house and premises where—

(a) his tenancy is a long tenancy and,—

(i) if the tenancy was entered into before 1st April 1990, or on or after 1st April 1990 in pursuance of a contract made before that date, and the house and premises had a rateable value at the date of commencement of the tenancy or else at any time before 1st April 1990, subject to subsections (5) and (6) below, the rateable value of the house and premises on the appropriate day was not more than £200 or, if it is in Greater London, than £400; and

(ii) if the tenancy does not fall within sub-paragraph (i) above, on the date the contract for the grant of the tenancy was made or, if there was no such contract, on the date the tenancy was entered into R did not exceed £25,000 under the formula—

$$R = \frac{P \times I}{1 - (1 + I)^{-T}}$$

where—

P is the premium payable as a condition of the grant of the tenancy (and includes a payment of money's worth) or, where no premium is so payable, zero,

I is 0.06, and

T is the term, expressed in years, granted by the tenancy (disregarding any right to terminate the tenancy before the end of the term or to extend the tenancy); and

(aa) in the case of a right to acquire an extended lease, his long tenancy is a tenancy at a low rent; and

(b) at the relevant time (that is to say, at the time when he gives notice in accordance with this Act of his desire to have the freehold or to have an extended lease, as the case may be) he has—

 (i) in the case of a right to acquire the freehold, been tenant of the house under a long tenancy for the last two years; and

 (ii) in the case of a right to acquire an extended lease, been tenant of the house under a long tenancy at a low rent for the last two years;

and to confer the like right in the other cases for which provision is made in this Part of this Act.

(1ZA) Where a house is for the time being let under two or more tenancies, a tenant under any of those tenancies which is superior to that held by any tenant on whom this Part of this Act confers a right does not have any right under this Part of this Act.

(1ZB) Where a flat forming part of a house is let to a person who is a qualifying tenant of the flat for the purposes of Chapter 1 or 2 of Part 1 of the Leasehold Reform, Housing and Urban Development Act 1993 (c. 28), a tenant of the house does not have any right under this Part of this Act unless, at the relevant time, he has been occupying the house, or any part of it, as his only or main residence (whether or not he has been using it for other purposes)—

(a) for the last two years; or

(b) for periods amounting to two years in the last ten years.

(1ZC) The references in subsection (1)(a) and (b) to a long tenancy do not include a tenancy to which Part 2 of the Landlord and Tenant Act 1954 (business tenancies) applies unless—

(a) it is granted for a term of years certain exceeding thirty-five years, whether or not it is (or may become) terminable before the end of that term by notice given by or to the tenant or by re-entry, forfeiture or otherwise,

(b) it is for a term fixed by law under a grant with a covenant or obligation for perpetual renewal, unless it is a tenancy by sub-demise from one which is not a tenancy which falls within any of the paragraphs in this subsection,

(c) it is a tenancy taking effect under section 149(6) of the Law of Property Act 1925 (c. 20) (leases terminable after a death or marriage or the formation of a civil partnership), or

(d) it is a tenancy which—

(i) is or has been granted for a term of years certain not exceeding thirty-five years, but with a covenant or obligation for renewal without payment of a premium (but not for perpetual renewal), and

(ii) is or has been once or more renewed so as to bring to more than thirty-five years the total of the terms granted (including any interval between the end of a tenancy and the grant of a renewal).

(1ZD) Where this Part of this Act applies as if there were a single tenancy of property comprised in two or more separate tenancies, then, if each of the separate tenancies falls within any of the paragraphs of subsection (1ZC) above, that subsection shall apply as if the single tenancy did so.

(1A) The references in subsection (1) to a long tenancy do not include a tenancy excluded from the operation of this Part by section 33A of and Schedule 4A to this Act.

(1B) This Part of this Act shall not have effect to confer any right on the tenant of a house under a tenancy to which Part 2 of the Landlord and Tenant Act 1954 (c. 56) (business tenancies) applies unless, at the relevant time, the tenant has been occupying the house, or any part of it, as his only or main residence (whether or not he has been using it for other purposes)—

(a) for the last two years; or
(b) for periods amounting to two years in the last ten years.

(2) [...]

(3) This Part of this Act shall not confer on the tenant of a house any right by reference to his being a tenant of it at any time when—

(a) it is let to him with other land or premises to which it is ancillary; or
(b) it is comprised in—
  (i) an agricultural holding within the meaning of the Agricultural Holdings Act 1986 held under a tenancy in relation to which that Act applies, or
  (ii) the holding held under a farm business tenancy within the meaning of the Agricultural Tenancies Act 1995.

or, in the case of any right to which subsection (3A) below applies, at any time when the tenant's immediate landlord is a charitable housing trust and the house forms part of the housing accommodation provided by the trust in the pursuit of its charitable purposes.

(3A) For the purposes of subsection (3) above this subsection applies as follows—

(a) where the tenancy was created after the commencement of Chapter III of Part I of the Leasehold Reform, Housing and Urban Development Act 1993, this subsection applies to any right to acquire the freehold of the house and premises; but

(b) where the tenancy was created before that commencement, this subsection applies only to any such right exercisable by virtue of any one or more of the provisions of sections 1A, 1AA and 1B below;

and in that subsection "charitable housing trust" means a housing trust within the meaning of the Housing Act 1985 which is a charity [...].

(4) In subsection (1)(a) above, "the appropriate day", in relation to any house and premises, means the 23rd March 1965 or such later day as by virtue of section 25(3) of the Rent Act 1977 would be the appropriate day for purposes of that Act in relation to a dwelling house consisting of that house.

(4A) Schedule 8 to the Housing Act 1974 shall have effect to enable a tenant to have the rateable value of the house and premises reduced for purposes of this section in consequence of tenant's improvements.

(5) If, in relation to any house and premises, the appropriate day for the purposes of subsection (1)(a) above falls on or after 1st April 1973 that subsection shall have effect in relation to the house and premises,—

(a) in a case where the tenancy was created on or before 18th February 1966, as if for the sums of £200 and £400 specified in that subsection there were substituted respectively the sums of £750 and £1,500; and

(b) in a case where the tenancy was created after 18th February 1966, as if for those sums of £200 and £400 there were substituted respectively the sums of £500 and £1,000.

(6) If, in relation to any house and premises,—

(a) the appropriate day for the purposes of subsection (1)(a) above falls before 1st April 1973, and

(b) the rateable value of the house and premises on the appropriate day was more than £200 or, if it was then in Greater London, £400, and

(c) the tenancy was created on or before 18th February 1966,

subsection (1)(a) above shall have effect in relation to the house and premises as if for the reference to the appropriate day there were substituted a reference to 1st April 1973 and as if for the sums of £200 and £400 specified in that subsection there were substituted respectively the sums of £750 and £1,500.

(7) The Secretary of State may by order replace the amount referred to in subsection (1)(a)(ii) above and the number in the definition of "I" in that subsection by such amount or number as is specified in the order; and such an order shall be made by statutory instrument which shall be subject to annulment in pursuance of a resolution of either House of Parliament.

[1A.—Right to enfranchisement only in cases of houses whose value or rent exceeds limit under s.1 or 4.

729   Add to footnote 18: In the case of a lease granted since September 7, 2009, ss. 1A(2) is repealed by the Housing and Regeneration Act 2008, s.300(2)(b).

[1AA.—Additional right to enfranchisement only in cases of houses whose value or rent exceeds applicable limit under section 4.]

Add to Footnote 21: In the case of a lease granted since September 7, 2009, ss. 1AA is repealed by the Housing and Regeneration Act 2008, s.300(2)(b).   **729**

[4A.—Alternative rent limits for purposes of section 1A(2)].

Add to Footnote 42: In the case of a lease granted since September 7, 2009, s. 4A is repealed by the Housing and Regeneration Act 2008, s.300(2)(b).   **736**

9.—Purchase price and costs of enfranchisement, and tenant's right to withdraw.

Add to Footnote 68: In the case of a lease granted since September 7, 2009, in s. 9(1C) ", 1AA" is repealed by the Housing and Regeneration Act 2008, Sch.16.   **745**

[9A.—Compensation payable in cases where right to enfranchisement arises by virtue of section 1A or 1B].

Add to Footnote 75: In the case of a lease granted since 7 September 2009, in s. 9A(1) "or 1AA" is repealed by the Housing and Regeneration Act 2008, Sch.16.   **747**

11.—Exoneration from, or redemption of, rentcharges etc.

The heading at the top of the page should read: LEASEHOLD REFORM ACT 1967, S. 11   **751**

18.—Residential rights (exclusion of enfranchisement or extension).

The heading at the top of the page should read: LEASEHOLD REFORM ACT 1967, S. 18   **763**

20.—Jurisdiction and special powers of county court.

Replace subsections (4) and (4A) with the following: **768**

(4) Where it is made to appear to the court that the landlord or the tenant has been guilty of any unreasonable delay or default in the performance of obligations arising from a tenant's notice of his desire to have the freehold or an extended lease under this Part of this Act, then (without prejudice to any right to damages) the court may—

    (a) by order revoke or vary, and direct repayment of sums paid under, any provision made by a previous order as to payment of the costs of proceedings in the court in relation to the matter, or, where costs have not been awarded, award costs;

    (b) certify particulars of the delay or default to the [Upper Tribunal][98A] with a view to enabling the Tribunal to exercise a like discretion in relation to costs of proceedings before the Tribunal.

[(4A)Where the court certifies particulars of delay or default to the [Upper Tribunal][98A] under subsection (4)(b) above, the [Upper Tribunal][98A] may make any order as to costs of proceedings before the [Upper Tribunal][98A] which the court may make in relation to proceedings in the court.][99]

Add new Footnote 98A: Words substituted by SI 2009/1307, art. 5(1), (2), Sch. 1, para 83, with effect from June 1, 2009.

21.—Jurisdiction of Lands Tribunal.

Replace the heading to s. 21 with the following text: **769**

21.—Jurisdiction of leasehold valuation tribunals.[99A]

Add new Footnote 99A: Heading substituted by SI 2009/1307, art. 5(1), (2), Sch. 1, para 84, with effect from June 1, 2009.

23.—Agreements excluding or modifying the rights of tenant

772   In section 23(4), replace "section 36 of the Charities Act 1993" with "sections 117 to 121 of the Charities Act 2011". Words substituted by the Charities Act 2011 (c. 25), Sch. 7, Pt 2, para. 15, with effect from March 14, 2012.

28.—Retention or resumption of land required for public purposes.

780–783   Replace section 28(5)(a) with the following:

> [(a) to any local authority, that is to say, the Mayor and commonalty [. . .][122] citizens of the City of London, [. . .][123] any county council, borough council or district council, [[. . .][124] any joint authority established by Part IV of the Local Government Act 1985[, [any economic prosperity board established under section 88 of the Local Democracy, Economic Development and Construction Act 2009, any combined authority established under section 103 of that Act][124A] [, any authority established for an area in England by an order under section 207 of the Local Government and Public Involvement in Health Act 2007 (joint waste authorities),][125] the London Fire and Emergency Planning Authority][126],][127] any joint board in which all the constituent authorities are local authorities within this paragraph [. . .][128] [any police authority established under [section 3 of the Police Act 1996][129] [and the [Mayor's Office for Policing and Crime][129A][130] and][131;][132]

Add new Footnote 124A: Words added by the Local Democracy, Economic Development and Construction Act 2009, s. 119, Sch. 6, para. 5, with effect from December 17, 2009.
Add new footnote 129A: Words substituted by the Police Reform and Social Responsibility Act 2011. Sch.16, Pt 3, para.85, with effect from January 16, 2012.

Replace section 28(5)(d) with the following:

> [(d) to [the National Health Service Commissioning Board, any clinical commissioning group,][138A] [. . .][139] any [[Local Health Board][140], any Special Health Authority][141][. . .][142[, any National Health Service trust and any NHS foundation trust][143; and][144

Add new footnote 138A: Words inserted by the Health and Social Care Act 2012. Sch. 5, Pt 1, para. 10, with effect from October 1, 2012.
Add to footnote 139: Words subsequently omitted by the Health and Social Care Act 2012. Sch. 5, Pt 1, para. 10, with effect from October 1, 2012.
Add to footnote 142: Words subsequently omitted by the Health and Social Care Act 2012. Sch. 5, Pt 1, para. 10, with effect from October 1, 2012.

In section 28(6), omit the second paragraph (a) (which appears after "However—").

Paragraph omitted by the Police Reform and Social Responsibility Act 2011. Sch.16, Pt 3, para.85, with effect from January 16, 2012.

Replace section 28(6)(c) with the following:

> [(c) in the case of [the National Health Service Commissioning Board, a clinical commissioning group,][150A] [...][151] [[Local Health Board][140], Special Health Authority][152][...][153][, National Health Service trust or NHS foundation trust][154], the purposes of [the National Health Service Act 2006 or the National Health Service (Wales) Act 2006][155] shall be substituted for the purposes of the body.][156]

Add new footnote 150A: Words inserted by the Health and Social Care Act 2012. Sch. 5, Pt 1, para. 10, with effect from October 1, 2012.

Add to footnote 151: Words subsequently omitted by the Health and Social Care Act 2012. Sch. 5, Pt 1, para. 10, with effect from October 1, 2012.

Add to footnote 153: Words subsequently omitted by the Health and Social Care Act 2012. Sch. 5, Pt 1, para. 10, with effect from October 1, 2012.

31.—Ecclesiastical property.

Replace section 31(2)(a) with the following text: **786**

> (a) the provisions to be contained in a conveyance in accordance with section 10 above, or in a lease granting a new tenancy under section 14, and the price or rent payable, except as regards matters determined by the court [a leasehold valuation tribunal][174] or the [Upper Tribunal][174A];

Add new Footnote 174A: Words substituted by SI 2009/1307, art. 5(1), (2), Sch. 1, para 85, with effect from June 1, 2009.

Replace subsection 31(4)(a) with the following text:

> (a) no consent or concurrence other than that of the Church Commissioners under subsection (2) above shall be required to a disposition under this Part of this Act of the [interest of the diocesan board of finance][177] (including a grant of a tenancy in satisfaction of the right to an extended lease);

[32A.—Property transferred for public benefit etc.

Add to footnote 183: In the case of a lease granted since September 7, 2009, in s. 32A(1)(b) the words   **788**
"or if section 1AA above were not in force" are repealed by the Housing and Regeneration Act 2008, Sch.16.

37.—Interpretation of Part 1.

Replace section 37(1)(ba)(i) with the following: **792**

> (i) in relation to England, the Homes and Communities Agency so far as exercising functions in relation to anything transferred (or to be transferred) to it as mentioned in section 52(1)(a) to (d) of the Housing and Regeneration Act 2008[or the Greater London Authority so far as exercising its new towns and urban development functions][188A]; and

Add new footnote 188A: Words inserted by the Localism Act 2011, Sch. 19, para. 2, with effect from April 1, 2012.

SCHEDULE 2

PROVISIONS SUPPLEMENTARY TO SECTIONS 17 AND 18 OF THIS ACT

802   Replace Schedule 2 paragraph 8 with the following:

8.—(1) Where a landlord makes an application for possession, and it is made to appear to the court that in relation to matters arising out of that application (including the giving up of possession of the house and premises or the payment of compensation) the landlord or the tenant has been guilty of any unreasonable delay or default, the court may—

(a) by order revoke or vary, and direct repayment of sums paid under, any provision made by a previous order as to payment of the costs of proceedings taken in the court on or with reference to the application, or, where costs have not been awarded, award costs;
(b) certify particulars of the delay or default to the [Upper Tribunal][222A] with a view to enabling the Tribunal to exercise a like discretion in relation to costs of proceedings before the Tribunal.

[(1A) Where the court certifies particulars of delay or default to the [Upper Tribunal][222A] under sub-paragraph (1)(b) above, the [Upper Tribunal][222A] may make any order as to costs of proceedings before the [Upper Tribunal][222A] which the court may make in relation to proceedings in the court.][223]

(2) [...][224]

(3) Where an application for possession is dismissed or withdrawn, and it is made to appear to the court—

(a) that the application was not made in good faith; or
(b) that the landlord had attempted in any material respect to support by misrepresentation or the concealment of material facts a request to the tenant to deliver up possession without an application for possession; the court may order that no further application for possession of the house and premises made by the landlord shall be entertained if it is made within the five years beginning with the date of the order. [...][223]

Add new Footnote 222A: Words substituted by SI 2009/1307, art. 5(1), (2), Sch. 1, para 86, with effect from June 1, 2009.

SCHEDULE 3

VALIDITY OF TENANTS' NOTICES, EFFECT ON LANDLORD AND TENANT ACT 1954 ETC. AND PROCEDURE GENERALLY

805   Add to Footnote 238: In the case of a lease granted since 7 September 2009, Sch.3 para.6(1A) is repealed by the Housing and Regeneration Act 2008 c. 17, Sch.16.

[SCHEDULE 4A

EXCLUSION OF CERTAIN SHARED OWNERSHIP LEASES]

811–814   Replace Schedule 4A, paragraphs 1 and 2 with the following text:

[Leases granted in pursuance of right to be granted a shared ownership lease]

1. A lease granted in pursuance of the right to be granted a shared ownership lease under Part V of the Housing Act 1985 is excluded from the operation of this Part of this Act.

Certain leases granted by certain public authorities

2.—(1) A lease which—

(a) was granted at a premium by a body mentioned in sub-paragraph (2), and

(b) complies with the conditions set out in sub-paragraph (3), is excluded from the operation of this Part at any time when the interest of the landlord belongs to such a body [relevant housing provider][262] [or to a person who acquired that interest in exercise of the right conferred by Part IV of the Housing Act 1988][264].

(2) The bodies are—

(a) a county, [county borough,][265] district or London borough council, the Common Council of the City of London or the Council of the Isles of Scilly;

(b) ... [266] a joint authority established by Part IV of the Local Government Act 1985;

[(bb) the London Fire and Emergency Planning Authority;][267]

[(bc) a Mayoral development corporation;][267A]

(c) the [new towns residuary body][268] or a development corporation established by an order made, or having effect as made, under the New Towns Act 1981;

(d) an urban development corporation within the meaning of Part XVI of the Local Government, Planning and Land Act 1980;

(e) [...][269]

[(f) a housing action trust established under Part III of the Housing Act 1988][270]

(3) The conditions are that the lease—

(a) provides for the tenant to acquire the freehold for a consideration which is to be calculated in accordance with the lease and which is reasonable, having regard to the premium or premiums paid by the tenant under the lease, and

(b) states the landlord's opinion that by virtue of this paragraph the tenancy will be excluded from the operation of this Part of this Act at any time when the interest of the landlord belongs to a body mentioned in sub-paragraph (2) above [or to a relevant housing provider][262].

(4) If, in proceedings in which it falls to be determined whether a lease complies with the condition in sub-paragraph (3)(a), the question arises whether the consideration payable by the tenant on acquiring the freehold is reasonable, it is for the landlord to show that it is. [...][263]

[(5) In this paragraph "relevant housing provider" means—

(a) in relation to a lease of social housing within the meaning of Part 2 of the Housing and Regeneration Act 2008, a private registered provider of social housing, or

(b) a registered social landlord within the meaning of Part 1 of the Housing Act 1996.][262]

Delete Footnotes 260–261 and 271.
Replace Footnote 262 with the following: Amendments made by the Housing and Regeneration Act 2008 (September 7, 2009 (SI 2009/2096)).
Add new footnote 267A: Inserted by the Localism Act 2011, Sch. 22, para. 1, with effect from January 15, 2012.

Replace paragraph 4 with the following text:

[Certain leases for the elderly.][279]

[**4.**—(1)A lease for the elderly granted by [a relevant housing provider][280A] and which complies with the conditions set out in sub-paragraph (2) is excluded from the operation of this Part of this Act at any time when the interest of the landlord belongs to [a relevant housing provider][280A].

(2) The conditions are that the lease—

- (a) is granted at a premium which is calculated by reference to a percentage of the value of the house or of the cost of providing it,
- (b) complies, at the time when it is granted, with such requirements as may be prescribed, and
- (c) states the landlord's opinion that by virtue of this paragraph the lease will be excluded from the operation of this Part of this Act at any time when the interest of the landlord belongs to [a relevant housing provider][280A].

(3) In this paragraph—

"lease for the elderly" has such meaning as may be prescribed; and

["relevant housing provider" means—

- (a) in relation to a lease of social housing within the meaning of Part 2 of the Housing and Regeneration Act 2008, a private registered provider of social housing, or
- (b) a registered social landlord within the meaning of Part 1 of the Housing Act 1996][280A].][280]

Add Footnote 280A: Amendments made by SI 2010/866, Sch. 2, para. 2 with effect from April 1, 2010.

In Footnotes 282–291 insert the words September 7, 2009 in place of not yet in force otherwise.

APPENDIX 1B

Housing Act 1974

SCHEDULE 8

REDUCTION OF RATEABLE VALUE IN CASE OF CERTAIN IMPROVEMENTS

Replace paragraph 2(2)(d) with the following: **818**

(d) what proportion his contribution, if any, bears to the whole cost;

the county court may on the application of the tenant determine that matter [. . .]²

Replace paragraphs 2 and 3 of the Form with the following text:

2 It has been [agreed in writing between me and my landlord] [determined by the **819** county court] that the improvement[s] specified in the First Schedule hereto [is an improvement] [are improvements] to which [Schedule 8 to the Housing Act 1974] applies, and that I or a previous tenant under the tenancy made the improvement[s] or contributed to [its] [their] cost, and that the works specified in the Second Schedule hereto were involved in the improvement[s].

3 It has not been agreed between me and my landlord whether any or what reduction is to be made under said Schedule [8] in the rateable value of the premises for the purposes of the Leasehold Reform Act 1967, and I hereby make application to you for a certificate under paragraph 3(2) of the said Schedule [8] (Note 4).

APPENDIX 1F

Housing and Planning Act 1986

SCHEDULE 4

FURTHER PROVISIONS WITH RESPECT TO SHARED OWNERSHIP LEASES

826   Please note: in Schedule 4A (Exclusion of certain shared ownership leases) the heading to para.2 "Certain leases granted by certain public authorities" should be centred in italics and not in bold

At the end of para.2 insert heading to para.3—*"Certain leases granted by housing associations"*

APPENDIX 1G

Leasehold Reform, Housing and Urban Development Act 1993

1.—The right to collective enfranchisement.
The heading at top of the page should read: LEASEHOLD REFORM ETC. ACT   **829**
1993, s. 1

[4A RTE Companies]
Replace section 4A with the following text: **834**
    (1) A company is a RTE company in relation to premises if—

    (a) it is a private company limited by guarantee, and
    (b) its [articles of association state][11A] of association states that its object, or one of its objects, is the exercise of the right to collective enfranchisement with respect to the premises.

    (2) But a company is not a RTE company if it is a commonhold association (within the meaning of Part 1 of the Commonhold and Leasehold Reform Act 2002).
    (3) And a company is not a RTE company in relation to premises if another company which is a RTE company in relation to—

    (a) the premises, or
    (b) any premises containing or contained in the premises,

has given a notice under section 13 with respect to the premises, or any premises containing or contained in the premises, and the notice continues in force in accordance with subsection (11) of that section][12]

Add new Footnote 11A: Words substituted by the Companies Act 2006 (Consequential Amendments, Transistional Provisions and Savings) Order (SI 2009/1941, Sch. 1 para. 140, October 1, 2009).

[4C RTE companies: regulations
Replace section 4(C) with the following text: **836**
    (1) The Secretary of State shall by regulations make provision about the content and form of the memorandum of association and articles of association of RTE companies.
    (2) A RTE company may adopt provisions of the regulations for its [articles][13A].
    (3) The regulations may include provision which is to have effect for a RTE company whether or not it is adopted by the company.
    (4) A provision of the [articles][13A] of a RTE company has no effect to the extent that it is inconsistent with the regulations.
    (5) The regulations have effect in relation to [articles][13A]—

(a) irrespective of the date of [the articles][13A], but

(b) subject to any transitional provisions of the regulations.

(6) [Section 20 of the Companies Act 2006 (default application of model articles) does not apply to a RTE company][11A].][14]

Add new Footnote 13A: Words substituted by the Companies Act 2006 (Consequential Amendments, Transistional Provisions and Savings) Order(SI 2009/1941, Sch.1 para.140, October 1, 2009).

5.—Qualifying tenants.

836 In section 5(2) omit the words "within the meaning of the Charities Act 1993".

Words omitted by SI 2011/1396, Sch. 1, Pt 4, para. 37, with effect from March 14, 2012.

837 Replace subsection (6) with the following text:

(6) For the purposes of subsection (5) in its application to a body corporate any flat let to an associated company (whether alone or jointly with any other person or persons) shall be treated as if it were so let to that body; and for this purpose "associated company" means another body corporate which is (within the meaning of [section 1159 of the Companies Act 2006][15A]) that body's holding company, a subsidiary of that body or another subsidiary of that body's holding company. [...][15]

Insert Footnote 15A: Words substituted by the Companies Act 2006 (Consequential Amendments, Transistional Provisions and Savings) Order(SI 2009/1941, Sch.1 para.140, October 1, 2009).

9.—The reversioner and other relevant landlords for the purposes of this Chapter.

840 Replace section 9(2)(b) with the following text:

(2) (b) the person who owns the freehold of the premises [every person who owns any freehold interest which it is proposed to acquire by virtue of section 1(2)(a),][27] and every person who owns any leasehold interest which it is proposed to acquire under or by virtue of section 2(1)(a) or (b), shall be a relevant landlord for those purposes.

846 **13.—Notice by qualifying tenants of claim to exercise right.**

In s. 13(2)(a)(ii) replace "section 9(2)" with "section 9(2A)".

93.—Agreements excluding or modifying rights of tenant under Chapter I or II.

929 Replace section 93(6) with the following:

[(6) The provisions referred to in subsection (5) are—

(a) [sections 117 to 121 of the Charities Act 2011][107A] (restrictions on disposition of charity land); and

(b) paragraph 8(2)(c) of Schedule 2 to this Act.]

Add new footnote 107A: Words substituted by the Charities Act 2011, Sch. 7, Pt 2, para. 67, with effect from March 14, 2012.

SCHEDULE 6

PURCHASE PRICE PAYABLE BY NOMINEE PURCHASER

Replace para. 3(2) of Sch. 6 with the following text: **954**

(2) It is hereby declared that the fact that sub-paragraph (1) requires assumptions to be made as to the matters specified in paragraphs (a) to (d) of that sub-paragraph does not preclude the making of assumptions as to other matters where those assumptions are appropriate for determining the amount which at [the relevant date][193] the freeholder's interest in the specified premises might be expected to realise if sold as mentioned in that sub-paragraph.

In para. 3(4), omit "the" before [the relevant date]

SCHEDULE 10

ACQUISTION OF INTERESTS FROM LOCAL AUTHORITIES ETC.

Replace para.1(2)(b) with the following text: **973**

[(b) sections 148 and 172 of the Housing and Regeneration Act 2008 (disposals by registered providers of social housing);

(ba) sections 9 and 42 of the Housing Act 1996 (disposals by registered social landlords);

(bb) section 9 of the Housing Associations Act 1985 (disposals by unregistered housing associations);][240]

Replace Footnote 240 with the following: Substituted by SI 2010/866, Sch.2 para.79 (April 1, 2010).

APPENDIX 1H

Commonhold and Leasehold Reform Act 2002

175 Appeals

994–995 Replace section 175 with the following text:

(1) A party to proceedings before a leasehold valuation tribunal may appeal to the [Upper Tribunal][1] from a decision of the leasehold valuation tribunal.

(2) But the appeal may be made only with the permission of—

(a) the leasehold valuation tribunal, or

(b) the [Upper Tribunal][1].

(3) [. . .][1]

(4) On the appeal the [Upper Tribunal][1] may exercise any power which was available to the leasehold valuation tribunal.

(5) And a decision of the [Upper Tribunal][1] on the appeal may be enforced in the same way as a decision of the leasehold valuation tribunal.

(6) [. . . .][2]

(7) [. . . .][2]

(8) No appeal lies from a decision of a leasehold valuation tribunal to the High Court by virtue of section 11(1) of the Tribunals and Inquiries Act 1992 (c. 53).

(9) And no case may be stated for the opinion of the High Court in respect of such a decision by virtue of that provision.

(10) [. . .][1]

Add new Footnote 1: Words substituted and subss repealed by SI 2009/1307, art.5, Sch.1 para. 269 from June 1, 2009.

Add new Footnote 2: Subss. omitted by SI 2010/22, art.5(1), Sch.2 para. 73 from January 18, 2010.

STATUTORY INSTRUMENTS

APPENDIX 2A

Leasehold Reform (Enfranchisement and Extension) Regulations 1967

SCHEDULE 1

PART 1

ENFRANCHISEMENT

Footnotes 9 and 12 should be omitted.   **1024–**
1025

APPENDIX 2C

Leasehold Reform (Collective Enfranchisement and Lease Renewal) Regulations 1993

SCHEDULE 1

COLLECTIVE ENFRANCHISEMENT

1031 Footnote 10 should be substituted to read:
Revoked by SI 2003/1990, reg. 3(a) with effect from September 30, 2003.

SCHEDULE 2

LEASE RENEWAL

1033 Footnote 10 should be substituted to read:
Substituted by SI 2003/1990, reg. 3(b) with effect from September 30, 2003.

APPENDIX 2E

Lands Tribunal Rules 1996

The Lands Tribunal Rules 1996 have been revoked and replaced by the Tribunal **1037–**
Procedure (Upper Tribunal) (Lands Chamber) Rules 2010 (SI 2010/2600), which **1067**
are reproduced at Appendix 2Z.

APPENDIX 2H

The Leasehold Reform (Notices) Regulations 1997

1128– These forms should not have been included. The following are the correct
1135 forms:

FORM 1

LEASEHOLD REFORM ACT 1967

Notice of tenant's claim to acquire the freehold or an extended lease

To *[Name and address of person on whom this notice is served]* **(see Note 1 below)**

[and]

To: *[Name and address of any recipient of a copy of this notice*]* **(see Note 1 below, in addition, your attention is drawn to paragraphs 8 to 10 of this notice)**

(*Delete if paragraphs 5 to 10 are deleted)

1. I am the tenant of the house and premises of which particulars are given in the Schedule to this notice.

2. In exercise of my rights under Part 1 of the Leasehold Reform Act 1967, I give you notice of my desire—

[to have the freehold of the house and premises.]*
[to have an extended lease of the house and premises.]*

(*Delete whichever is inapplicable.)

3. The particulars on which I rely are set out in the Schedule to this notice.

4. If you are both my immediate landlord and the freeholder, you must give me, within two months of the service of this notice, a notice in reply in Form 3 set out in the Schedule to the Leasehold Reform (Notices) Regulations 1997 (or in a form substantially to the same effect), stating whether or not you admit my right [to have the freehold of the house and premises]* [to have an extended lease of the house and premises]* (*delete whichever is inapplicable*) (subject to any question as to the correctness of the particulars of the house and premises) and, if you do not admit my right, stating the grounds on which you do not admit it. **(see Note 2 below)**

(The remaining paragraphs of this form should be deleted where the claimant's immediate landlord is known to be the freeholder of the house and premises.)

5. If you are not my immediate landlord, or if you are my immediate landlord but not the freeholder, you must comply with the requirements of paragraphs 7 and 8, but you need only give me the notice mentioned in paragraph 4 if you are the person designated as "the reversioner" in accordance with paragraph 2 of Schedule 1 to the Act. If you are the reversioner, you must give the notice mentioned in paragraph 4 within two months of the first service of this notice on any landlord. **(see Note 3 below)**

6. I have served a copy of this notice on the following person[s] whom I know or believe to have an interest in the house and premises superior to my tenancy—*[insert name and address of each person on whom a copy of the notice has been served.]*

7. You must now serve a copy of this notice on any other person whom you know or believe to have an interest in the house and premises superior to my tenancy, and you must record on that copy the date on which you received this notice. If you serve a copy on any person you must add his name and, if you know it, his address to the list at the end of paragraph 6, and give me written notice of the name, and address (if known).

8. If you know who is, or believe yourself or another person to be, the reversioner, you must give me written notice stating the name and address (if known) of the person who you think is the reversioner, and serve copies of it on every person whom you know or believe to have an interest superior to my tenancy, stating on each copy the date on which you received this notice.

9. Anyone who receives a copy of this notice must, without delay, serve a further copy of it on any person whom he knows or believes to have an interest in the house and premises superior to my tenancy but who is not named in the notice, unless he knows that that person has already received a copy of it, and he must also record on each further copy the date on which he received this notice. For each further copy served, you must add the name of the person served and, if you know it, his address to the list at the end of paragraph 6, and give me written notice of the name and (if known) the address of that person.

10. Anyone who receives a copy of this notice and who knows who is, or believes himself to be, the reversioner, must notify me in writing of the name and (if known) the address of the person known or believed by him to be the reversioner, and serve a copy of this notification on every person whom he knows or believes to have an interest superior to my tenancy.

[Insert date.]

Signed

....

(Tenant)

of [*insert address*]

....

....

[The name and address of my solicitor or agent, to whom further communications may be sent is

....

]* (**Delete if inapplicable.*)

The Schedule

Particulars Supporting Tenant's Claim

1. *The address of the house.*

2. *Particulars of the house and premises sufficient to identify the property to which your claim extends.* **(see Note 4 below)**

3. *Particulars of the tenancy of the house and premises sufficient to identify the instrument creating the tenancy and to show that the tenancy is and has at the material times been a long tenancy or treated as a long tenancy.* **(see Note 5 below)**

4. *Particulars sufficient to show the date on which you acquired the tenancy.* **(see Note 6 below)**

5. (a) *Particulars of the tenancy of the house and premises sufficient to show that the tenancy is and has at the material times been a tenancy at a low rent or treated as a tenancy at a low rent.* **(see Note 7 below)**

OR

(b) *If your claim is based on section 1AA (additional right to enfranchisement only in case of houses whose rent exceeds applicable limit under section 4), particulars of the tenancy sufficient to show that the tenancy is one in relation to which section 1AA has effect to confer a right to acquire the freehold of the house and premises.* (**see Note 8 below**)

6. *Particulars of any other long tenancy of the house or a flat forming part of the house held by any tenant.* (**see Note 9 below**)

7. *Where either—*

(a) *a flat forming part of the house is let to a person who is a qualifying tenant of a flat for the purposes of Chapter 1 or 2 of Part 1 of the Leasehold Reform, Housing and Urban Development Act 1993; or*

(b) *your tenancy is a business tenancy,*

the following particulars:

(i) *the periods for which in the last ten years, and since acquiring the tenancy, you have and have not occupied the house as your residence; and*

(ii) *during those periods what parts (if any) of the house have not been in your own occupation and for what periods, and*

(iii) *what other residence (if any) you have had and for what periods, and which was your main residence.* (**see Note 10 below**)

8. *Additional particulars sufficient to show that the value of the house and premises does not exceed the applicable financial limit specified in section 1(1)(a)(i) or (ii), (5) or (6) of the Act. (These are not required where the right to have the freehold is claimed in reliance on any one or more of the provisions in section 1A, 1AA or 1B of the Act, or where the tenancy of the house and premises has been extended under section 14 and the notice under section 8(1) was given (whether by a tenant or a sub-tenant) after the original term date of the tenancy).* (**see Note 11 below**)

9. *Additional particulars sufficient to show whether the house and premises are to be valued in accordance with section 9(1) or section 9(1A) of the Act. (These are not required where the right to have the freehold is claimed in reliance on any one or more of the provisions in section 1A, 1AA or 1B of the Act, or where the tenancy of the house and premises has been extended under section 14 and the notice under section 8(1) was given (whether by a tenant or a sub-tenant) after the original term date of the tenancy).*

10. *Additional particulars where you rely on section 6 (rights of trustees), 6A (rights of personal representatives) or 7 (rights of members of family succeeding to tenancy on death) of the Act.* (**see Note 12 below**)

Notes

1. (a) Where the tenant's immediate landlord is not the freeholder, the claim may, in accordance with the Leasehold Reform Act 1967, as amended, be served on him or any superior landlord, and copies of the notice must be served by the tenant on anyone else known or believed by him to have an interest superior to his own (Schedule 3, paragraph 8(1)).

(b) Where the landlord's interest is subject to a mortgage or other charge and the mortgagee or person entitled to the benefit of the charge is in possession of that interest, or a receiver appointed by him or by the court is in receipt of the rents and profits, the notice may be served either on the landlord or on the person in possession or the receiver (Schedule 3, paragraph 9(1)).

(c) Any landlord whose interest is subject to a mortgage or other charge (not being a rent-charge) to secure the payment of money must (subject to special provisions applicable to debenture-holders' charges) on receipt of the claim inform the mortgagee or person entitled to the benefit of the charge (Schedule 3, paragraph 9(2)).

2. The landlord must (unless note 3 applies) serve a notice in reply in Form 3 set out in the Schedule to the Leasehold Reform (Notices) Regulations 1997 (or in substantially the same form) within two months of the service on him of this notice. If he does not admit the tenant's right to have the freehold or an extended lease, the notice in reply must state the grounds on which the right is not admitted. If the landlord intends to apply to the court for possession of the house and premises in order to redevelop it (section 17) or to occupy it (section 18), his notice must say so. If he does not so intend, but he objects under subsection (4) or (5) of section 2 to the inclusion in the claim of a part of the house and premises which projects into other property, or to the exclusion from the claim of property let with the house and premises but not occupied with and used for the purposes of the house by any occupant of it, he must give notice of his objection with or before his notice in reply; unless in his notice in reply he reserves the right to give it later, in which case it must still be given within two months of the service on him of the tenant's notice. If the landlord admits the claim, the admission is binding on him, unless he shows that he was misled by misrepresentation or conceal-ment of material facts, but it does not conclude any question of the correctness of the particulars of the house and premises as set out in the claim (Schedule 3, paragraph 7).

3. Where the tenant's immediate landlord is not the freeholder, any proceedings arising out of the tenant's notice, whether for resisting or for giving effect to the claim, must be conducted by the person who is designated as "the reversioner" in accordance with paragraph 2 of Schedule 1 to the Act and he must give the notice in reply. The reversioner is the landlord whose tenancy carries an expectation of possession of the house and premises of 30 years or more after the expiration of all inferior tenancies and, if there is more than one such landlord, it means the landlord whose tenancy is nearest to that of the tenant; if there is no such landlord, it means the owner of the freehold. The tenant will be informed in the notice in reply if it is given by a landlord acting as the reversioner.

4. "Premises" to be included with the house in the claim are any garage, outhouse, garden, yard and appurtenances which at the time of the notice are let to the tenant with the house.

5. In respect of a house, "long tenancy" has the meaning given by section 3 of the Act. (Special provisions apply in relation to business tenancies—see section 1(1ZC) of the Act inserted by section 140 of the Commonhold and Leasehold Reform Act 2002). Where there have been successive tenancies, particulars should be given of each tenancy. In the case of a lease already extended under the Act, the date of the extension and the original term date should be given. In addition to section 3 of the Act, section 174(a) of the Housing Act 1985 provides for certain tenancies granted pursuant to the right to buy to be treated as long tenancies. Section 1B of the Act also provides for certain tenancies terminable on death or marriage to be long tenancies for the limited right described in note 11. Under Schedule 4A to the Act, certain shared ownership leases granted by public authorities, housing associations, **private registered providers of social housing**[1] and registered social landlords carry neither the right to enfranchise nor the right to obtain an extended lease.

6. The claimant must have owned the lease for two years prior to the date of the application for enfranchisement or lease extension (section 1(1)(b) of the Act, as amended by sections 138 and 139 of the Commonhold and Leasehold Reform Act 2002).

7. In addition to the provision of section 4 of the Act (meaning of "low rent"), section 1A(2) of the Act provides for tenancies falling within section 4A(1) of the Act to be treated as tenancies at a low rent for the limited right described in note 11.

8. Section 1AA confers a limited right to enfranchisement (described in note 11) in the case of leases which would qualify but for the fact that the tenancy is not a tenancy at a low rent, with two exceptions. The first is where the lease is excluded from the right under section 1AA(3): i.e. where the house is in an area designated as a rural area, the freehold of the house is owned together with adjoining land which is not occupied for residential purposes, and the tenancy was either granted on or before 1st April 1997 or was granted after that date but before the coming into force of section 141 of the Commonhold and Leasehold Reform Act 2002, for a term of 35 years or less. Information as to the location of designated rural areas is held at the offices of leasehold valuation tribunals. The second exception applies to any shared ownership lease (as defined by section 622 of the Housing Act 1985) originally granted by a housing association or a registered social landlord.

9. Section 1(1ZA) of the Act (inserted by section 138(2) of the Commonhold and Leasehold Reform Act 2002) provides that head lessees do not have rights to enfranchise or a lease extension where there exist inferior tenancies which confer on the tenant the right to enfranchise and a lease extension under the Act. Under section 1(1ZB) of the Act, where there exists an inferior long tenancy (as defined under section 7 of the Leasehold Reform, Housing and Urban Development Act 1993) of a flat which confers on the tenant the right to enfranchise or a new lease under that Act the head lessee only has the right to enfranchise or a lease extension under the Act where he meets the residence requirement (see note 10 below). It is therefore necessary to provide details of any other long ten-ancies.

10. Particulars of residence and occupation are required in relation to those cases specified in paragraph 7 of the Schedule to this notice (see section 1(1ZB) and (1B) of the Act as inserted, respectively, by sections 138 and 139 of the Commonhold and Leasehold Reform Act 2002). The residence requirement in these specified cases is that the tenant has lived in the property as his only or main residence for the last two years or for periods amounting to two years in the last ten years.

11. A claimant who relies on any one or more of the provisions in section 1A, 1AA or 1B of the Act, (or where the tenancy of the house and premises has been extended under section 14 and the notice under section 8(1) was given (whether by a tenant or a sub-tenant) after the original term date of the tenancy), has the right to have the freehold at a price determined in accordance with section 9(1C) of the Act, but not the right to have an extended lease.

Section 1A(1) applies to a tenancy of a house and premises the value of which exceeds the applicable financial limit. Sections 1A(2) and 1B are described in notes 7 and 5 respectively. Section 1AA (described in note 8) applies to certain cases where the long lease fails the low rent test.

12. (a) Where the claimant is giving the notice by virtue of section 6, 6A or 7 he is required (Schedule 3, paragraph 6(2)) to adapt the notice and show under paragraphs 4 and 7 of the Schedule to the notice the particulars that bring the claim within section 6, 6A or, as the case may be, section 7.

    (b) Where the tenancy is or was vested in trustees the claimant should, for the purposes of a claim made in reliance on section 6, state the date when the tenancy was acquired by the trustees, and, where the case falls within paragraphs 7(a) or (b) of the Schedule to the notice, the date when the beneficiary occupied the house by virtue of his interest under the trust, and the particulars of any period of occupation by the beneficiary which are relied upon as bringing the case within section 6.

    (c) Section 6A of the Act (inserted by section 142 of the Commonhold and Leasehold Reform Act 2002) provides that where a tenant dies and immediately before his death he qualified for the right to enfranchise or a lease extension, those rights can be exercised (up to two years after the date of probate or letters of administration) by his personal representatives. Where the tenancy is vested in personal representatives, they should, for the purposes of making a claim under section 6A, provide evidence that the deceased tenant qualified for the relevant right immediately before his death, state the date when the tenancy became vested in them, and provide evidence to show that probate or letters of administration have been granted no more than two years before the date of the claim for extension of the lease or enfranchisement.

    (d) Where the claimant was a member of the previous tenant's family and became the tenant on the latter's death, for the purposes of a claim made in reliance upon section 7, the claimant should state the date on which the previous tenant acquired the tenancy, particulars of his relationship to the previous tenant and his succession to the tenancy, and particulars in respect of any period of occupation by himself on which the claimant relies as bringing the case within section 7.

Notes

[1] The words in paragraph 5 of the notes to the schedule were inserted by SI 2010/671, Sch. 1, para. 20(a) with effect from April 1, 2010.

FORM 2

LEASEHOLD REFORM ACT 1967

Notice of tenant's claim under section 28(1)(b)(ii)

To: *[Name and address of landlord]*

1. I am the tenant of the house and premises of which particulars are given in the Schedule to this notice.

2. I claim to be entitled under the Leasehold Reform Act 1967 ("the Act") to acquire—

[the freehold of the house and premises.]*
[an extended lease of the house and premises.]*

(*Delete whichever is inapplicable.)

3. The particulars on which I rely are set out in the Schedule to this notice.

4. On [*insert date of service of copy certificate*] you served on me a copy of a certificate given under [section 28 of the Act, certifying that the house and premises will in ten years or less be required for relevant development]* [section 57 of the Landlord and Tenant Act 1954, certifying that it is requisite that the use or occupation of the whole or a part of the house and premises should be changed]* (**delete whichever is inapplicable*), and I am making this claim in the exercise of my rights under section 28 of the Act. (**see Note 1 below**)

5. You must give me, within two months of the service of this notice, a notice in reply in Form 3 set out in the Schedule to the Leasehold Reform (Notices) Regulations 1997 (or in a form substantially to the same effect), stating whether or not you admit my claim (subject to any question as to the correctness of the particulars of the house and premises given in the Schedule to this notice) and, if you do not admit my claim, stating the grounds on which you do not admit it. (**see Note 2 below**)

(Insert date.)

(Signature)

....

(Tenant)
of (*insert address*)

....

....

[The name and address of my solicitor or agent, to whom further communications may be sent is

....

]* (**Delete if inapplicable.*)

The Schedule

Particulars Supporting Tenant's Claim

1. The address of the house.

2. Particulars of the house and premises sufficient to identify the property to which your claim extends. (**see Note 3 below**)

3. Particulars of the tenancy of the house and premises sufficient to identify the instrument creating the tenancy and to show that the tenancy is and has at the material times been a long tenancy or treated as a long tenancy. (**see Note 4 below**)

4. Particulars sufficient to show the date on which you acquired the tenancy. (**see Note 5 below**)

5. (a) Particulars of the tenancy of the house and premises sufficient to show that the tenancy is and has at the material times been a tenancy at a low rent or treated as a tenancy at a low rent. (**see Note 6 below**)

OR

(b) If your claim is based on section 1AA (additional right to enfranchisement only in case of houses whose rent exceeds applicable limit under section 4), particulars of the tenancy sufficient to show that the tenancy is one in relation to which section 1AA has effect to confer a right to acquire the freehold of the house and premises. (**see Note 7 below**)

6. Particulars of any other long tenancy of the house or a flat forming part of the house held by any tenant. (**see Note 8 below**)

7. Where either—

(a) *a flat forming part of the house is let to a person who is a qualifying tenant of a flat for the purpose of Chapter 1 or 2 of Part 1 of the Leasehold Reform, Housing and Urban Development Act 1993; or*
(b) *your tenancy is a business tenancy,*

the following particulars:

(i) *the periods for which in the last ten years, and since acquiring the tenancy, you have and have not occupied the house as your residence; and*
(ii) *during those periods what parts (if any) of the house have not been in your own occupation and for what periods, and*
(iii) *what other residence (if any) you have had and for what periods, and which was your main residence.* (**see Note 9 below**)

8. Additional particulars sufficient to show that the value of the house and premises does not exceed the applicable financial limit specified in section 1(1)(a)(i) or (ii), (5) or (6) of the Act. (These are not required where the right to have the freehold is claimed in reliance on any one or more of the provisions in section 1A, 1AA or 1B of the Act, or where the tenancy of the house and premises has been extended under section 14 and the notice under section 8(1) was given (whether by a tenant or a sub-tenant) after the original term date of the tenancy). (**see Note 10 below**)

9. Additional particulars sufficient to show whether the house and premises are to be valued in accordance with section 9(1) or section 9(1A) of the Act. (These are not required where the right to have the freehold is claimed in reliance on any one or more of the provisions in section 1A, 1AA or 1B of the Act, or where the tenancy of the house and premises has been extended under section 14 and the notice under section 8(1) was given (whether by a tenant or sub-tenant) after the original term date of the tenancy).

10. Additional particulars where you rely on section 6 (rights of trustees), 6A (rights of personal representatives) or 7 (rights of members of family succeeding to tenancy on death) of the Act. (**see Note 11 below**)

Notes

1. In accordance with section 28(1)(b)(ii) of the Leasehold Reform Act 1967, this notice may not be served later than two months after a copy of the certificate has been served on the tenant.

2. (a) The landlord must serve a notice in reply in Form 3 set out in the Schedule to the Leasehold Reform (Notices) Regulations 1997 (or in substantially the same form) within two months of service on him of this notice. If he does not admit the tenant's claim to be entitled to acquire the freehold or an extended lease the notice in reply must state the grounds on which the claim is not admitted. If the landlord admits the claim, the admission is binding on him, unless he shows that he was misled by misrepresentation or concealment of material facts, but it does not conclude any question of the correctness of the particulars of the house and premises as set out in the claim (Schedule 3, paragraph 7).

(b) If the landlord admits the claim the tenant will not be entitled to a grant of the freehold or a new tenancy of the house and premises but, if the landlord obtains an order of the court under section 17 of the Act for possession of the house and premises in order to redevelop it, the tenant will become entitled to be paid compensation for the loss of the house and premises in accordance with Schedule 2 to the Act.

3. "Premises" to be included with the house in the claim are any garage, outhouse, garden, yard and appurtenances which at the time of the notice are let to the tenant with the house.

4. In respect of a house, "long tenancy" has the meaning given by section 3 of the Act. (Special provisions apply in relation to business tenancies—see section 1(1ZC) of the Act inserted by section 140 of the Commonhold and Leasehold Reform Act 2002). Where there have been successive tenancies, particulars should be given of each tenancy. In the case of a lease already extended under the Act, the date of the extension and the original term date should be given. In addition to section 3 of the Act, section 174(a) of the Housing Act 1985 provides for certain tenancies granted pursuant to the right to buy to be treated as long tenancies. Section 1B of the Act also provides for certain tenancies terminable on death or marriage to be long tenancies for the limited right described in note 10. Under Schedule 4A to the Act, certain shared ownership leases granted by public authorities, housing associations, **private registered providers of social housing**[1] and registered social landlords carry neither the right to enfranchise nor the right to obtain an extended lease.

5. The claimant must have owned the lease for two years prior to the date of the application for enfranchisement or lease extension (section 1(1)(b) of the Act, as amended by sections 138 and 139 of the Commonhold and Leasehold Reform Act 2002).

6. In addition to the provision of section 4 of the Act (meaning of "low rent"), section 1A(2) of the Act provides for tenancies falling within section 4A(1) of the Act to be treated as tenancies at a low rent for the limited right described in note 10.

7. Section 1AA confers a limited right to enfranchisement (described in note 10) in the case of leases which would qualify but for the fact that the tenancy is not a tenancy at a low rent, with two exceptions. The first is where the lease is excluded from the right under section 1AA(3): i.e. where the house is in an area designated as a rural area, the freehold of the house is owned together with adjoining land which is not occupied for residential purposes, and the tenancy was either granted on or before 1st April 1997 or was granted after that date but before the coming into force of section 141 of the Commonhold and Leasehold Reform Act 2002, for a term of 35 years or less. Information as to the location of designated rural areas is held at the offices of leasehold valuation tribunals. The second exception applies to any shared ownership lease (as defined by section 622 of the Housing Act 1985) originally granted by a housing association or a registered social landlord.

8. Section 1(1ZA) of the Act (inserted by section 138(2) of the Commonhold and Leasehold Reform Act 2002) provides that head lessees do not have rights to enfranchise or a lease extension where there exist inferior tenancies which confer on the tenant the right to enfranchise and a lease extension under the Act. Under section 1(1ZB) of the Act, where there exists an inferior long tenancy (as defined under section 7 of the Leasehold Reform, Housing and Urban Development Act 1993) of a flat which confers on the tenant the right to enfranchise or a new lease under that Act, the head lessee only has the right to enfranchise or a lease extension where he meets the residence requirements (see note 9 below). It is therefore necessary to provide details of any other long tenancies.

9. Particulars of residence and occupation are required in relation to those cases specified in paragraph 7 of the Schedule to this notice (see section 1(1ZB) and (1B) as inserted, respectively, by sections 138 and 139 of the Commonhold and Leasehold Reform Act 2002). The residence requirement in these specified cases is that the tenant has lived in the property as his only or main residence for the last two years or for periods amounting to two years in the last ten years.

10. A claimant who relies on any one or more of the provisions in section 1A, 1AA or 1B of the Act, (or where the tenancy of the house and premises has been extended under section 14 and the notice under section 8(1) was given (whether by a tenant or a sub-tenant) after the original term date of the tenancy), has the right to have the freehold at a price determined in accordance with section 9(1C) of the Act, but not the right to have an extended lease. Section 1A(1) applies to a tenancy of a house and premises the value of which exceeds the applicable financial limit.

Sections 1A(2) and 1B are described in notes 7 and 5 respectively. Section 1AA (described in note 8) applies to certain cases where the long lease fails the low rent test.

11. (a) Where the claimant is giving the notice by virtue of section 6, 6A or 7 he is required (Schedule 3, paragraph 6(2)) to adapt the notice and show under paragraph 4 or 7 of the Schedule to the notice the particulars that bring the claim within section 6, 6A or, as the case may be, section 7.

(b) Where the tenancy is or was vested in trustees the claimant should, for the purposes of a claim made in reliance on section 6, state the date when the tenancy was acquired by the trustees, and, where the case falls within paragraphs 7(a) or (b) to the Schedule to this notice, the date when the beneficiary occupied the house by virtue of his interest under the trust, and the particulars of any period of occupation by the beneficiary which are relied upon as bringing the case within section 6.

(c) Section 6A of the Act (inserted by section 142 of the Commonhold and Leasehold Reform Act 2002) provides that where a tenant dies and immediately before his death he qualified for the right to enfranchise or a lease extension, those rights can be exercised (up to two years after the date of probate or letters of administration) by his personal representatives. Where the tenancy is vested in personal representatives, they should, for the purposes of making a claim under section 6A, provide evidence that the deceased tenant qualified for the relevant right immediately before his death, state the date when the tenancy became vested in them, and provide evidence to show that probate or letters of administration have been granted no more than two years before the date of the claim for extension of the lease or enfranchisement.

(d) Where the claimant was a member of the previous tenant's family and became the tenant on the latter's death, for the purposes of a claim made in reliance upon section 7, the claimant should state the date on which the previous tenant acquired the tenancy, particulars of his relationship to the previous tenant and his succession to the tenancy, and particulars in respect of any period of occupation by himself on which the claimant relies as bringing the case within section 7.

Notes

[1] The words in paragraph 4 of the notes to the schedule were inserted by SI 2010/671, Sch. 1, para. 20(b) with effect from April 1, 2010.

FORM 3

LEASEHOLD REFORM ACT 1967

Notice in reply to Tenant's Claim

To: [*Name and address of claimant*]

1. I have received [a copy of]* your notice dated

....

(insert date) claiming the right to have [the freehold]* [an extended lease]* *(*delete as appropriate)* of the house and premises described in your notice. (**see Note 1 below**).

2. [I admit your right (subject to any question as to the correctness of the particulars given in your notice of the house and premises).]* *(*delete if inapplicable)* (**see Note 2 below**).

3. [I do not admit your right on the following grounds:

(state grounds on which the tenant's right is not admitted)

....

....

....

....

]*

(*delete if inapplicable).

4. [The house and premises are within an area of a scheme approved under [section 19 of the Act]* [section 70 of the Leasehold Reform, Housing and Urban Development Act 1993[4]]*]* *(*delete as appropriate or delete entire paragraph if paragraph 2 has been deleted)* (**see Note 3 below**).

5. [In my opinion the house should be valued in accordance with section [9(1)]*, [9(1A)]*, [9(1C)]* of the Act.]* *(*delete as appropriate or delete the entire paragraph if paragraph 2 has been deleted)* (**see Note 4 below**).

6. [I intend]* [intends]* to apply to the court for possession of the house and premises under [section 17]* [section 18]* of the Act.]* (*delete the entire paragraph, if inapplicable, or delete whichever of the first alternatives does not apply and the reference to section 17 or section 18 as the circumstances require) (**see Note 5 below**).

7. [I reserve the right to give notice under section 2 of the Act of my objection to the exclusion from the house and premises claimed by you of property let with the house and premises but which is not subject to a tenancy vested in you, or to the continued inclusion in the house and premises of parts lying above or below other premises in which I have an interest.]* (*delete the entire paragraph if inapplicable) (**see note 6 below**).

8. [This notice is given by me as the person designated by paragraph 2 of Schedule 1 to the Act as the reversioner of the house and premises.]* (*delete the entire paragraph, if you are the claimant's immediate landlord and also the freeholder) (**see note 7 below**).

(Signature)

....

(Date)

....

[The name and address of my solicitor or agent, to whom further communications may be sent is

....

]* (*delete if inapplicable.)

Notes

(References in this Form and these Notes to "the Act" are references to the Leasehold Reform Act 1967)

1. This notice must be given within two months of the service of the notice of the tenant's claim. Where there is a chain of landlords, the time limit runs from the date of the first service of the claimant's notice on any landlord (Schedule 3, paragraphs 7(1) and 8(1)(a) to the Act).

2. If the landlord admits the claim he will not later be able to dispute the claimant's right to have the freehold or an extended lease, unless he shows that he was misled by misrepresentation or concealment of material facts, but the admission does not conclude any question as to the correctness of the particulars of the house and premises as set out in the claim (Schedule 3, paragraph 7(4) to the Act).

3. Schemes approved under section 19 of the Act (retention of management powers for general benefit of neighbourhood) and section 70 of the Leasehold Reform, Housing and Urban Development Act 1993 (approval by leasehold valuation tribunal of estate management scheme) provide that within a specified area the landlord will retain powers of management and rights against leasehold houses and premises in the event of the tenants acquiring the freehold.

4. Where section 9(1) of the Act applies, the purchase price and cost of enfranchisement is determined on the basis of the value of the land and there is no element of marriage value.

Where section 9(1A) of the Act applies, the purchase price and cost of enfranchisement is determined on the basis of the land and the house including fifty percent of any marriage value (see new section 9(1D) of the Act inserted by section 145 of the Commonhold and Leasehold Reform Act 2002[5]). No marriage value is payable if the unexpired term of the lease exceeds eighty years (see new section 9(1E) of the Act inserted by section 146 of the Commonhold and Leasehold Reform Act 2002). The fact that the tenant has security of tenure will be taken into account in determining the price.

Where section 9(1C) of the Act applies, the purchase price and cost of enfranchisement is determined on the same basis as that under section 9(1A) of the Act, except that there is no security of tenure at the end of the lease, and additional compensation may be payable if the sale of the freehold results in the diminution of value of or any other loss or damage in relation to any interest of the landlord in any other property.

5. If the landlord (on the assumption, where this is not admitted, that the claimant has the right claimed) intends to apply to the court for an order for possession of the premises for redevelopment under section 17 or use as a residence under section 18 of the Act, the notice must say so (Schedule 3, paragraph 7(3) to the Act). (Where a claim is to have a freehold, only certain public authorities or bodies can resist it on the grounds of an intention to redevelop the property).

6. If the landlord intends to object (under subsection (4) or (5) of section 2 of the Act) to the exclusion from the claim of property let with the house and premises to the tenant but not at the relevant time subject to a tenancy vested in him (see amendment to section 2(4) made by section 138(4) of the Commonhold and Leasehold Reform Act 2002), or to the inclusion of part of the house and premises which projects into other property of the landlord's, notice of his objection must be given before or with this notice, unless the right to give it later is reserved by this notice (Schedule 3, paragraph 7(2) to the Act). In any case, notice of the objection must be given within two months of the service of the claimant's notice.

7. Where there is a chain of landlords, this notice must be given by the landlord who is designated as "the reversioner" (see paragraphs 1 and 2 of Schedule 1 to the Act). For this purpose the reversioner is either the landlord whose tenancy carries an expectation of possession of the house and premises of 30 years or more after the expiration of all the inferior tenancies (or, if there is more than one such landlord, the one whose tenancy is nearest to that of the tenant) or, if there is no such landlord, the freeholder.

APPENDIX 2P

The Leasehold Valuation Tribunals (Procedure) (England) Regulations 2003

Regulation 20 is amended to read as follows: **1170**

20. Permission to appeal

Where a party makes an application to a tribunal for permission to appeal to the [*Lands Tribunal*] **Upper Tribunal**[182A]—

   (a) the application shall be made to the tribunal within the period of 21 days starting with the date on which the document which records the reasons for the decision under regulation 18 was sent to that party; and

   (b) a copy of the application shall be served by the tribunal on every other party.

Add new footnote 182A: The words in reg. 20 were substituted by SI 2009/1307, Sch. 2, para. 95 with effect from June 1, 2009.

APPENDIX 2U

The Land Registry Practice Guide is updated to read as follows:

Land Registry Practice Guide 27

July 2012

Update

This edition of the guide replaces the October 2011 edition. A correction has been made to section 6.4.4. The prohibition against disposals by a landlord once an initial notice in respect of a claim for collective enfranchisement has been served and registered applies to certain leases, not all leases.

Scope of this guide

This guide gives advice on the land registration aspects of the exercise of rights under leasehold reform legislation. The guide is aimed at conveyancers and you should interpret references to 'you' accordingly. Land Registry staff will also use the guide and it contains some information specifically for their use.

1 Abbreviations and terms used

This guide deals with the relevant legislation contained in:

- the Leasehold Reform Act 1967, as amended by the Commonhold and Leasehold Reform Act 2002 (1967 Act)
- the Leasehold Reform, Housing and Urban Development Act 1993, as amended by the Commonhold and Leasehold Reform Act 2002 (1993 Act)
- the Landlord and Tenant Act 1987 (1987 Act)
- the Land Registration Act 2002 (LRA 2002)
- the Land Registration Rules 2003 (LRR 2003)
- the Land Registration (Amendment) (No 2) Rules 2005.

In this guide:

- 'conveyancer' means an authorised person within the meaning of s.18, Legal Services Act 2007 who is entitled to provide the conveyancing services referred to in paragraphs 5(1)(a) and (b) of Schedule 2 to that Act, or a person carrying out those activities in the course of their duties as a public officer. It also includes an individual or body who employs or has among their managers such an authorised person who will undertake or supervise those conveyancing activities (r.217A, LRR 2003)
- 'CRE' followed by a number means a Land Registry computerised register entry code

- 'prescribed clauses lease' means any lease, granted on or after 19 June 2006, which is required by r.58A, LRR 2003 to contain the prescribed clauses set out in Schedule 1A, LRR 2003.

2 Scope and further information
Note that the following are outside the scope of this guide.

- The amendments and provisions of the Commonhold and Leasehold Reform Act 2002 not in force at 1 May 2003.
- The extension of leases by agreement—see Practice Guide *28—Extension of leases*.
- The enfranchisement of places of worship under the Places of Worship (Enfranchisement) Act 1920.
- Deeds of enlargement under section 153 of the Law of Property Act 1925.

In relation to leasehold enfranchisement and extension of leases of houses and flats, the Department for Communities and Local Government and the Welsh Assembly Government publish booklets covering various aspects of the legislation and procedures for exercising rights.

Land Registry publishes a range of guides. Some are referred to in the relevant sections. The following contain information relevant to a variety of applications covered by this guide and should be consulted as necessary.

- Practice Guide *19—Notices, restrictions and the protection of third party interests in the register* gives more detailed information on applications for the entry and removal of these entries.
- Practice Guide *46—Land Registry forms* gives details of the forms that must be used for various applications.
- Practice Guide *64—Prescribed clauses leases* gives more detailed information about prescribed clauses leases.

These can be obtained free of charge from Customer Support (see *Contact details*), or you can download them from our website.

3 Fees
Calculate fees in accordance with the current Land Registration Fee Order.

4 Preliminaries

4.1 Search of the index map
A tenant interested in acquiring the freehold reversion of their property or extending their lease should discover at the outset whether the title to the reversionary interest, or interests, is registered.

Do this by applying for an official search of the index map. The procedure is described in Practice Guide *10—Official searches of the index map* .

It is inadvisable to apply for an official copy of the register without knowing the title number, as described in Practice Guide *11—Inspection and applications for official copies*, as this could result in an unwanted official copy being supplied.

The lessor's title number, if shown on the register of the applicant's title, is not always up to date. That title may of course be inspected—see section *4.2 Inspection of register of superior registered titles* but check the schedule of notices of leases carefully to ensure that it includes the applicant's lease. It is not enough to check the property register description as that too may be out of date if land has been removed from the title.

Land Registry portal customers may be able to obtain all or some of the relevant title numbers by means of the property or postal description, but this is not a substitute for an official search of the index map.

4.2 Inspection of register of superior registered titles

Anyone may apply for an official copy of the entries on the register, the title plan and any documents referred to in the register that are kept by the registrar. These facilities are described in Practice Guide *11—Inspection and applications for official copies*.

5 Houses: enfranchisement and extension of leases under the Leasehold Reform Act 1967

5.1 Generally

The 1967 Act confers on a tenant of a house for the last two years under a long tenancy at a low rent the right to either:

- acquire, on enfranchisement, the freehold, or
- obtain an extended lease of the house and premises expiring 50 years after the date on which the existing term is due to expire—s.1AA, 1967 Act (as amended).

There is an additional right to enfranchisement in relation to tenancies that fail the low rent test. 'House' does not include flats in a horizontally divided building and 'premises' includes any garage, outhouse, garden, yard and appurtenances, let and occupied, and used for the purpose of the house (s.2(1) to (3), 1967 Act). 'Long tenancy' means any tenancy originally granted for a term exceeding 21 years whether or not it is determinable by notice or re-entry (s.3, 1967 Act (as amended)).

Business tenants of a house must meet a residency requirement and hold under a tenancy originally granted for 35 years or more.

The personal representatives of a deceased tenant now have limited rights of enfranchisement.

There are further conditions and exceptions that apply in particular circumstances.

Even if the original lease included the mines and minerals they will not be included in the enfranchisement if the landlord requires them to be excepted and provision is made for support of the property (s.2(6), 1967 Act). A note of any exception will be entered in the register.

There are a variety of statutory provisions that apply to enfranchisement under the 1967 Act. If the deed or the application does not contain a clear statement, such as that set out below, the registrar will be unable to recognise it. There are a large number of applications to register the purchase of reversions and new leases entirely unconnected with the 1967 Act. If the applicant wishes to ensure that the application is completed quickly and accurately without requisitions:

- in the case of transfers, conveyances or other leases a statement along the following lines should appear prominently in the deed:

  "This [transfer] [conveyance] [lease] is made under the provisions of the Leasehold Reform Act 1967.", or

- in the case of a prescribed clauses lease, clause LR5.2 should refer to the 1967 Act.

The low-rent test in respect of the right to enfranchise (but not the right to a lease extension) does not apply to long leases in England granted on or after 7 September 2009 unless arising from an agreement for lease made prior to 7 September 2009[1].

[1] S.300 of the Housing and Regeneration Act 2008 which came into force on 7 September 2009.

5.2 Protection of claims by notice

When a tenant has given notice of their desire to have the freehold or to have an extended lease, that notice may be protected as if it were an estate contract. If the reversionary title(s) affected are registered, this may be done by application for the entry of a notice under s.34, LRA 2002. The tenant's right cannot constitute an interest that overrides within Schedules 1 or 3, LRA 2002.

An application for an agreed notice should be made in form AN1 together with a certified copy of the notice (which will be filed at Land Registry). We will make the following entry in the charges register:

> *"Notice entered pursuant to section 5(5) of the Leasehold Reform Act 1967 that a notice dated _____ has been served under that Act by _____ of*
>
> _____
>
>   *NOTE: Copy filed."*

(There is no CRE for this entry.)

Alternatively, application may be made for a unilateral notice by applying in form UN1.

If any of the reversionary titles affected are unregistered, the notice may be protected by a class C (iv) entry at the Land Charges Department.

5.3 Enfranchisement

On completion of the acquisition of the freehold title, application should be made in the usual way for registration of the transfer, if the title is already registered, or for the first registration of the land, if it is not.

If the tenant's or any superior leasehold interest is to be merged in the freehold, a request for merger should be included in the application, as described in *Appendix 1 Merger of leases on acquisition of the freehold.*

Where a deed of substituted security transferring a legal charge on a merged lease to the freehold is lodged, the charge will normally be registered against the freehold title. If the charge is only to be noted, lodge form AN1 or UN1, depending on whether the application is for an agreed or a unilateral notice.

NB: Where two or more charges are being registered their priorities must be clearly apparent. The following special provisions apply on the acquisition of the freehold of the house and will be reflected on the register.

5.3.1 Rights and burdens passing under the 1967 Act

S.10(2), 1967 Act provides that certain rights that affect the leasehold interest shall automatically continue on enfranchisement for and against the freehold but without prejudice to any rights that may be expressly granted or reserved.

The rights passing under s.10(2) that take effect "so far as the landlord is capable of granting them" are rights of support, rights of access of light and air and rights to the passage, use or maintenance of the usual common services, such as water, gas or other piped fuel, drainage, electricity, telephone and so on.

Entries will always be made in the register in respect of the land transferred, whether or not the lease is merged:

In the property register

> *"The land _____ has the benefit of such easements and rights as the ____ dated _____ referred to in the Charges Register has had the effect of granting by virtue of section 10(2)(i) of the Leasehold Reform Act 1967____."* [2]

Or

> *"The land _____ has the benefit of such easements and rights as the _____ dated ____ referred to above has had the effect of granting by virtue of section 10(2)(i) of the Leasehold Reform Act 1967_____."* [3]

[2] CRE AK211 contains fields in the order *1*, *2*, *3*, *9*.
[3] CRE AK130 contains fields in the order *1*, *2*, *3*, *9*.

If the conveyance or transfer expressly excludes or restricts any of the appurtenant rights, which would otherwise be deemed to pass by statutory implication, this will be reflected at the end of the above entry.

In the charges register

> *"The land _____ is subject to such easements and rights as by a ____ dated _____ made between _____it was made subject to by virtue of section 10(2)(ii) of the Leasehold Reform Act 1967."* [4]

Or

> *"The land _____ is subject to such easements and rights as by the _____*
> *dated _____ referred to above it was made subject to by virtue of section*
> *10(2)(ii) of the Leasehold Reform Act 1967."*[5]

[4] CRE CK795 contains fields in the order *1*, *2*, *3*, *4*.
[5] CRE CK355 contains fields in the order *1*, *2*, *3*.

No reference will normally be made to any deed (whether it be the lease or otherwise) that contains a grant or reservation of rights granted by virtue of s.10(2) of the 1967 Act. If, however, specific application is made, an entry will be made on the following lines:

> *"In relation to the effect of section 10(2)(i) [or (ii)] of the Leasehold Reform*
> *Act 1967 a lease/transfer/deed dated _____ made between _____ granted/*
> *reserved the following rights [or rights of drainage, or as the case may*
> *be]."*

(There is no CRE for this entry.)

If the conveyance or transfer expressly excludes or restricts any of the appurtenant rights, which would otherwise be deemed to pass by statutory implication, an entry of this provision will be made in the property register.

If the conveyance or transfer contains new easements or restrictive covenants under s.10(3) and (4), 1967 Act, entries relating to them will be made in the register in accordance with normal practice.

Applicants should ensure that either:

- if the reversion over which the easement is granted is registered in the name of the landlord but under a different title to that of the house, application is also made against the servient title, or
- where the land is unregistered that good title is deduced.

Where a transfer of part of a registered title is made pursuant to the 1967 Act, the rights created under s.10(2) will call for entries to be made on the transferor's title as well.

Where the transferor's title comprises no more than three properties, specific entries on the lines of those referred to above will be made, but where it comprises more properties an entry in the following terms will be made in the property register:

> *"Such transfers of the parts edged and numbered in green on the title plan*
> *as were made under the Leasehold Reform Act 1967 took effect with the*
> *benefit of and subject to easements and other rights as prescribed by section*
> *10(2) of that Act."*[6]

[6] CRE AK164 contains no fields.

5.3.2 Discharge of charges on landlord's estate (whether registered or unregistered)

No difficulty will arise if any registered or noted charge, or any mortgage against the landlord's title, can be discharged or released in the normal way when the tenant acquires the freehold. However, the 1967 Act provides additional mechanisms for the discharges of charges or mortgages where necessary, which may mean that the conventional evidence or receipt may be inappropriate. The following paragraphs describe what evidence will be accepted in these cases.

- The purchasing tenant may have paid sufficient money to the landlord's mortgagee direct in order to discharge the land from the mortgage (s.12, 1967 Act). If the mortgagee has accepted payment of the whole or a sufficient part of the purchase money in full discharge of the property from their mortgage, a copy of the receipt, so worded, must be lodged with the application.
- If the money has been paid into court under s.13, 1967 Act, the tenant must supply a copy of the affidavit, which they will have made for that purpose, and also a copy of the court's official receipt.

We may serve a notice after the application for registration has been lodged. The notice will be served on the registered mortgagee and any other party appearing by the register to have an interest in the mortgage, and will give details of:

- the mortgage
- the applicants and the nature of the application
- the intended closure of the relevant part of the title if the transfer is of part
- how any objection to the application can be made.

If no reply to the notice is received within the time allowed, registration will be completed free from any reference to the charge. If the mortgagee shows prima facie grounds for objection in reply to the notice (for example, because an insufficient part of the purchase money has been paid into court), it may be agreed that the entry of the mortgage will remain on the register of the purchaser's title until proper evidence of a full discharge is produced, or the matter is otherwise settled.

5.3.3 Landlord's estate subject to a rentcharge

The transfer or conveyance will normally take effect subject to any pre-existing rentcharges affecting the title[7]. However, where the rentcharge is more than the amount payable as rent under the lease, the tenant can require the landlord to discharge the house and premises from the rentcharge to the extent of the excess. Where difficulties arise in paying the redemption price, provision is made for payment into court (s.11(4), 1967 Act). The evidence we require for the discharge of the rentcharge will be similar to that mentioned in section *5.3.2 Discharge of charges on landlord's estate (whether registered or unregistered)*.

The landlord may either:

- procure a release of the rentcharge from the rentcharge owner. The normal conveyancing evidence will be required including the production of any relevant certificates, or
- require, subject to the reasonable consent of the tenant[8], that the rentcharge shall be charged exclusively on other land so as to exonerate the land conveyed or else that it shall be apportioned. The normal conveyancing evidence of formal or informal exoneration or apportionment must be produced.

[7] Ss.8(2) and (4)(b), 1967 Act (as amended by the Rentcharges Act 1977, s.17(1); Schedule 1, paragraph 4).
[8] S.11(1), 1967 Act (as amended by the Rentcharges Act 1977, s.17(1); Schedule 1, paragraph 4(2)).

5.4 Extended leases

Because the 1967 Act allows individual leaseholders to acquire the freehold of their properties, few applications for registration of extended leases under that Act have been received. However, since the provisions are still available for use, and if used can create difficulties for us, applications for registration of such leases are dealt with in the following paragraphs.

5.4.1 Registration of new lease—Land Registry requirements

On completion of the acquisition of a new lease granted in substitution for an existing lease pursuant to s.14, 1967 Act, make an application for registration of the lease. If necessary, also lodge an application to give effect on the register to the deemed surrender of the existing lease, which will have taken place by operation of law.

Appendix 2—Applications for registration of extended leases explains Land Registry's requirements in connection with these applications.

5.4.2 Entries in the register

Where appropriate, the following entry will be made on the new title.

> *"The land is subject to such rights as may be subsisting in favour of the persons interested under a Charge dated _____ and made between _____of the leasehold interest under a Lease dated _____ in substitution of which, pursuant to the Leasehold Reform Act 1967, the registered lease was granted."*[9]

[9] CRE CK889 contains fields in the order *3*, *4*, *3*.

If it is not possible to make the type of entry described above (for example, because the original lease is unregistered and no evidence as to any mortgages affecting it has been produced), the following entry will be made.

> *"The land is subject to such rights as may be subsisting in favour of the persons interested under any charge of the leasehold interest under a Lease*

dated _____ in substitution for which pursuant to the Leasehold Reform Act 1967, the registered lease was granted." [10]

[10] CRE CK179 contains field *3*.

5.5 Sub-leases

There are complicated provisions in Schedule 1, 1967 Act to determine which lessor is to act as reversioner on behalf of all the lessors where there are sub-leases.

It is important to note that the sub-lessee does not necessarily have to serve the notice under s.5, 1967 Act on all persons interested (see paragraph 8 of Schedule 3, 1967 Act).

5.6 Miscellaneous

5.6.1 Consent by Charity Commissioners not required

Where the landlord's title is held by a charity then the transfer or lease will not be affected by any restriction in the register in Form E to Schedule 4, LRR 2003. However, any disposition of registered or unregistered land must contain the appropriate statement and where the lease is a prescribed clauses lease, the statement must be included in clause LR5.1.

5.6.2 Rights of future development and pre-emption

On enfranchisement or extension of a lease, certain landlords, including local authorities and the Commission for the New Towns, may require the tenant to enter into:

- covenants to restrain the tenant from developing or clearing the land in case the lessor may need it for future development
- a covenant that they will not grant a tenancy of the property without the consent of the landlord and that they will not sell it without first offering it to the landlord.

We will make an appropriate entry in the register if a conveyance, transfer, or extended lease contains covenants of this nature (paragraph 1(3) of Schedule 4, 1967 Act as amended).

6 Flats: enfranchisement and extension of leases of flats under the Leasehold Reform, Housing and Urban Development Act 1993

6.1 Generally

Part I of the 1993 Act gives qualifying tenants of flats either:

- a collective right to buy the freehold of the block (collective enfranchisement) if the flats are contained in premises that satisfy certain conditions, or
- an individual right to a new lease expiring 90 years after the termination of an existing lease.

Neither of these rights can be exercised when the National Trust owns any interest or when the flat is within the precinct of a cathedral. A precinct is defined under the Care of Cathedrals Measure 1990 by reference to the plans kept by the Cathedrals Fabric Commission for England. Where the Crown is not the immediate landlord but is a superior landlord, then, in some cases, there will be a right to a new lease (s.94, 1993 Act).

6.2 Tenants' right to collective enfranchisement

6.2.1 Generally

This is the right of tenants to acquire the freehold of their block whether or not the landlord wishes to sell.

The 1993 Act lays down a framework within which negotiations take place with the aim of entering into a contract for sale in the normal way. The 1993 Act does not contain any provision for the grant of statutory easements, unlike the 1967 Act described in section *5 Houses: enfranchisement and extension of leases under the Leasehold Reform Act 1967*. Instead, the 1993 Act says that the parties must include, in the conveyance or transfer, any necessary easements, such as rights of support, so the parties have to decide what is required in their particular situation.

In acquiring the freehold any intermediate lease between the tenants' leases and the freehold is also acquired. This means that even if the tenants already have a flat management company holding an intermediate lease, that lease will be acquired under s.2(1), 1993 Act. It would not appear that there is any way this can be avoided since s. 2(1)(a) and (2) appear to be mandatory.

In these circumstances the tenants should perhaps consider not using the procedure in the 1993 Act.

Where tenants acquire the premises outside the legislation, by independent negotiation, the provisions of the 1993 Act do not apply.

It is, therefore, a requirement that the conveyance or transfer must contain a statement in the following terms where the 1993 Act procedure is used.

> *"This conveyance [or transfer] is executed for the purposes of Chapter I of Part I of the Leasehold Reform, Housing and Urban Development Act 1993."*[11]

[11] S.34(10), 1993 Act and r.196, LRR 2003.

Chapter I of Part I of the 1993 Act confers on qualifying tenants of flats the right to have the freehold of the premises, in which the flats are contained, acquired on their behalf by a person appointed by them for the purpose.

A person so appointed is known as the nominee purchaser (s.1, 1993 Act).

A person is a qualifying tenant if they are a tenant under a long lease for a term exceeding 21 years.

6.2.2 Protection of tenants' rights—notices

The procedures whereby qualifying tenants assert their collective rights to have the freehold acquired are outside the scope of this guide. See section *6.4 Notices* for the procedure for protecting a notice of claim to exercise such rights.

6.2.3 Completion of acquisition

When all matters have been agreed between the parties, or otherwise resolved, a binding contract is entered into for the acquisition of the freehold and superior leasehold interests by the nominee purchaser with the reversioner (s.34(2) and paragraph 6(1)(b)(ii) of Schedule 1, 1993 Act). Precisely who is the reversioner may be complex, particularly where there are intermediate leasehold titles.

The acquisition is then completed by a conveyance or transfer of the freehold to the nominee purchaser, subject only to such incumbrances as may have been agreed or determined. The 1993 Act makes provision for the kind of matters that should be included in any sale, without being prescriptive as to their exact content. Where the purchase involves the acquisition of a superior leasehold interest, title will need to be deduced, if it is not registered, to all interests acquired, as will title to land over which any party grants easements in favour of the land acquired by the nominee purchaser. Where the leasehold or freehold interests, or any adjacent land over which easements are granted, are registered, application against the respective titles is required.

If the freeholder is granting easements and the land over which they are being granted is held in lease by a leaseholder, part of whose interest is also being sold to the nominee purchaser, for the easements to be effective as against that leaseholder the leaseholder will have to be a party to the grant of the freehold easements so that they are binding on it during the term of the lease. This will involve an entry being made on the leaseholder's title so that subsequent owners will have notice of the rights.

The conveyance or transfer is effective to overreach any incumbrances that are capable of being overreached (s.34(3), 1993 Act), which means most incumbrances that would be overreached on a sale at arm's length. The main exception is some rentcharges that are covered below. Mortgages on the freehold or intermediate titles are also discussed later.

The person who executes the transfer or conveyance will normally be the freeholder, whom the 1993 Act designates as the reversioner. Where there are intermediate leasehold titles the reversioner will act on behalf of the other landlords in the transfer or conveyance and execute the deed on their behalf, although they should be described as being parties to the deed for the purpose of the sale and any concurrence to the grant of easements or other rights (paragraph 6(1)(iii) of Schedule 1, 1993 Act). However, the other landlords can opt out of this procedure and can transfer or convey the interest themselves, as indeed can the nominee purchaser (paragraph 7 of Schedule 1, 1993 Act).

Where an intermediate leasehold title is unregistered, it would be advisable for a note of any transfer of part or grant of an easement to be endorsed on the lease.

The registrar will assume, where an intermediate landlord is described as party to the transfer, that no opt out has taken place. However, if the transfer is silent, a requisition will be raised requiring a separate transfer, conveyance or assignment of the intermediate interest.

Where the reversioner, being the person making the transfer to the nominee purchaser, is shown on the title as the registered proprietor of the freehold, or is shown as having the legal estate in fee simple absolute in an unregistered title, no further evidence as to the power of the reversioner to convey the block will be needed. Where, however, the court has appointed any other person to be the reversioner, a certified copy of the court order will be required. A person so appointed acts as if they were the freehold reversioner (Schedule 1, Part I, 1993 Act).

6.2.4 Registration of nominee purchaser

The nominee purchaser can be any person or persons (which includes a company) appointed by the participating tenants. Although the 1993 Act calls the purchaser a 'nominee' it may well be the case that they are not, in fact, a nominee at law. If a company or other body corporate is used as a vehicle to buy the land it seems likely that the company will be beneficially entitled with the qualifying tenants exercising their rights through their shareholding. Whether the nominee purchaser is a true nominee, or perhaps some other type of trustee, an application for a suitable restriction should accompany the application for registration of the nominee purchaser.

NB: The registrar will not enter a restriction unless one is applied for appropriately or the LRA 2002 or the LRR 2003 otherwise require it.

In almost all cases, the existing tenants' leases will be incumbrances to which the sale is subject. Counterparts of these leases, and any new lease back, must be produced with the application if they are not already noted as incumbrances in the charges register of the title affected by the sale.

Subject to the points mentioned in this section, the application should be made in the usual way in form AP1 or FR1 depending on whether the reversioner's title is registered or unregistered. Applications for merger of an intermediate lease with the freehold should be dealt with in accordance with *Appendix 1—Merger of leases of acquisition of the freehold*.

6.2.5 Unpaid vendor's lien

A vendor's lien is capable of arising on the transfer to the nominee purchaser, where an amount remains outstanding in any of the following categories (s.32(2), 1993 Act).

- The price payable.
- Amounts due from tenants (not just those who are participating in the purchase) in respect of their leases or under or in respect of agreements collateral thereto.
- Any amount payable to the vendor by virtue of s.18(2), 1993 Act (where the valuation has been reduced by a failure of the nominee purchaser to reveal the existence of a relevant agreement or shareholding).
- Any costs payable by the nominee purchaser (s.33, 1993 Act).

The lien is not capable of substantive registration, but can be the subject of an application for protection by way of notice in the register. However, since the lien does not arise automatically, but depends upon the circumstances of the particular case, we will take no action except on receipt of a specific application to note the lien.

6.2.6 Discharge of mortgages on the landlord's estate (and any leaseholder's estate that is being acquired) on transfer to the nominee purchaser (whether registered or unregistered)

It is preferable for any registered or noted charge or any mortgage against the landlord's title or any intermediate lessee's title to be discharged, cancelled or receipted in the normal way when the tenant acquires the freehold. This is because, despite the provisions of s.35, 1993 Act referred to below, it will never be clear that its provisions apply, unless the money has been paid into court, because of the severely limiting effect of paragraph 2 of Schedule 8, 1993 Act (Duty of nominee purchaser to redeem mortgages).

Unless a form DS1, form DS3, Electronic Discharge, application to cancel a notice, or evidence of payment into court is produced with the application the registrar will either requisition for a statutory declaration or statement of truth serve notice, where possible, on the person having the benefit of the mortgage or charge.

The following describes what evidence will be satisfactory for our purposes and what action we will take.

Under the 1993 Act the transfer or conveyance has the effect of discharging all the land acquired, including any intermediate leasehold interest, from any charge on it (s.35(1), 1993 Act) without the mortgagee or chargee having to execute the transfer or conveyance or becoming parties to the conveyance. The parties can, however, agree that the land will be subject to the mortgage. If the parties intend this to happen then the transfer or conveyance should make this absolutely clear, otherwise the charges may be cancelled.

The nominee purchaser may have paid sufficient money to the landlord's chargee direct in order to discharge the land from the charge. If the chargee has accepted payment of the whole, or a sufficient part of the purchase money, in full discharge of the property from the charge, a copy of the receipt must be lodged with the application.

If the money has been paid into court under s.35 of, and Schedule 8 to, the 1993 Act, the purchaser must supply a copy of the affidavit or statement of truth which they will have made to the court for that purpose, and also a copy of the court's official receipt. We may serve notice of the application on the registered chargee and any other person appearing by the register to be interested in the charge.

It will give details of:

- the charge
- the applicants and the nature of the application
- the intended closure of the relevant part of the title where it is a transfer of part
- how any objection to the application can be made.

If no reply to the notice is received within the time allowed, registration will be completed free from any reference to the charge.

If the chargee shows prima facie grounds for objection in reply to the notice, for example, because an insufficient part of the purchase money has been paid into court, it may be agreed that the entry of the charge will remain on the register of the purchaser's title until proper evidence of a full discharge is produced or the matter is otherwise settled.

6.2.7 Landlord's estate subject to a rentcharge

The transfer or conveyance will normally take effect subject to any preexisting rentcharge affecting the title (s.34(6), 1993 Act). The landlord may either:

- procure a release of the rentcharge from the rentcharge owner. The normal conveyancing evidence will be required, or
- require, subject to the reasonable consent of the tenant (s.34(8), 1993 Act), that the rentcharge shall be charged exclusively on other land so as to exonerate the land conveyed or else that it shall be apportioned. The normal conveyancing evidence of formal or informal exoneration or apportionment must be produced.

6.2.8 Lease back to the former freeholder

On acquiring the freehold in the whole of the building the nominee purchaser is required in certain circumstances to grant leases back to the former freeholder of those units or flats in the building not leased by the qualifying tenants and which they are not acquiring. Such leases will be for terms of 999 years at a peppercorn rent (s.36 of, and Schedule 9 to, the 1993 Act).

The application for registration of such a lease must be made in form AP1 or FR1 depending on whether the reversioner's title is registered. Furthermore, the position with regard to the status of the lease will differ depending on whether or not the freehold is already registered.

Registered freehold

The new lease will be a disposition of registered land and will, therefore, take effect in equity only until registered. It would seem that the potential lessee is a purchaser within the meaning of r.131, LRR 2003 in order to be able to make a protecting search. Since the 1993 Act provides that the nominee purchaser must grant the lease back, the transaction is one where any contemporaneous mortgagee of the freehold will be subject to the right to a new lease. An official search will secure the priority to which the intended lessee is entitled.

The lessee should also make the nature of the transaction clear in a letter accompanying the application for registration.

This is because since the lessee has no control over the timing of the application for registration of the freehold disposal, it is possible that the application for registration of the lease will be made before that of the freehold. It will then appear that the freeholder is attempting to grant a lease to themselves, which is not possible, and we would reject the application. Where this 'mistiming' occurs we will hold the leasehold application, but when we receive the application for the freehold transfer it will be entered on the day list of pending applications and the leasehold application will then be reentered on the day list after the transfer so that the priorities are correct.

Unregistered land

Where the freehold is unregistered it will be subject to first registration and the new lease will take effect as a legal estate whether or not the purchaser makes the application for registration before the new lease application is lodged. Again, it would be helpful if there could be an accompanying letter setting out the circumstances. When the freehold application is lodged the application should reveal the existence of the lease back and the counterpart should be lodged with the application.

The usual conveyancing evidence of the freehold title will be required, including the appropriate Land Charges searches.

6.2.9 Vesting orders

Chapter I of Part I, 1993 Act gives power to the court to make vesting orders where:

- the terms of acquisition are in dispute
- there is a failure to enter into a contract (s.24, 1993 Act), or
- the reversioner fails to give a counter-notice (s.25, 1993 Act) or cannot be found or identified (s.26, 1993 Act).

As to the protection of such orders see sections *6.4.2 Vesting orders made under ss.26(1) or 50(1), 1993 Act (where the relevant landlord cannot be found or identified)* and *6.4.3 Orders made under ss.24, 25, 48 or 49, 1993 Act (where there is a dispute)*.

6.2.10 Variation of flat leases

Nothing in the collective enfranchisement procedure has any effect on the length of the tenants' leases. Where the tenants wish to take advantage of their new found freedom to 'extend' their leases they may do so by agreement, or possibly by exercising rights under Chapter II of Part I, 1993 Act. They should, however, be aware of the traps the law contains in this area and note Land Registry's requirements in connection with the voluntary extension of leases as set out in Practice Guide *28—Extension of leases*.

6.3 Right of a tenant to acquire a new lease

Chapter II of Part I, 1993 Act confers on a qualifying tenant of a flat for the last two years an individual right to acquire a new lease of the flat on payment of a premium determined in accordance with a statutory formula.

NB: A person is a qualifying tenant if they are (subject to certain exceptions) a tenant under a long lease of a flat (s.39(3), 1993 Act). The right is suspended if the tenants collectively seek to buy the freehold.

As a result of the decision in Cadogan & Ors v 26 Cadogan Square Ltd, Howard de Walden Estates Ltd v Aggio & Ors [2008] UKHL 44, a head lessee is entitled, under the 1993 Act, to an extended lease of an individual flat which comprises part of the land demised by the head lease. This guide should be read and interpreted accordingly.

6.3.1 Procedure on tenant's claim to new lease

The procedures whereby a qualifying tenant asserts their claim to a new lease are beyond the scope of this guide except that the procedure for protecting a notice of claim to exercise such a right is discussed in section *6.4 Notices*.

6.3.2 Terms of the new lease

The new lease, which takes effect in substitution for the existing lease, will be for a term expiring 90 years after the term date of the existing lease at the rent of a peppercorn (s.56(1), 1993 Act). The new lease is to be on the same terms as the existing lease but with such modifications as may be required or appropriate (s.57, 1993 Act).

Although the right is a right to have a new lease of the land demised to the tenant, under the existing lease it is clear that variations in extent and in the rights granted are permitted (s.57(1), 1993 Act). Very careful examination of the extents of any existing flats and of the terms of easements will, therefore, be required to ensure that the landlord has power to grant the new lease. It is quite likely that some new leases will not be of the same extent since over a long period there are informal arrangements between tenants that 'vary' the terms of their leases in practice. This may cause problems on the grant of new leases, for example the switching of use of car parking spaces, dustbin areas and other common facilities. Landlords will need to ensure that the extent granted and the terms of the new lease (including any easements) are compatible with any other leases that exist.

6.3.3 Statement to be contained in new lease

The lease must contain a statement in the following terms:

> "This lease is granted under section 56 of the Leasehold Reform, Housing and Urban Development Act 1993." (s.57(11), 1993 Act and r.196, LRR 2003).

Where the lease is a prescribed clauses lease this statement must be inserted in clause LR5.1 or reference made to the clause, paragraph or schedule in the lease that contains this statement in full.

If the lease does not contain such a statement the registrar will assume that it is not made pursuant to the 1993 Act. Although there is no prescribed form of statement where the lease is granted under s.93(4), 1993 Act (leases granted on terms approved by the court) it would be helpful if it did contain such a statement because of the consequences that flow from that section as mentioned in the following paragraphs. In those circumstances a certified copy of the court order under that section should also be produced.

6.3.4 Reversionary titles

If the qualifying tenant's immediate landlord does not have a sufficient interest (ie is not the freeholder and does not have a leasehold interest of sufficient duration to enable such landlord to grant a new lease) then the new lease will be granted by the nearest landlord whose interest is sufficient, and they will be the 'competent landlord' for the purposes of the 1993 Act (s.40(1) and (2), 1993 Act). The intermediate landlord's title may be registered but the competent landlord's title unregistered.

The early identification of the competent landlord is important in order to determine what evidence of their title to grant the lease is required (see *Appendix 2—Applications for registration of extended leases*).

This raises certain problems in relation to an existing intermediate lease.

The competent landlord's title

The new lease will be a disposition by the competent landlord. If the competent landlord's title is registered, the following note will be made in the schedule of notice of leases.

> "*NOTE: The lease was made under the provisions of section 56 or 93(4) of the Leasehold Reform, Housing and Urban Development Act 1993.*"

(There is no CRE for this entry.)

If a lease that includes the flat is noted on the competent landlord's title then an additional entry will be made against it along the following lines.

> "*The lease dated _____ to _____ [referred to above] was deemed to have been surrendered and regranted following the grant of a lease or leases under section 56 or 93(4) of the Leasehold Reform, Housing and Urban Development Act 1993 with the effect provided for by paragraph 10 of Schedule 11 to that Act.*"

(There is no CRE for this entry.)

Applicants and their advisers will need to consider what conveyancing evidence and memoranda, if any, should be endorsed on or placed with the deeds.

Intermediate leasehold title(s)

The 1993 Act makes special provision for the situation where there are intermediate leases (s.40(3) of, and Schedule 11 to, the 1993 Act).

An intermediate lessor has a reversionary interest which does not have enough years left to grant a new lease. There may be more than one intermediate lessor. The right to grant the new lease is vested only in the competent landlord but the 1993 Act provides that any intermediate lease is deemed to have been surrendered and regranted. This is a device to ensure that the integrity of intermediate leases of the whole block and any service charge arrangements contained in them are preserved. The registrar has concluded that this provision does not have the effect of actually effecting a surrender and regrant that would require intermediate lessees to apply for the closure of their title and an application to register it again. The intermediate lessor is bound by the terms of the new lease as it is granted pursuant to a statutory power. Notice that the new lease has been registered should be served on any registered intermediate lessor.

An entry will be made in the property register along the following lines.

"The registered lease is deemed to have been surrendered and regranted following the grant of a lease or leases under section 56 or 93(4) of the Leasehold Reform, Housing and Urban Development Act 1993 with the effect specified in paragraph 10 of Schedule 11 to that Act."

(There is no CRE for this entry.)

Any lease granted under these provisions will be noted in the schedule of notice of leases and a note to the entry will be made along the following lines.

"NOTE: This lease was granted under the provisions of section 56 or 93(4) of the Leasehold Reform, Housing and Urban Development Act 1993 and the provisions of paragraph 10 of Schedule 11 to that Act apply."

(There is no CRE for this entry.)

The only circumstance where these provisions in relation to intermediate leases do not apply is where an intermediate lease is owned by the tenant or is held on trust for them (paragraph 10(3) of Schedule 11, 1993 Act). Where this is the case the tenant's application will need to make this clear and include an application to close (perhaps as to part) any registered title affected, since the effect of the grant of the new lease is to bring about the immediate surrender of the intermediate lease.

6.3.5 Registration of new lease—Land Registry requirements

When a new lease is acquired in substitution for an existing lease, pursuant to s.56, 1993 Act, make an application for registration of the lease. If necessary also lodge an application to give effect to the deemed surrender of the existing lease, which will have taken place by operation of law. *Appendix 2—Application for registration of extended leases* explains our requirements in connection with these applications.

6.3.6 Entries in the register

The following entry will be made in the property register immediately after the entry relating to the registered lease.

"The registered lease was granted under the provisions of section 56 or 93(4) of the Leasehold Reform, Housing and Urban Development Act 1993."

(There is no CRE for this entry.)

The reason for this entry is that under s.56, 1993 Act, if the registered proprietor grants a new long lease out of the title, the subtenant has no right to claim a new lease from the competent landlord under that act.

Where a charge is brought forward from the surrendered leasehold estate, its date of registration will be that of the application to register the new lease. The following entry will be made on the registration or reregistration of the charge.

"This charge, [which] takes effect against this title under the provisions of section 58(4) of the Leasehold Reform, Housing and Urban Development Act 1993, [was formerly registered against title number(s)_____]"

(There is no CRE for this entry.)

If the charge is merely being noted, there will be an entry on similar lines.

"This charge, [which] takes effect against this title under the provisions of section 58(4) of the Leasehold Reform, Housing and Urban Development Act 1993, [was formerly noted against title number(s)_____]"

(There is no CRE for this entry.)

Unless postponed, all charges and other entries brought forward will have the same priority as they had on the old title[12].

---

[12] See s.58A, 1993 Act, inserted by the Housing Act 1996.

6.3.7 Possession of lease and certificate where mortgagee held deeds of surrendered lease

Where a new lease takes effect, subject to a mortgage and the mortgage is at that time entitled to possession of title documents relating to the surrendered lease, the mortgagee becomes similarly entitled to possession of the documents of title relating to the new lease. In such a case, the tenant is bound to deliver the new lease to the mortgagee within one month of the date on which it is received from Land Registry following its registration.

6.3.8 Vesting orders

The court has power to make vesting orders where the terms of acquisition are in dispute or there is failure to enter into a lease (s.48, 1993 Act) or where the reversioner fails to give a counter-notice (s.49, 1993 Act) or cannot be found or identified (s.50, 1993 Act). As to the protection of such orders see sections *6.4.2 Vesting orders made under s.26(1) or 50(1), 1993 Act* and *6.4.3 Orders made under ss.24, 25, 48 or 49, 1993 Act (where there is a dispute)*.

6.4 Notices

6.4.1 Notice of claim to exercise right of collective enfranchisement or right to a new lease

The extended period over which negotiations will often take place under the 1993 Act makes it very desirable that the rights of the parties are protected in the register. The general rule is that registration by the tenants or tenant will be against the title of the freeholder or, in the case of a tenant claiming a new lease, against the competent landlord, who may or may not be the freeholder. However, it may also be desirable to register against other persons as well and this section considers when this might be done.

Any right of a tenant arising from a notice given under s.13, 1993 Act (notice by qualifying tenants of flats of claim to exercise the right of collective enfranchisement) or s.42, 1993 Act (notice by qualifying tenant of a flat of claim to exercise the right to a new lease) ('the 1993 Act notice') is not an interest with overriding status within the meaning of the LRA 2002 but may be protected on the register by a notice as if it were an estate contract (s.97(1), 1993 Act).

If an application is made to enter an agreed notice under r.81, LRR 2003, the evidence in support should normally consist of a certified copy of the notice (which will be filed).

The entry in the charges register will be as follows.

> *"Notice entered pursuant to section 97(1) of the Leasehold Reform, Housing and Urban Development Act 1993 that a notice dated _____ has been served under section 13 [or 42] of that Act by _____ of _____.*
> NOTE: Copy filed."

(There is no CRE for this entry.)

If the application is for a unilateral notice the statement or conveyancer's certificate given in form UN1 will need to state that a notice was served by or on behalf of the beneficiary on the registered proprietor (who should be named) in accordance with ss.13 or 42, 1993 Act on a stated date.

6.4.2 Vesting orders made under ss.26(1) or 50(1), 1993 Act (where the relevant landlord cannot be found or identified)

The LRA 2002 applies to such an order as it applies to an order affecting land that is made by the court for the purpose of enforcing a judgment (s.97(2)(a), 1993 Act). You can, therefore, apply for such an order or application to the court for such an order to be protected by notice. A person who has applied for such an order who applies for a restriction in Form N to Schedule 4, LRR 2003 and a person who has obtained an order who applies for a restriction in Form L or N is regarded as having sufficient interest to apply for the restriction (rr.93(q) and (o), LRR 2003 respectively).

6.4.3 Orders made under ss.24, 25, 48 or 49, 1993 Act (where there is a dispute)

There are no express provisions in the 1993 Act relating to the protection of such an order or an application to the court for such an order. However, in view of its nature, such an order or application to the court for such an order can be protected by a notice.

6.4.4 Protection against persons other than the freeholder or competent landlord

Collective enfranchisement

The 1993 Act provides that, after any initial notice has been served and registered, the freeholder cannot "make any disposal severing his interest in the premises or" in any property specified in the notice nor may they grant certain leases. Similarly, any intermediate lessee cannot grant certain leases, although the leasehold interest itself can be sold or mortgaged (s.19(1), 1993 Act). Any such grant or disposal that contravenes s.19(1) is void.

Where the registrar is uncertain whether or not a disposition is caught by these provisions, they will require a certificate to be given by the solicitors to the freeholder or intermediate lessee (as the case may be) that the transaction is not one to which the 1993 Act applies. This includes any disposition by a mortgagee under any power of sale. For these reasons, the registrar considers that the nominee purchaser should apply against all titles affected by the notice, not just that of the reversioner. Where any interest is not registered, a land charge should be registered.

Individual new flat leases

A tenant's notice severely restricts the right of the landlord and competent landlord to terminate the tenant's lease (Schedule 12, 1993 Act). Since it would seem undesirable for a purchaser from an intermediate lessee to be unaware of the position of the tenant, such a tenant should consider protecting the notice on any intermediate landlord's title, or at the Land Charges Department.

Generally

The 1993 Act makes considerable provision for the service of notices or counter notices. Most of these would not seem to be pending land actions. However, where there are specific applications to the court or to a tribunal, it would seem that they very well may be, for example an application to the court to defeat a tenant's claim on the grounds of redevelopment under s.47(1), 1993 Act. In those cases, reversioners, intermediate landlords and tenants should consider carefully against whom the registration should be made.

6.4.5 Cancellation generally
Application for cancellation should be made in either form CN1 or UN4 and an application to remove a unilateral notice should be made in form UN2. In accordance with normal Land Registry practice, there will be no automatic cancellation of notices where an application is received to register a transfer of the freehold or new lease. Where the notice under the 1993 Act was protected by a caution, a withdrawal in form WCT should be lodged.

6.4.6 Later application to register a disposition where a notice made under s.13, 1993 Act is protected in the register
Any application to register a disposition must include a certificate that the disposition is not one involving a disposal or grant of a lease within s.19(1), 1993 Act. (This requirement also applies to a transfer by a mortgagee in exercise of their power of sale.) It does not matter whether the disposition is dated before or after the notice in the register.

Once you have supplied this certificate, we will then serve notice of your application on the beneficiary of the unilateral notice or the applicant for the agreed notice. If we receive no objection to the notice, we will complete the registration, but will not cancel the entry of the s.13 notice on the register.

6.4.7 Later application for agreed or unilateral notice where a notice made under s.13, 1993 Act is protected in the register
We will generally ignore a s.13 notice where the later application is one to enter a unilateral or agreed notice. The exception to this general rule is where we have

had to satisfy ourselves as to the validity of the applicant's claim under s.34(3)(c), 1993 Act. In that case, where it appears that the application may be to register a notice protecting an interest arising under a disposition falling with s.19(1), 1993 Act, we will require a certificate and serve notice as referred to in section *6.4.6 Later application to register a disposition where a notice made under s.13, 1993 Act is protected in the register.*

9 Enquiries and comments

If you have a particular concern that is not covered by this guide, please contact Land Registry in advance of the transaction—see *Contact details*. If the transaction is particularly complex, it may be better to make your enquiry in writing at the Land Registry office that will process your application.

If you have any comments or suggestions about our guides, please send them to:

Central Operations Group
Land Registry
Trafalgar House
1 Bedford Park
Croydon
CR0 2AQ
(DX 8888 Croydon 3)

You can obtain further copies of this and all our guides free of charge from Customer Support (see *Contact details*) or you can download them from our website in English or Welsh.

Appendix 1—Merger of leases on acquisition of the freehold

When a person is entitled, in the same capacity, to the leasehold and any superior leasehold and the freehold titles to a property, the leasehold titles will be merged if the registered proprietor or their practitioner makes an application for merger and any entries on the inferior title(s) that would prevent merger are cancelled or removed.

The mechanics of the application depend on the circumstances of the case, as explained below. If you cannot produce the lease for any reason (for example where the lease is not in the lessee's possession because it affects also other land) a short letter stating the reason for its non-production should be lodged.

Merger of registered leases

When the freehold title is already registered, the request for closure of the leasehold title(s) may be made in panel 4 of form AP1, which should refer to the title numbers of the titles to be closed.

When the freehold title is the subject of an application for first registration, the request for merger should be made in panel 5 of form FR1 and in addition form AP1 should be lodged for closure of the leasehold title(s). The lease should accompany the application. The registered leasehold title can only be closed when all entries on the register have been satisfactorily dealt with.

Any restriction on the register must normally be withdrawn by means of a form RX3 signed by the restrictioner or their conveyancer, unless a corresponding restriction is to be entered against the freehold title.

A restriction in favour of a chargee will be cancelled automatically when the title is closed (and re-entered on the new title if the charge is to be registered against it).

A Form A restriction on dispositions by a sole proprietor will also be cancelled automatically on closure of the title.

An inhibition resulting from an injunction or restraint order may prevent the closure of the title, or a restriction may be entered on the freehold title, depending on the terms of the court order on which the entry is founded. It may be cancelled on production of an official copy of the court order that puts an end to the original order.

Application should be made for the cancellation or removal of any notice on forms CN1, UN4 or UN2 as appropriate.

Evidence to support certain applications is listed below.

When a registered charge appears on the title a discharge of the charge, or a deed of substituted security, must be produced.

Where a noted charge appears on the title it must be produced with a receipt endorsed or other evidence of discharge, or a deed of substituted security.

A creditor's notice on the leasehold title will normally be entered on the freehold title. If no longer required, the notice may be cancelled on application accompanied by an office copy of the court order dismissing or withdrawing the petition in bankruptcy or rescinding or annulling the subsequent bankruptcy order.

A bankruptcy inhibition registered under the Land Registration Act 1925, or a restriction registered under s.86, LRA 2002, may be cancelled on production of an official copy of the court order under which the bankruptcy order was rescinded or annulled.

An inhibition resulting from an injunction or restraint order may prevent the closure of the title, or a restriction may be entered on the freehold title, depending on the terms of the court order on which the entry is founded. It may be cancelled on production of an official copy of the court order that puts an end to the original order.

A (matrimonial) homes rights notice that no longer affects the title may be withdrawn by means of an application in form HR4. If not withdrawn or cancelled, the notice will be carried forward onto the freehold title.

A notice of an access order under the Access to Neighbouring Land Act 1992 may be cancelled on production of the appropriate evidence, and if not cancelled will likewise be carried forward onto the freehold title.

A caution may be withdrawn by means of form WCT.

Merger of unregistered lease noted against a registered superior title
Make the application in form CN1, supported by the lease and all deeds and documents relating to the leasehold title. The documents lodged should include an up-to-date land charges search.

Merger of unregistered lease not noted against a registered superior title

If the superior title is being registered or is the subject of an application in form CN1, the lease should be referred to in the application.

If the superior title is already registered and the lease is not noted against it, no application for merger is required. In either case the original lease and all deeds and documents relating to the title to it should be lodged. The documents lodged should include an up-to-date land charges search.

Appendix 2—Applications for registration of extended leases
Registration of new lease

The application for registration of the new lease should be made in form FR1 if the reversionary title is unregistered, or form AP1 if the reversionary title is registered.

The application should be accompanied by:

- the lease being registered, and (if you wish us to return the original) a certified copy
- stamp duty land tax certificate, if required
- evidence of the lessor's title to grant the lease, if required
- consent of lessor's mortgagee, if required
- any consent required by a restriction affecting the lessor's title
- particulars of any leases intermediate between the lessor's title and the new lease (see section *6.3.4 Reversionary titles, Intermediate leasehold titles*)
- application to give effect to the deemed surrender of the existing lease and any intermediate lease held by or in trust for the applicant
- application for any necessary restriction or notice on the title to the new lease
- fees.

The new lease may either be a complete, full-length lease, or it may be drawn by reference to the terms of the lease being surrendered. Avoid using a deed of variation. The effect of the procedure may appear to be the variation of the length of the term of the original lease but this is not the case. The new lease takes effect in substitution for the existing lease.

Lessor's title

If the lessor's title is unregistered, an examined abstract or epitome of the lessor's title, and a current search in Land Charges Department, should be obtained and lodged with the application, with a view to the grant of an absolute leasehold title. Normally an absolute leasehold title can be granted only if the lessor's title and any superior titles have previously been approved by Land Registry on an application for first registration or are lodged with the application.

Consent of lessor's mortgagee

If there is a restriction in favour of the lessor's mortgagee on the lessor's title, the mortgagee's consent must be lodged to comply with s.41(1), LRA 2002, unless the registrar makes an order to disapply the restriction under s.41(2).

Even if there is no such restriction on the lessor's title, the consent of the lessor's mortgagee (and any other person interested in the mortgage) should be lodged where the old lease:

- was granted on or after 1 November 1993 (for applications under the 1993 Act) or 1 January 1968 (for applications under the 1967 Act)
- was made subsequent to the date of the lessor's mortgage, and
- would not have been binding on the persons interested in the mortgage (ie it was outside the mortgagor's leasing powers and they did not concur in it).

Where, however, the consent is not lodged, the following entry will be made in the property register of the new title:

> *"The title to the lease is, during the subsistence of the charge dated . . . . in favour of . . . . affecting the landlord's title (and to the extent permitted by law, any charge replacing or varying this charge or any further charge in respect of all or part of the sum secured by this charge), subject to any rights that may have arisen by reason of the absence of chargee's consent, unless the lease is authorised by section 99 of the Law of Property Act 1925."*

This entry will not be made if a copy of the mortgage deed is lodged together with confirmation that the granting of the lease was permitted by the terms of the mortgage (by referring to the relevant clause in the deed) and that the mortgagee's consent was not required.

In other cases the power of the lessor to grant the lease cannot be questioned on account of the existence of a mortgage on its title.

Application to give effect to the deemed surrender of the existing lease

The form of this application will depend on whether the existing lease is registered, whether the surrendered lease is noted on any reversionary title, and whether the application is under the 1967 Act or the 1993 Act.

If the applicant's existing leasehold title is registered, application should be made to give effect to the surrender of the existing lease by closing that title. If the applicant's leasehold title is not registered but notice of it is entered on any reversionary title, you must make an application for the cancellation of the notice.

Even if the surrendered lease is neither registered nor noted on any reversionary title, it is still necessary for the surrendered lease and the applicant's title to it to be lodged, together with a current Land Charges Department search. Any mortgages affecting the lease should also be lodged.

Any mortgagees of the applicant's existing lease should be contacted prior to completion of the new lease and the necessary arrangements made.

Any other interest affecting the existing lease should also be carefully considered.

If it is protected in the register of the existing lease but does not affect the new lease, lodge an application for the withdrawal of the restriction, or notice of deposit or intended deposit, or the cancellation of the notice. If it, or a corresponding interest, affects the new lease, an application to protect it by means of a suitable entry in the register should be included in, or accompany, the application to register the new lease.

Closure of existing leasehold title

Make the application to close the applicant's existing title on form AP1 and describe the application in panel 4 as 'Closure of leasehold title'. The original lease should accompany the application.

Cancellation of notice of existing lease on reversionary title (when existing lease is unregistered)

Make the application in form CN1. The surrendered lease and the applicant's title to it should be lodged, together with a current Land Charges Department search. Any mortgages affecting the lease should also be lodged.

Arrangements with mortgagees

Where the new lease is being granted under the 1993 Act, any charges on the surrendered lease will transfer automatically. The applicant should apply for registration of the charge in panels 4 and 10 of form AP1 or panels 5 and 10 of form FR1, the form used depending on whether the reversioner's title is registered. It is only necessary to arrange for the charge to be lodged if the surrendered lease is unregistered. If the charge is to be protected by notice only, and the reversioner's title is registered, you should complete either form AN1 or UN1, as appropriate.

Where, however, the new lease is being granted under the 1967 Act, a mortgage does not transfer automatically to the new lease and should, therefore, either be discharged and replaced, or transferred to the new lease by deed. If the mortgage is discharged, the discharged mortgage and evidence of discharge and the new mortgage, if any, with a certified copy if the new mortgage is to be registered, should be lodged with the application. If a deed of substituted security is used, the mortgage should be lodged together with the deed and, if the mortgage is to be registered against the new title, a certified copy.

If the mortgagee's cooperation cannot be secured, Land Registry will endeavour to serve a special notice on them, and any other person appearing to be interested in the mortgage, giving details of:

- the mortgage
- the applicants and the nature of the application
- the intended closure of the title to the existing lease (if registered)
- the intended cancellation of the notice of the existing lease on a superior title (if the existing lease is not registered but is noted on such a title)
- the effect of the application, if completed, on the mortgage
- how any objection to the application can be made; and requesting the lodging of the original mortgage.

If there is no response to the notice, the application will be completed. In the case of a lease granted under the 1993 Act, the mortgage may be registered or noted against the new title in the normal way. In the case of a lease granted under the 1967 Act, a special entry will be made, as described in section *5.4.2 Entries in the register*.

If, in response to the notice, the recipient lodges the original mortgage, it will either be registered or noted. If notice has to be served in respect of more than one subsisting mortgage, separate entries will be made in the register according to the respective priorities of the mortgages concerned.

Other entries on existing leasehold title

A restriction in favour of a chargee will be cancelled automatically when the old title is closed (and re-entered on the new title if the charge is registered against it). A form A restriction against dispositions by a sole proprietor will also be cancelled on closure of the title. A voluntary restriction in the register of the old title must normally be withdrawn by means of a form RX4 signed by the restrictioner or their conveyancer, unless a corresponding restriction is applied for against the new lease.

Application should be made for the cancellation or removal of any notices other than one protecting a monetary charge, on forms CN1, UN4 or UN2 as appropriate.

Evidence to support certain applications is set out below. A creditor's notice will normally be entered on the new title. If no longer required, application should be accompanied by an office copy of the court order dismissing or withdrawing the petition in bankruptcy or rescinding or annulling the subsequent bankruptcy order. A bankruptcy restriction may be cancelled on production of an official copy of the court order under which the bankruptcy order was rescinded or annulled.

A homes rights notice that no longer affects may be withdrawn by means of an application in form HR4. If not withdrawn or cancelled, the notice will be carried forward onto the new title.

A notice of an access order under the Access to Neighbouring Land Act 1992 requires production of the appropriate evidence, and if not cancelled will be carried forward onto the new title.

A caution may be withdrawn by means of a form WCT.

An inhibition resulting from an injunction or restraint order may prevent the closure of the title or a restriction may be entered on the freehold title, depending on the terms of the court order on which the entry is founded. It may be cancelled on production of an official copy of the court order that puts an end to the original order.

We will consider any entry affecting the old title that is not withdrawn or cancelled and is not carried forward onto, or replaced by a corresponding entry on, the new title on a case-by-case basis. In some cases it may be possible to deal with the matter by the service of notice.

Protection of interests affecting the new lease

As with all applications for registration of a lease, full particulars of all third party interests affecting the lease must be entered in the appropriate panel of the application form AP1/FR1 and separate applications made for their entry on the register where appropriate. In addition to this, any restriction required must be applied for in form RX1.

APPENDIX 2W

The Housing and Regeneration Act 2008 (Commencement No. 6 and Transitional and Savings Provisions) Order 2009

(SI 2009/2096)

Arts 1, 2(2), 3(1) and (2)

The Secretary of State, in exercise of the powers conferred by sections 322 and 325(1) and (4) of the Housing and Regeneration Act 2008, makes the following Order: **1228W**

Citation and interpretation

1.—(1) This Order may be cited as the Housing and Regeneration Act 2008 (Commencement No. 6 and Transitional and Savings Provisions) Order 2009.

(2) In this Order—

"the 2008 Act" means the Housing and Regeneration Act 2008; and

"the commencement date" means 7th September 2009.

Commencement of certain provisions of the Act

2.— . . .

(2) The following provisions of the 2008 Act shall come into force, in relation to England, on the commencement date, subject to article 3(1) and (2)—

(a) section 300 (right to acquire freehold: abolition of low rent test);

(b) sections 301 (shared ownership leases: protection for certain leases) and 302 (shared ownership leases: protection for hard to replace houses), in so far as they are not already in force; and

(c) except as mentioned in section 325(2)(b) of the 2008 Act, section 321(1) (consequential amendments and repeals) and Schedule 16 (repeals and revocations), in so far as they relate to the repeal of such provisions of the 1967 Act as are listed in Schedule 16.

. . .

Transitional and savings provisions

3.—(1) Subject to paragraph (2), the amendments made in consequence of article 2(2)(a) and (c) shall not have effect as regards any long tenancy within the meaning of Part 1 of the Leasehold Reform Act 1967 (enfranchisement and extension of long leaseholds)—

(a) granted before the commencement date; or

(b) granted after the commencement date but arising from a written agreement for the grant of that tenancy made before the commencement date.

(2) Section 1AA of the Leasehold Reform Act 1967 (additional right to enfranchisement only in case of houses whose rent exceeds applicable limit under section 4) shall continue to have effect as regards a tenancy granted—

    (a) before the commencement date; and

    (b) in respect of a house that is within an area described in the Housing (Right to Enfranchise) (Designated Protected Areas) (England) Order 2009,

and for the purpose of the application of that section the areas described in that Order shall be treated as areas designated as rural areas under subsection (3)(a) of that section.

. . .

APPENDIX 2X

The Housing (Shared Ownership Leases) (Exclusion from Leasehold Reform Act 1967) (England) Regulations 2009

(SI 2009/2097)

The Secretary of State for Communities and Local Government, in exercise of the **1228X** *powers conferred by paragraphs 3A(1) and (2), 4A(1) and (2) and 5 of Schedule 4A to the Leasehold Reform Act 1967, makes the following Order:*

Citation, commencement and application

1.—(1) These Regulations may be cited as the Housing (Shared Ownership Leases) (Exclusion from Leasehold Reform Act 1967) (England) Regulations 2009 and shall come into force on 7th September 2009.

(2) These Regulations apply in relation to the granting of a long tenancy for a house in England at any time after the coming into force of these Regulations except where such tenancy arises from a written agreement for the grant of that tenancy made before the coming into force of these Regulations.

Interpretation

2. In these Regulations "the Act" means the Leasehold Reform Act 1967.

Meaning of "market value price", etc

3.—(1) For the purposes of these Regulations, "market value price" means the amount which the interest in the house of the tenant would fetch, if sold on the open market by a willing vendor, on the assumption that the tenant had previously purchased 100 per cent of the shares in the house, disregarding the following matters—

(a) any mortgage of the tenant's interest;
(b) any interest in or right over the house created by the tenant;
(c) any improvement made by the tenant or any predecessor in title of the tenant; and
(d) any failure by the tenant or any predecessor in title of the tenant to carry out any repairing obligations under the lease.

(2) Subject to paragraph (3), the market value price shall be agreed between the landlord and the tenant, or determined in a manner agreed between them.

(3) Where the landlord and tenant are unable to agree the manner in which the market value price should be determined they may appoint an independent expert to determine the price.

(4) If the landlord and tenant are unable to agree on the person to be appointed, either party may apply to the President of the Royal Institution of Chartered

Surveyors for the market value price to be determined by the President or such person as he may nominate.

Prescribed condition under paragraph 3A(1)(b) of Schedule 4A to the Act

4. The condition prescribed under paragraph 3A(1)(b) of Schedule 4A to the Act is that the lease must set out the amount of any rent payable and the basis for calculating or determining any increase in the rent payable.

Acquisition of additional shares in the house: requirements prescribed under paragraph 3A(2)(c) of Schedule 4A to the Act

5.—(1) The following requirements are prescribed under paragraph 3A(2)(c) of Schedule 4A to the Act for the purposes of paragraph 3A(1)(a) of that Schedule.

(2) The tenant is to be entitled to acquire additional shares in the house, up to a maximum of 100 per cent, in instalments of 25 per cent or such lesser percentage as may be specified in the lease.

(3) If the lease specifies the date after which the tenant may acquire additional shares in the house, such date must not be later than 12 months after the date the tenant first acquired shares in the house.

(4) The tenant is to be able to exercise the entitlement to acquire additional shares in the house by serving notice in writing on the landlord at any time during the term of the lease, stating the additional shares the tenant proposes to acquire.

(5) Where the tenant serves a notice under paragraph (4) the landlord must not act in a way that would unreasonably delay the acquisition by the tenant of the additional shares.

(6) The price for the additional shares is to be an amount no greater than the same percentage of the market value price at the date of service of the tenant's notice under paragraph (4) as is represented by the percentage of the additional shares being acquired.

(7) The rent payable by the tenant to the landlord under the lease (excluding amounts payable, directly or indirectly, for services, repairs, maintenance, insurance, or management costs) is to be reduced, on the tenant's acquisition of additional shares, in the same proportion as is represented by the reduction in the percentage of shares remaining un-acquired by the tenant.

Payment for outstanding shares in the house: circumstances prescribed under paragraph 3A(2)(e) of Schedule 4A to the Act

6.—(1) (1) The circumstances prescribed under paragraph 3A(2)(e) of Schedule 4A to the Act for the purposes of paragraph 3A(1)(a) of that Schedule are that the lease must provide—

(a) that there shall have been a disposal, other than an exempt disposal, of any interest in the house by the tenant; and

(b) that the amount payable by the tenant to the landlord is to be an amount no greater than the same percentage of the market value price at the date of the disposal as is represented by the percentage of the shares in the house remaining un-acquired by the tenant.

(2) In paragraph (1) "exempt disposal" means—

(a) a disposal under a will or intestacy;

(b) a disposal under section 24 of the Matrimonial Causes Act 1973 or section 2 of the Inheritance (Provision for Family and Dependants) Act 1975;

(c) a grant of a sub-tenancy in respect of which a notice has been given under section 52(1)(b) of the Housing Act 1980 (notice that a tenancy is to be a protected shorthold tenancy) or of a kind mentioned in any of Cases 11 to 18 or 20 in Schedule 15 to the Rent Act 1977;

(d) a grant of a sub-tenancy of part of the house, if any other part of the house remains in the possession of the tenant; or

(e) a grant of a mortgage.

Acquisition of the landlord's interest in the house: requirements prescribed under paragraph 3A(2)(f) of Schedule 4A to the Act

7.—(1) The following requirements are prescribed under paragraph 3A(2)(f) of Schedule 4A to the Act for the purposes of paragraph 3A(1)(a) of that Schedule.

(2) The lease must provide that the tenant may not acquire the landlord's interest until the tenant has acquired 100 per cent of the shares in the house.

(3) If the lease specifies the date after which the tenant may acquire the landlord's interest, such date must not be later than 12 months after the date the tenant first acquired shares in the house.

(4) Where the lease does not provide for the landlord's interest to be transferred automatically to the tenant once the tenant has acquired 100 per cent of the shares in the house, it must provide for the tenant to acquire the landlord's interest—

(a) by serving notice in writing on the landlord at any time during the term of the lease; and

(b) requiring the landlord's interest to be transferred to the tenant as soon as practicable after the coming into effect of the notice referred to in sub-paragraph (a).

(5) The lease must not make provision entitling the landlord to make any charge for the conveyance or assignment of his interest in the house.

Protected areas: conditions prescribed under paragraph 4A(1)(c) of Schedule 4A to the Act[2]

8.—(1) The following conditions are prescribed under paragraph 4A(1)(c) of Schedule 4A to the Act.

---

[2] Regulation 8 was amended by SI 2010/671, Sch. 1, para. 78 and Sch. 3 with effect from April 1, 2010.

(2) The lease must contain a condition enabling the tenant to acquire at least 80 per cent of the total shares in the house.

(3) If the lease enables the tenant to acquire more than 80 per cent of the shares in the house the lease must also contain conditions to the effect that where the tenant holds more than 80 per cent of the shares and wants to sell those shares—

(a) except in the circumstances described in paragraph (4)(h), the tenant must sell the shares to the landlord, or to a housing association or [*registered social landlord*] **private registered provider of social housing** nominated by the landlord; and

(b) on a sale of the shares the landlord, nominated housing association or nominated [*registered social landlord*] **private registered provider of social housing**, as the case may be, must pay to the tenant an amount no greater than the same percentage of the market value price at the date of service of the tenant's notice under sub-paragraph (4)(e) as is represented by the percentage of the shares being sold.

(4) Where the lease contains conditions to the effect specified in paragraph (3) the lease must also—

(a) specify the circumstances in which the tenant may notify the landlord of the tenant's intention to sell the shares in the house;

(b) require the tenant to notify the landlord that the tenant intends to sell those shares;

(c) specify the time by which the landlord must respond to the tenant's notice of intended sale, which must be no later than 3 months after the date of receipt by the landlord of the tenant's notice;

(d) specify that the landlord's response—

    (i) will confirm that the landlord will purchase the shares; or

    (ii) will state the name, address and contact details of the housing association or [*registered social landlord*] **private registered provider of social housing** nominated by the landlord to purchase the shares;

(e) specify that the landlord, the nominated housing association or the [*registered social landlord*] **private registered provider of social housing** will complete the purchase of the tenant's shares no later than 6 months after the date of receipt by the landlord, the nominated housing association or the nominated [*registered social landlord*] **private registered provider of social housing** of the tenant's notice that the tenant is ready to sell the tenant's shares specified in the notice referred to in sub-paragraph (b);

(f) prohibit the tenant from giving the notice referred to in sub-paragraph (e) until the market value price has been ascertained in accordance with regulation 3;

(g) specify the manner in which notices referred to in this regulation may be served, including any circumstances in which service shall be deemed to have taken place; and

(h) specify the remedies available to the tenant in the event of a failure by the landlord, the nominated housing association or the nominated [*registered social landlord*] **private registered provider of social housing** to complete the purchase of the tenant's shares in the house in accordance with the conditions of the lease, which must include enabling the tenant—

  (i) to dispose of the shares as the tenant sees fit; and
  (ii) to recover from the landlord compensation for any loss occasioned by the tenant as a result of delay or failure on the part of the landlord, the nominated housing association or the nominated [*registered social landlord*] **private registered provider of social housing** to complete the purchase in accordance with the conditions of the lease.

(5) The lease must contain conditions to the effect that—

(a) the landlord may not nominate a housing association or [*registered social landlord*] **private registered provider of social housing** to purchase the tenant's shares unless that housing association or [*registered social landlord*] **private registered provider of social housing** has confirmed in writing to the landlord that it wishes to be nominated to purchase the tenant's shares; and

(b) where a housing association or [*registered social landlord*] **private registered provider of social housing** has been nominated by the landlord, the housing association or [*registered social landlord*] **private registered provider of social housing** will be substituted for the landlord during the process of acquiring the tenant's shares (whether or not the tenant's shares are acquired by the nominated association or landlord) and, in particular, will be subject to the same conditions as would apply to the landlord if the landlord were purchasing the shares, with the exception of that referred to in paragraph (4)(h)(ii).

(6) A lease granted by a person other than a housing association or [*registered social landlord*] **private registered provider of social housing** must set out the amount of any rent payable and the basis for calculating or determining any increase in the rent payable.

(7) [. . .]

**Protected areas: acquisition of additional shares in the house—
requirements prescribed under paragraph 4A(2)(c) of Schedule 4A to the Act**

9.—(1) The following requirements are prescribed under paragraph 4A(2)(c) of Schedule 4A to the Act for the purposes of paragraph 4A(1)(a) of that Schedule.

(2) The tenant is to be entitled to acquire additional shares in the house, up to the maximum specified in the lease (being not less than 80 per cent of the total shares in the house), in instalments of 25 per cent or such lesser percentage as may be specified in the lease.

(3) If the lease specifies the date after which the tenant may acquire additional shares in the house, such date must not be later than 12 months after the date the tenant first acquired shares in the house.

(4) The tenant is to be able to exercise the entitlement to acquire additional shares in the house by serving notice in writing on the landlord at any time during the term of the lease, stating the additional shares the tenant proposes to acquire.

(5) Where the tenant serves a notice under paragraph (4) the landlord must not act in a way that would unreasonably delay the acquisition by the tenant of the additional shares.

(6) The price for the additional shares is to be an amount no greater than the same percentage of the market value price at the date of service of the tenant's notice under paragraph (4) as is represented by the percentage of the additional shares being acquired.

(7) The rent payable by the tenant to the landlord under the lease (excluding amounts payable, directly or indirectly, for services, repairs, maintenance, insurance, or management costs) is to be reduced, on the tenant's acquisition of additional shares, in the same proportion as is represented by the reduction in the percentage of shares remaining un-acquired by the tenant.

Protected areas: payment for outstanding shares in the house—circumstances prescribed under paragraph 4A(2)(e) of Schedule 4A to the Act

10.—(1) The circumstances prescribed under paragraph 4A(2)(e) of Schedule 4A to the Act for the purposes of paragraph 4A(1)(a) of that Schedule are that the lease must provide—

    (a) that there shall have been a disposal, other than an exempt disposal, of any interest in the house by the tenant; and

    (b) that the amount payable by the tenant to the landlord is to be an amount no greater than the same percentage of the market value price at the date of the disposal as is represented by the percentage of the shares in the house remaining un-acquired by the tenant.

(2) In paragraph (1) "exempt disposal" means—

    (a) a disposal under a will or intestacy;

    (b) a disposal under section 24 of the Matrimonial Causes Act 1973 or section 2 of the Inheritance (Provision for Family and Dependants) Act 1975;

    (c) a grant of a sub-tenancy in respect of which a notice has been given under section 52(1)(b) of the Housing Act 1980 (notice that a tenancy is to be a protected shorthold tenancy) or of a kind mentioned in any of Cases 11 to 18 or 20 in Schedule 15 to the Rent Act 1977;

    (d) a grant of a sub-tenancy of part of the house, if any other part of the house remains in the possession of the tenant; or

    (e) a grant of a mortgage.

APPENDIX 2Y

The Housing (Right to Enfranchise) (Designated Protected Areas) (England) Order 2009

(SI 2009/2098)

The Secretary of State for Communities and Local Government, in exercise of the **1228Y** *powers conferred by paragraphs 4A(3) of Schedule 4A to the Leasehold Reform Act 1967; having published the criteria to be taken into account when deciding whether to designate an area as a protected area as required by paragraph 4A(4) of that Schedule; and having taken steps to consult those likely to be affected by the Order as required by paragraph 4A(5) of that Schedule, makes the following Order:*

Citation and commencement and interpretation

1.—(1) This Order may be cited as the Housing (Right to Enfranchise) (Designated Protected Areas) (England) Order 2009 and shall come into force on 7th September 2009.

(2) In this Order "the 1967 Act" means the Leasehold Reform Act 1967.

Designated protected areas in the West Midlands

2. The following areas in the West Midlands region are designated protected areas for the purposes of paragraph 4A(1) of Schedule 4A to the 1967 Act (certain leases in protected areas)—

- (a) those parishes in the district of Herefordshire and in the counties of Shropshire, Staffordshire, Warwickshire, West Midlands and Worcestershire specified in Schedule 1 to this Order; and
- (b) those areas in the parishes and the unparished areas in the district of Herefordshire and in the counties of Shropshire, Staffordshire, Warwickshire, West Midlands and Worcestershire specified in Schedule 2 to this Order each shown bounded with a black line and crossed hatched on one of the maps contained in the volume entitled "Maps of the Protected Areas in the West Midlands designated as protected areas by the Housing (Right to Enfranchise) (Designated Protected Areas) (England) Order 2009 (SI No: 2009/2098) and referred to in article 2(b) and Schedule 2 to the Order", which volume is—
    - (i) signed by a member of the Senior Civil Service in the Department for Communities and Local Government; and
    - (ii) deposited and available for inspection at the principal office of the Secretary of State for Communities and Local Government.

Designated protected areas in the South West

3. The following areas in the South West region are designated protected areas for the purposes of paragraph 4A(1) of Schedule 4A to the 1967 Act—

(a) those parishes in the districts of Bath and North East Somerset, North Somerset and South Gloucestershire and in the counties of Cornwall, Devon, Dorset, Gloucestershire, Somerset and Wiltshire specified in Schedule 3 to this Order; and

(b) those areas in the parishes and the unparished areas in the districts of Bath and North East Somerset, North Somerset and South Gloucestershire and in the counties of Cornwall Devon, Dorset, Gloucestershire, Somerset and Wiltshire specified in Schedule 4 to this Order each shown bounded with a black line and cross hatched on one of the maps contained in the volume entitled "Maps of the Protected Areas in the South West designated as protected areas by the Housing (Right to Enfranchise) (Designated Protected Areas) (England) Order 2009 (SI No: 2009/2098) and referred to in article 3(b) and Schedule 4 to the Order", which volume is—

   (i) signed by a member of the Senior Civil Service in the Department for Communities and Local Government; and

   (ii) deposited and available for inspection at the principal office of the Secretary of State for Communities and Local Government.

Designated protected areas in the North West

4. The following areas in the North West region are designated protected areas for the purposes of paragraph 4A(1) of Schedule 4A to the 1967 Act—

(a) those parishes in the districts of Cheshire East, Cheshire West and Chester, Halton and Warrington and in the counties of Cumbria, Greater Manchester, Lancashire and Merseyside specified in Schedule 5 to this Order; and

(b) those areas in the parishes and the unparished areas in the districts of Cheshire East, Cheshire West and Chester and Warrington and in the counties of Cumbria, Greater Manchester, Lancashire and Merseyside specified in Schedule 6 to this Order each shown bounded with a black line and cross hatched on one of the maps contained in the volume entitled "Maps of the Protected Areas in the North West designated as protected areas by the Housing (Right to Enfranchise) (Designated Protected Areas) (England) Order 2009 (SI No: 2009/2098) and referred to in article 4(b) and Schedule 6 to the Order", which volume is—

   (i) signed by a member of the Senior Civil Service in the Department for Communities and Local Government; and

   (ii) deposited and available for inspection at the principal office of the Secretary of State for Communities and Local Government.

Designated protected areas in the East of England

5. The following areas in the East of England region are designated protected areas for the purposes of paragraph 4A(1) of Schedule 4A to the 1967 Act—

(a) those parishes in the district of Bedford and in the counties of Cambridgeshire, Essex, Hertfordshire, Norfolk and Suffolk specified in Schedule 7 to this Order; and

(b) those areas in the parishes and the unparished areas in the district of Beford and in the counties of Cambridgeshire, Essex, Hertfordshire, Norfolk and Suffolk specified in Schedule 8 to this Order each shown bounded with a black line and cross hatched on one of the maps contained in the volume entitled "Maps of the Protected Areas in the East of England designated as protected areas by the the Housing (Right to Enfranchise) (Designated Protected Areas) (England) Order 2009 (SI No: 2009/2098) and referred to in article 5(b) and Schedule 8 to the Order", which volume is—

(i) signed by a member of the Senior Civil Service in the Department for Communities and Local Government; and

(ii) deposited and available for inspection at the principal office of the Secretary of State for Communities and Local Government.

Designated protected areas in the North East

6. The following areas in the North East region are designated protected areas for the purposes of paragraph 4A(1) of Schedule 4A to the 1967 Act—

(a) the parishes in the districts of Hartlepool, Middlesborough, Redcar and Cleveland, and Stockton-on-Tees and in the counties of Durham, Northumberland and Tyne and Wear specified in Schedule 9 to this Order; and

(b) those areas in the parishes and the unparished areas in the districts of Hartlepool and Redcar and Cleveland and in the counties of Durham, Northumberland and Tyne and Wear specified in Schedule 10 to this Order each shown bounded with a black line and cross hatched on one of the maps contained in the volume entitled "Maps of the Protected Areas in the North East designated as protected areas by the Housing (Right to Enfranchise) (Designated Protected Areas) (England) Order 2009 (SI No: 2009/2098) and referred to in article 6(b) and Schedule 10 to the Order", which volume is—

(i) signed by a member of the Senior Civil Service in the Department for Communities and Local Government; and

(ii) deposited and available for inspection at the principal office of the Secretary of State for Communities and Local Government.

Designated protected areas in the South East

7. The following areas in the South East region are designated protected areas for the purposes of paragraph 4A(1) of Schedule 4A to the 1967 Act—

(a) those parishes and the unparished area in the district of West Berkshire and in the counties of Buckinghamshire, East Sussex, Hampshire, the Isle of Wight, Kent, Oxfordshire, Surrey and West Sussex specified in Schedule 11 to this Order; and

(b) those areas in the parishes and the unparished areas in the district of West Berkshire and in the counties of Buckinghamshire, East Sussex, Hampshire, the Isle of Wight, Kent, Oxfordshire, Surrey and West Sussex specified in Schedule 12 to this Order each shown bounded with a black line and cross hatched on one of the maps contained in the volume entitled "Maps of the Protected Areas in the South East designated as protected areas by the Housing (Right to Enfranchise) (Designated Protected Areas) (England) Order 2009" (SI No: 2009/2098) and referred to in article 7(b) and Schedule 12 to the Order, which volume is—

   (i) signed by a member of the Senior Civil Service in the Department for Communities and Local Government; and
   (ii) deposited and available for inspection at the principal office of the Secretary of State for Communities and Local Government.

Designated protected areas in the East Midlands

8. The following areas in the East Midlands region are designated protected areas for the purposes of paragraph 4A(1) of Schedule 4A to the 1967 Act—

(a) those parishes in the counties of Derbyshire, Leicestershire, Lincolnshire, Northamptonshire and Nottinghamshire specified in Schedule 13 to this Order; and

(b) those areas in the parishes and the unparished areas in the counties of Derbyshire, Leicestershire, Lincolnshire, Northamptonshire and Nottinghamshire specified in Schedule 14 to this Order each shown bounded with a black line and crossed hatched on one of the maps contained in the volume entitled "Maps of the Protected Areas in the East Midlands designated as protected areas by the Housing (Right to Enfranchise) (Designated Protected Areas) (England) Order 2009" (SI No: 2009/2098) and referred to in article 8(b) and Schedule 14 to the Order, which volume is—

   (i) signed by a member of the Senior Civil Service in the Department for Communities and Local Government; and
   (ii) deposited and available for inspection at the principal office of the Secretary of State for Communities and Local Government.

Designated protected areas in Yorkshire and the Humber

9. The following areas in Yorkshire and the Humber region are designated protected areas for the purposes of paragraph 4A(1) of Schedule 4A to the 1967 Act—

(a) those parishes in the districts of the East Riding of Yorkshire, North East Lincolnshire and North Lincolnshire and in the counties of North Yorkshire, South Yorkshire and West Yorkshire specified in Schedule 15 to this Order; and

(b) those areas in the parishes and the unparished areas in the districts of the East Riding of Yorkshire and North Lincolnshire and in the counties of

North Yorkshire, South Yorkshire and West Yorkshire specified in Schedule 16 to this Order each shown bounded with a black line and crossed hatched on one of the maps contained in the volume entitled "Maps of the Protected Areas in Yorkshire and the Humber designated as protected areas by the Housing (Right to Enfranchise) (Designated Protected Areas) (England) Order 2009 (SI No: 2009/2098) and referred to in article 9(b) and Schedule 16 to the Order", which volume is—

   (i) signed by a member of the Senior Civil Service in the Department for Communities and Local Government; and

   (ii) deposited and available for inspection at the principal office of the Secretary of State for Communities and Local Government.

SCHEDULES   Regulation 2(a)

SCHEDULE 1 DESIGNATED PROTECTED AREAS IN THE WEST MIDLANDS—ENTIRE PARISHES

PART 1 HEREFORDSHIRE

Abbey Dore, Aconbury, Acton Beauchamp, Adforton, Allensmore, Almeley, Ashperton, Aston Ingham, Avenbury, Aylton, Aymestrey,

Bacton, Ballingham, Bartestree, Birley with Upper Hill, Bishops Frome, Bishopstone, Blakemere, Bodenham, Bolstone, Bosbury, Brampton Abbotts, Brampton Bryan, Bredenbury, Bredwardine, Breinton, Bridge Sollers, Bridstow, Brilley, Brimfield, Brinsop and Wormsley, Brobury with Monnington on Wye, Brockhampton, Brockhampton (in the district of South Herefordshire), Bromyard and Winslow, Buckton and Coxall, Burghill, Burrington, Byford, Byton,

Callow, Canon Frome, Canon Pyon, Castle Frome, Clehonger, Clifford, Coddington, Collington, Colwall, Combe, Cradley, Craswall, Credenhill, Croft and Yarpole, Cusop,

Dewsall, Dilwyn, Dinedor, Dinmore, Docklow and Hampton Wafer, Donnington, Dormington, Dorstone, Downton, Dulas,

Eardisland, Eardisley, Eastnor, Eaton Bishop, Edvin Loach and Saltmarshe, Edwyn Ralph, Eggleton, Elton, Evesbatch, Ewyas Harold, Eye Moreton and Ashton, Eyton,

Felton, Ford and Stoke Prior, Fownhope, Foy,

Ganarew, Garway, Goodrich, Grafton, Grendon Bishop,

Hampton Bishop, Hampton Charles, Harewood, Hatfield and Newhampton, Haywood, Hentland, Holme Lacy, Hope Mansell, Hope under Dinmore, How Caple, Humber,

Kenchester, Kenderchurch, Kentchurch, Kilpeck, Kimbolton, Kings Pyon, Kings Caple, Kingsland, Kingstone, Kington (in the district of Leominster), Kington Rural, Kinnersley, Kinsham, Knill,

Laysters, Lea, Leinthall Starkes, Leintwardine, Letton, Lingen, Linton, Linton (in the district of South Herefordshire), Little Birch, Little Cowarne, Little Dewchurch, Little Hereford, Little Marcle, Llancillo, Llandinabo, Llangarron, Llanrothal, Llanveynoe, Llanwarne, Longtown, Lower Harpton, Lucton, Lugwardine, Luston, Lyonshall,

Madley, Mansell Gamage, Mansell Lacy, Marden, Marstow, Mathon, Michaelchurch Escley, Middleton on the Hill, Moccas, Monkland and Stretford, Mordiford, Moreton Jeffries, Moreton on Lugg, Much Birch, Much Cowarne, Much Dewchurch, Much Marcle, Munsley,

Newton (in the district of South Herefordshire), Newton (in the district of Leominster), Norton Canon, Norton,

Ocle Pychard, Orcop, Orleton,

Pembridge, Pencombe with Grendon Warren, Pencoyd, Peterchurch, Peterstow, Pipe and Lyde, Pipe Aston, Pixley, Preston on Wye, Preston Wynne, Pudlestone, Putley,

Richards Castle (Hereford), Rodd, Nash & Little Brampton, Ross Rural, Rowlstone, Sarnesfield, Sellack, Shobdon, Sollers Hope, St Devereux, St Margarets, St Weonards, Stanford Bishop, Stapleton, Staunton on Arrow, Staunton on Wye, Stoke Edith, Stoke Lacy, Stretton Grandison, Stretton Sugwas, Sutton,

Tarrington, Tedstone Delamere, Tedstone Wafer, Thornbury, Thruxton, Titley, Tretire with Michaelchurch, Treville, Turnastone, Tyberton,

Ullingswick, Upper Sapey, Upton Bishop,

Vowchurch,

Wacton, Walford, Letton and Newton, Walterstone, Wellington, Wellington Heath, Welsh Bicknor, Welsh Newton, Weobley, Westhide, Weston Beggard, Weston under Penyard, Whitbourne, Whitchurch, Whitney on Wye, Wigmore, Willersley and Winforton, Willey, Withington, Wolferlow, Woolhope, Wormbridge,

Yarkhill, Yatton, Yazor.

PART 2 SHROPSHIRE

Abdon, Acton Burnell, Acton Round, Acton Scott, Adderley, Alberbury with Cardeston, All Stretton, Alveley, Ashford Bowdler, Ashford Carbonel, Astley Abbotts, Astley, Aston Botterell, Aston Eyre, Atcham,

Badger, Barrow, Baschurch, Beckbury, Bedstone, Berrington, Bettws y Crwyn, Bicton, Billingsley, Bishops Castle, Bitterley, Boningale, Boraston, Boscobel, Bromfield, Bucknell, Buildwas, Burford, Burwarton,

Cardington, Caynham, Chelmarsh, Cheswardine, Chetton, Chetwynd Aston & Woodcote, Chetwynd, Childs Ercall, Chirbury with Brompton, Church Preen, Church Pulverbatch, Claverley, Clee St Margaret, Cleobury Mortimer, Cleobury North, Clive, Clun, Clunbury, Clungunford, Cockshutt cum Petton, Colebatch, Condover, Coreley, Cound, Craven Arms, Cressage, Culmington,

Deuxhill, Diddlebury, Ditton Priors,

Eardington, Easthope, Eaton under Heywood, Edgemond, Edgton, Ellesmere Rural, Ercall Magna, Eyton upon the Weald Moors,

Farlow, Ford, Frodesley,

Glazeley, Great Hanwood, Great Ness, Greete, Grinshill,

Hadnall, Harley, Heath , Hinstock, Hodnet, Hope Bagot, Hope Bowdler, Hopesay, Hopton Cangeford, Hopton Castle, Hopton Wafers, Hordley, Hughley,

Ightfield,

Kemberton, Kenley, Kinlet, Kinnerley, Knockin, Kynnersley,

Lawley and Overdale, Leebotwood, Leighton & Eaton Constantine, Little Ness, Little Wenlock, Llanfair Waterdine, Llanyblodwel, Llanymynech and Pant, Longden, Longnor, Loppington, Ludford, Lydbury North, Lydham,

Mainstone, Melverley, Middleton Scriven, Milson, Minsterley, Monkhopton, Montford, More, Moreton Corbet and Lee Brockhurst, Moreton Say, Morville, Much Wenlock, Munslow, Myddle and Broughton, Myndtown,

Nash, Neen Savage, Neen Sollars, Neenton, Newcastle on Clun, Norbury, Norton in Hales,

Onibury, Oswestry Rural,

Pimhill, Pitchford, Pontesbury, Prees, Preston upon the Weald Moors,

Quatt Malvern,

Ratlinghope, Richards Castle, Rodington, Romsley, Ruckley and Langley, Rudge, Rushbury, Ruyton XI Towns, Ryton,

Selattyn and Gobowen, Shawbury, Sheinton, Sheriffhales, Shipton, Sibdon Carwood, Sidbury, Smethcott St Martins, Stanton Lacy, Stanton Long, Stanton upon Hine Heath, Stockton, Stoke St Milborough, Stoke upon Tern, Stottesdon, Stowe, Sutton Maddock, Sutton upon Tern,

Tasley, The Gorge, Tibberton and Cherrington, Tong,

Uffington, Upton Cressett, Upton Magna,

Waters Upton, Welshampton and Lyneal, Wem Rural, Wentnor, West Felton, Westbury, Weston Rhyn, Weston under Redcastle, Wheathill, Whitchurch Rural, Whittington, Whitton, Whixall, Wistanstow, Withington, Woolstaston, Woore, Worfield, Worthen with Shelve, Wrockwardine, Wroxeter and Uppington.

PART 3 STAFFORDSHIRE

Abbots Bromley, Acton Trussell and Bednall, Adbaston, Alrewas, Alstonefield, Alton, Anslow,

Bagnall, Balterley, Barlaston, Berkswich, Betley, Blithfield, Blore with Swinscoe, Blymhill and Weston under Lizard, Bobbington, Bradley, Bradnop, Branston, Brewood, Brindley Heath, Brocton, Butterton,

Cannock Wood, Castle Church, Caverswall, Chapel and Hill Chorlton, Chebsey, Checkley, Church Eaton, Clifton Campville, Colton, Colwich, Consall, Coppenhall, Cotton, Croxden, Curborough and Elmhurst,

Denstone, Dilhorne, Draycott in the Clay, Draycott in the Moors, Drayton Bassett, Dunstall, Dunston,

Eccleshall, Edingale, Elford, Ellastone, Ellenhall, Enville, Essington,

Farewell and Chorley, Farley, Fawfieldhead, Featherstone, Fisherwick, Forton, Fradley and Streethay, Fradswell,

Gayton, Grindon, Gnosall,

Hamstall Ridware, Hanbury, Harlaston, Hatherton, Haughton, Heathylee, Heaton, High Offley, Hilderstone, Hilton, Himley, Hints, Hoar Cross, Hollinsclough, Horton,

Ilam, Ingestre, Ipstones,

Keele, Kings Bromley, Kingsley, Kingstone,

Lapley Stretton and Wheaton Aston, Leekfrith, Leigh, Loggerheads, Longdon, Longnor, Longsdon, Lower Penn,

Madeley, Maer, Marchington, Marston, Mavesyn Ridware, Mayfield, Milwich,

Newborough, Norbury,

Oakamoor, Okeover, Onecote,

Pattingham and Patshull, Perton,

Quarnford,

Ramshorn, Ranton, Rocester, Rushton,

Salt and Enson, Sandon and Burston, Saredon, Shareshill, Sheen, Standon, Stanton, Stone Rural, Stowe, Swindon, Swinfen and Packington,

Tatenhill, Teddesley Hay, Thorpe Constantine, Tittesworth, Tixall, Trysull and Seisdon, Uttoxeter Rural,

Wall, Warslow and Elkstones, Waterhouses, Weeford, Weston, Wetton, Whitgreave, Whitmore, Whittington, Wigginton, Wootton, Wychnor,

Yoxhall.

PART 4 WARWICKSHIRE

Admington, Alderminster, Ansley, Ansty, Arley, Arrow with Weethley, Ashow, Astley, Aston Cantlow, Atherstone on Stour, Austrey, Avon Dassett,

Baddesley Clinton, Baddesley Ensor, Baginton, Barcheston, Barford, Barton-on-the-Heath, Baxterley, Bearley, Beaudesert, Beausale, Haseley, Honiliey and Wroxall, Bentley, Billesley, Binley Woods, Binton, Birdingbury, Bishops Itchington, Bishops Tachbrook, Blackdown, Bourton and Draycote, Brailes, Brandon and Bretford, Brinklow, Bubbenhall, Budbrooke, Burmington, Burton Dassett, Burton Hastings, Bushwood, Butlers Marston, Caldecote, Chadshunt, Chapel Ascote, Charlecote, Cherington, Chesterton and Kingston, Church Lawford, Churchover, Claverdon, Clifford Chambers and Milcote, Clifton upon Dunsmore, Combe Fields, Combrook, Compton Verney, Compton Wynyates, Copston Magna, Corley, Cosford, Coughton, Curdworth,

Dorsington, Dunchurch,

Easenhall, Eathorpe, Ettington, Exhall,

Farnborough, Fenny Compton, Fillongley, Frankton, Fulbrook,
Gaydon, Grandborough, Great Alne, Great Packington, Great Wolford, Grendon,
Halford, Hampton Lucy, Harborough Magna, Harbury, Haselor, Hatton, Henley-in-Arden,
Hodnell and Wills Pastures, Honington, Hunningham,
Ildicote, Ilmington,
Kineton, Kings Newnham, Kinwarton,
Ladbroke, Langley, Lapworth, Lea Marston, Leamington Hastings, Leek Wootton and
Guys Cliffe, Lighthorne, Little Compton, Little Lawford, Little Packington, Little Wolford, Long Compton, Long Itchington, Long Lawford, Long Marston, Loxley, Luddington,
Marton, Maxstoke, Merevale, Middleton, Monks Kirby, Moreton Morrell, Morton
Bagot,
Napton on the Hill, Nether Whitacre, Newbold Pacey, Newton and Biggin, Newton Regis,
Norton Lindsey,
Offchurch, Old Milverton, Old Stratford and Drayton, Oldberrow, Over Whitacre,
Oxhill,
Pailton, Pillerton Hersey, Pillerton Priors, Preston Bagot, Preston on Stour, Princethorpe,
Priors Hardwick, Priors Marston,
Quinton,
Radbourn, Radford Semele, Radway, Ratley and Upton, Rowington, Ryton-on-Dunsmore,
Salford Priors, Sambourne, Seckington, Sherbourne, Shilton, Shotteswell, Shrewley,
Shustoke, Shuttington, Snitterfield, Spernall, Stockton, Stoneleigh, Stoneton, Stourton,
Stretton on Fosse, Stretton Baskerville, Stretton under Fosse, Stretton-on-Dunsmore,
Sutton-under-Brailes,
Tanworth-in-Arden, Temple Grafton, Thurlaston, Tidmington, Tredington, Tysoe,
Ufton, Ullenhall, Upper and Lower Shuckburgh,
Wappenbury, Warmington, Wasperton, Watergall, Welford-on-Avon, Weston under
Wetherley, Weston on Avon, Whatcote, Whichford, Whitchurch, Wibtoft, Willey, Willoughby, Wishaw, Withybrook, Wixford, Wolfhampcote, Wolston, Wolverton, Wolvey,
Wootton Wawden, Wormleighton.

PART 5 WEST MIDLANDS

Allesley,
Barston,
Hampton in Arden, Hockley Heath,
Keresley.

PART 6 WORCESTERSHIRE

Abberley, Abberton, Abbots Morton, Aldington, Alfrick, Ashton under Hill, Astley and
Dunley, Aston Somerville,
Badsey, Bayton, Beckford, Belbroughton, Bentley Pauncefoot, Beoley, Berrow, Besford,
Bickmarsh, Birlingham, Birtsmorton, Bishampton, Bockleton, Bransford, Bredicot, Bredon, Bredons Norton, Bretforton, Bricklehampton, Broadheath, Broadwas, Broadway,
Broome, Broughton Hackett, Bushley,
Castlemorton, Chaddesley Corbett, Charlton, Childswickham, Church Lench, Churchill
and Blakedown, Churchill, Cleeve Prior, Clifton upon Teme, Conderton, Cookhill,
Cotheridge, Croome D'Abitot, Cropthorne, Crowle,
Defford, Doddenham, Dodderhill, Dodford with Grafton, Dormston, Doverdale, Drakes
Broughton and Wadborough,
Earls Croome, Eastham, Eckington, Eldersfield, Elmbridge, Elmley Castle, Elmley
Lovett,
Feckenham, Fladbury, Flyford Flavell,
Grafton Flyford, Great Comberton, Great Witley, Grimley, Guarlford,

Hadzor, Hallow, Hampton Lovett, Hanbury, Hanley Castle, Hanley, Hartlebury, Harvington, Hill and Moor, Hill Croome, Hillhampton, Himbleton, Hindlip, Hinton on the Green, Holdfast, Holt, Honeybourne, Huddington, Hunnington,

Inkberrow

Kemerton, Kempsey, Kenswick, Kidderminster Foreign, Kington (in the district of Wychavon), Knighton on Teme, Knightwick, Kyre,

Leigh, Lindridge, Little Comberton, Little Malvern, Little Witley, Longdon, Lower Sapey, Lulsley,

Madresfield, Malvern Wells, Mamble, Martin Hussingtree, Martley,

Naunton Beauchamp, Netherton, Newland, North and Middle Littleton, North Piddle, Norton Juxta Kempsey,

Oddingley, Offenham, Ombersley, Overbury,

Pebworth, Pendock, Pensax, Peopleton, Pinvin, Pirton, Powick,

Queenhill,

Ribbesford, Ripple, Rochford, Rock, Rous Lench, Rushock, Rushwick,

Salwarpe, Sedgebarrow, Severn Stoke, Shelsley Beauchamp, Shelsley Kings, Shelsley Walsh, Shrawley, South Littleton, Spetchley, St Peter the Great County, Stanford with Orleton, Stapleton, Stock and Bradley, Stockton on Teme, Stoke Bliss, Stone, Stoulton, Strensham, Suckley,

Tenbury, Throckmorton, Tibberton, Tutnall and Cobley,

Upper Arley, Upton upon Severn, Upton Snodsbury, Upton Warren,

Warndon, Welland, Westwood, White Ladies Aston, Whittington, Wichenford, Wick, Wickhamford, Wolverley and Cookley, Wyre Piddle.

Regulation 2(b)

SCHEDULE 2 DESIGNATED PROTECTED AREAS IN THE WEST MIDLANDS—BY MAPS

PART 1 HEREFORDSHIRE

The parishes of—

Holmer,
Ledbury, Leominster, Lower Bullingham,

PART 2 SHROPSHIRE

The parishes of—

Bridgnorth,
Church Aston, Church Stretton,
Donington,
Hadley,
Lilleshall and Donnington,
Shifnal,
Whitchurch Urban.

PART 3 STAFFORDSHIRE

The parishes of—

Audley Rural,
Barton under Needwood, Biddulph, Bilbrook, Brown Edge,
Cheadle, Cheddleton, Codsall, Creswell,
Endon and Stanley,
Forsbrook, Fulford,

Hammerwich, Hopton and Coton,
Kidsgrove, Kinver,
Leek,
Penkridge,
Seighford, Shenstone, Swynnerton,
Werrington.

PART 4 WARWICKSHIRE

The parishes of—

Alcester,
Bidford on Avon,
Dordon,
Hartshill,
Kenilworth, Kingsbury,
Mancetter,
Polesworth,
Stratford upon Avon, Studley.

PART 5 WEST MIDLANDS

The parishes of—

Balsall, Berkswell, Bickenhill.

PART 6 WORCESTERSHIRE

The parishes of—

Alvechurch,
Bewdley,
Clent,
Frankley,
North Claines, Norton and Lenchwick,
Pershore,
Romsley,
Stoke Prior,
Wythall.

The unparished area bounded by the parishes of Cofton Hackett, Alvechurch, Tutnall &
Cobley, Stoke Prior, Dodford with Grafton, Belbroughton, Romsley; and by the borough
constituency of Birmingham Northfield in the West Midlands.
The unparished area bounded by the parishes of Cookhill, Inkberrow, Feckenham, Bentley
Pauncefoot, Tutnall & Cobley, Alvechurch, Beoley; and by the parishes of Studley and
Sambourne in the county of Warwickshire.

Regulation 3(a)

SCHEDULE 3 DESIGNATED PROTECTED AREAS IN THE SOUTH WEST—ENTIRE PARISHES

PART 1 BATH AND NORTH EAST SOMERSET

Bathampton, Batheaston, Bathford,
Cameley, Camerton, Charlcombe, Chelwood, Chew Magna, Chew Stoke, Claverton,
Clutton, Combe Hay, Compton Dando, Compton Martin, Corston,

Dunkerton,
East Harptree, Englishcombe,
Farmborough, Farrington Gurney, Freshford,
High Littleton, Hinton Blewett, Hinton Charterhouse,
Kelston,
Marksbury, Monkton Combe,
Nempnett Thrubwell, Newton St Loe, North Stoke, Norton Malreward,
Priston, Publow,
Shoscombe, Southstoke, St Catherine, Stanton Drew, Stowey-Sutton, Swainswick,
Timsbury,
Ubley,
Wellow, West Harptree, Whitchurch.

PART 2 CORNWALL

Advent, Altarnun, Antony,
Blisland, Boconnoc, Botusfleming, Boyton, Breage, Broadoak, Budock,
Calstock, Camelford, Cardinham, Carharrack, Carn Brea, Chacewater, Colan, Constantine, Crantock, Crowan, Cubert, Cuby, Cury,
Davidstow, Dobwalls and Trewidland, Duloe,
Egloshayle, Egloskerry,
Feock, Forrabury and Minster, Fowey,
Germoe, Gerrans, Grade Ruan, Grampound with Creed, Gunwalloe, Gweek, Gwennap, Gwinear, Gwithian,
Helland,
Jacobstow,
Kea, Kilkhampton,
Ladock, Landewednack, Landrake with St Erney, Landulph, Laneast, Lanhydrock, Lanivet, Lanlivery, Lanner, Lanreath, Lansallos, Lanteglos, Launcells, Lawhitton Rural, Lesnewth, Lewannick, Lezant, Linkinhorne, Lostwithiel, Ludgvan, Luxulyan,
Mabe, Madron, Maker with Rame, Manaccan, Marazion, Marhamchurch, Mawgan in Meneage, Mawgan in Pydar, Mawnan, Menheniot, Mevagissey, Michaelstow, Millbrook, Morvah, Morval, Morwenstow, Mullion, Mylor,
North Hill, North Petherwin, North Tamerton,
Otterham,
Padstow, Paul, Pelynt, Penryn, Perranarworthal, Perranuthnoe, Perranzabuloe, Philleigh, Pillaton, Porthleven, Portreath, Poundstock, Probus,
Quethiock,
Roche, Ruanlanihorne,
Sancreed, Sennen, Sheviock, Sithney, South Hill, South Petherwin, St Agnes, St Allen, St Anthony in Meneage, St Breock, St Breward, St Buryan, St Cleer, St Clement, St Clether, St Columb Major, St Day, St Dennis, St Dominick, St Endellion, St Enoder, St Erme, St Erth, St Ervan, St Eval, St Ewe, St Gennys, St Germans, St Gluvias, St Goran, St Hilary, St Issey, St Ive, St John, St Juliot, St Just, St Just in Roseland, St Keverne, St Kew, St Keyne, St Levan, St Mabyn, St Martin, St Martin in Meneage, St Mellion, St Merryn, St Mewan, St Michael Caerhays, St Michael Penkevil, St Michaels Mount, St Minver Highlands, St Minver Lowlands, St Neot, St Newlyn East, St Pinnock, St Sampson, St Stephen in Brannel, St Stephens by Launceston Rural, St Teath, St Thomas the Apostle Rural, St Tudy, St Veep, St Wenn, St Winnow, Stithians, Stokeclimsland,
Tintagel, Towednack, Tregoney, Tremaine, Treneglos, Tresmeer, Trevalga, Treverbyn, Trewen, Tywardreath,
Veryan,
Warbstow, Warleggan, Week St Mary, Wendron, Werrington, Whitstone, Withiel,
Zennor,
The Isles of Scilly.

Part 3 Devon

Abbots Bickington, Abbotsham, Abbotskerswell, All Saints, Alverdiscott, Alwington, Arlington, Ashburton, Ashcombe, Ashford, Ashprington, Ashreigney, Ashton, Ashwater, Atherington, Aveton Gifford, Awliscombe, Axmouth, Aylesbeare,

Bampton, Beaford, Beaworthy, Belstone, Beer, Bere Ferrers, Berrynarbor, Bickington, Bickleigh (in the district of South Hams), Bickleigh (in the district of Mid Devon), Bicton, Bigbury, Bishops Nympton, Bishops Tawton, Bishopsteignton, Bittadon, Black Torrington, Blackawton, Bondleigh, Bow, Bradford, Bradninch, Bradstone, Bradworthy, Brampford Speke, Branscombe, Bratton Clovelly, Bratton Fleming, Brayford, Brendon, Brentor, Bridestow, Bridford, Bridgerule, Brixton, Broad Clyst, Broadhembury, Broadhempston, Broadwoodkelly, Broadwoodwidger, Brushford, Buckerell, Buckfastleigh, Buckland Brewer, Buckland Filleigh, Buckland in the Moor, Buckland Monachorum, Buckland Tout Saints, Bulkworthy, Burlescombe, Burrington, Butterleigh,

Cadbury, Cadeleigh, Chagford, Challacombe, Chardstock, Charlton, Chawleigh, Cheriton Bishop, Cheriton Fitzpaine, Chittlehamholt, Chittlehampton, Chivelstone, Christow, Chulmleigh, Churchstow, Clannaborough, Clawton, Clayhanger, Clayhidon, Clovelly, Clyst Honiton, Clyst Hydon, Clyst St George, Clyst St Lawrence, Clyst St Mary, Coffinswell, Colaton Raleigh, Coldridge, Colebrooke, Colyton, Combe Martin, Combe Raleigh, Combpyne Rousdon, Cookbury, Copplestone, Cornwood, Cornworthy, Coryton, Cotleigh, Countisbury, Crediton, Crediton Hamlets, Cruwys Morchard, Culmstock,

Dalwood, Dartington, Dartmoor Forest, Dean Prior, Diptford, Dittisham, Doddiscombsleigh, Dolton, Dowland, Down St Mary, Drewsteighnton, Dunchideock, Dunkeswell, Dunsford, Dunterton,

East Allington, East and West Buckland, East Anstey, East Budleigh, East Down, East Portlemouth, East Putford, East Worlington, Eggesford, Ermington, Exbourne, Exminster,

Farringdon, Farway, Feniton, Filleigh, Frithelstock, Frogmore and Sherford,

George Nympton, Georgeham, Germansweek, Gidleigh, Gittisham, Goodleigh, Gulworthy,

Haccombe with Combe, Halberton, Halwell and Moreleigh, Halwill, Harberton, Harford, Hartland, Hatherleigh, Hawkchurch, Heanton Punchardon, Hemyock, Hennock, High Bickington, Highampton, Hittisleigh, Hockworthy, Holbeton, Holcombe Burnell, Holcombe Rogus, Hollacombe, Holne, Holsworthy, Holsworthy Hamlets, Horrabridge, Horwood, Lovacott and Newton Tracey, Huish, Huntsham, Huntshaw, Huxham,

Iddesleigh, Ide, Ideford, Ilsington, Instow, Inwardleigh, Ipplepen,
Jacobstowe,

Kelly, Kenn, Kennerleigh, Kentisbeare, Kentisbury, Kenton, Kilmington, Kings Nympton, Kingston, Kingswear, Knowstone,

Lamerton, Landcross, Landkey, Langtree, Lapford, Lewtrenchard, Lifton, Little Torrington, Littleham, Littlehempston, Loddiswell, Loxbeare, Loxhore, Luffincott, Luppitt, Lustleigh, Lydford, Lympstone, Lynton and Lynmouth,

Malborough, Mamhead, Manaton, Mariansleigh, Marldon, Martinhoe, Marwood, Mary Tavy, Marystow, Meavy, Meeth, Membury, Merton, Meshaw, Milton Abbot, Milton Damerel, Modbury, Molland, Monkleigh, Monkokehampton, Monkton, Morchard Bishop, Morebath, Moretonhampstead, Mortehoe, Musbury,

Nether Exe, Newton and Noss, Newton Poppleford and Harpford, Newton St Cyres, Newton St Petrock, North Bovey, North Huish, North Molton, North Tawton, Northcott, Northleigh, Northlew, Nymet Rowland,

Oakford, Offwell, Okehampton Hamlets, Otterton,

Pancrasweek, Parkham, Parracombe, Payhembury, Peter Tavy, Peters Marland, Petrockstow, Plymtree, Poltimore, Poughill, Powderham, Puddington, Pyworthy,
Queens Nympton,
Rackenford, Rattery, Rewe, Ringmore, Roborough, Rockbeare, Romansleigh, Rose Ash,

Sampford Courtenay, Sampford Peverell, Sampford Spiney, Sandford, Satterleigh and Warkleigh, Shaldon, Shaugh Prior, Shebbear, Sheepstor, Sheepwash, Sheldon, Shillingford St George, Shirwell, Shobrooke, Shute, Silverton, Slapton, Sourton, South Brent, South Huish, South Milton, South Pool, South Tawton, Southleigh, Sowton, Sparkwell, Spreyton, St Giles in the Wood, St Giles on the Heath, Starcross, Staverton, Sticklepath, Stockland, Stockleigh English, Stockleigh Pomeroy, Stoke Canon, Stoke Fleming, Stoke Gabriel, Stoke Rivers, Stokeinteignhead, Stokenham, Stoodleigh, Stowford, Strete, Sutcombe, Swimbridge, Sydenham Damerel,

Talaton, Tedburn St Mary, Teigngrace, Templeton, Tetcott, Thelbridge, Thornbury, Thorverton, Throwleigh, Thrushelton, Thurleston, Torbryan, Trentishoe, Trusham, Twitchen, Uffculme, Ugborough, Uplowman, Uplyme, Upottery, Upton Hellions, Upton Pyne, Virginstow,

Walkampton, Washfield, Washford Pyne, Weare Giffard, Welcombe, Wembury, Wembworthy, West Alvington, West Anstey, West Buckfastleigh, West Down, West Pilton, West Putford, Westleigh, Whimple, Whitchurch, Whitestone, Widecombe in the Moor, Widworthy, Willand, Winkleigh, Witheridge, Woodbury, Woodland, Woodleigh, Woolfardisworthy (in the Mid Devon district), Woolfardisworthy (in the district of Torridge),

Yarcombe, Yarnscombe, Yealmpton,

Zeal Monachorum.

PART 4 DORSET

Abbotsbury, Affpuddle, Alderholt, Allington, Alton Pancras, Anderson, Arne, Ashmore, Askerswell, Athelhampton,

Batcombe, Beaminster, Beer Hackett, Bere Regis, Bettiscombe, Bincombe, Bishop's Caundle, Blandford St Mary, Bloxworth, Bothenhampton, Bourton, Bradford Abbas, Bradford Peverell, Broadmayne, Broadwindsor, Bryanston, Buckhorn Weston, Buckland Newton, Burleston, Burstock, Burton Bradstock, Burton,

Cann, Castleton, Catherston Leweston, Cattistock, Caundle Marsh, Cerne Abbas, Chalbury, Chaldon Herring, Charlton Marshall, Charminster, Charmouth, Chedington, Cheselbourne, Chetnole, Chettle, Chideock, Child Okeford, Chilcombe, Compton Valence, Chilfrome, Church Knowle, Clifton Maybank, Compton Abbas, Coombe Keynes, Corfe Castle, Corscombe, Cranborne, Crossways,

Dewlish, Durweston,

East Chelborough, East Holme, East Lulworth, East Orchard, East Stoke, East Stour, Edmondsham, Evershot,

Farnham, Fifehead Magdalene, Fifehead Neville, Fleet, Folke, Fontmell Magna, Frampton, Frome St Quintin, Frome Vauchurch,

Glanvilles Wootton, Goathill, Godmanstone, Gussage All Saints, Gussage St Michael, Halstock, Hammoon, Hanford, Haydon, Hazelbury Bryan, Hermitage, Hilfield, Hilton, Hinton Martell, Hinton Parva, Hinton St Mary, Holnest, Holt, Holwell, Hooke, Horton, Hurn,

Ibberton, Iwerne Courtney or Shroton, Iwerne Minster, Iwerne Stepleton,

Kimmeridge, Kingston Russell, Kington Magna,

Langton Herring, Langton Long Blandford, Langton Matravers, Leigh, Leweston, Lillington, Littlebredy, Litton Cheney, Loders, Long Bredy, Long Crichel, Longburton, Lydlinch, Lytchett Matravers,

Maiden Newton, Manston, Mapperton, Mappowder, Margaret Marsh, Marnhull, Marshwood, Melbury Abbas, Melbury Bubb, Melbury Osmond, Melbury Sampford, Melcombe Horsey, Milborne St Andrew, Milton Abbas, Minterne Magna, Moor Crichel, Morden, Moreton, Mosterton, Motcombe,

Nether Cerne, Nether Compton, Netherbury, North Poorton, North Wootton,

Oborne, Okeford Fitzpaine, Osmington, Over Compton, Owermoigne,

Pamphill, Pentridge, Piddlehinton, Piddletrenthide, Pilsdon, Pimperne, Portesham, Portland, Powerstock, Poxwell, Poyntington, Puddletown, Pulham, Puncknowle, Purse Caundle,

Rampisham, Ryme Intrinseca,

Sandford Orcas, Seaborough, Shapwick, Shillingstone, Shipton Gorge, Silton, Sixpenny Handley, South Perrott, Spetisbury, Stalbridge, Stanton St Gabriel, Steeple, Stinsford, Stockwood, Stoke Abbott, Stoke Wake, Stour Provost, Stourpaine, Stourton Caundle, Stratton, Studland, Sturminster Marshall, Sturminster Newton, Sutton Waldron, Swyre, Sydling St Nicholas, Symondsbury,

Tarrant Crawford, Tarrant Gunville, Tarrant Hinton, Tarrant Keyneston, Tarrant Launceston, Tarrant Monkton, Tarrant Rawston, Tarrant Rushton, Thorncombe, Thornford, Tincleton, Todber, Toller Fratrum, Toller Porcorum, Tolpuddle, Trent, Turners Puddle, Turnworth, Tyneham,

Up Cerne,

Wareham St Martin, Warmwell, West Chelborough, West Compton, West Knighton, West Lulworth, West Orchard, West Stafford, West Stour, Whitcombe, Whitchurch Canonicorum, Wimborne St Giles, Winfrith Newburgh, Winterborne Came, Winterborne Clenston, Winterborne Herringston, Winterborne Houghton, Winterborne Kingston, Winterborne Monkton, Winter borne St Martin, Winterborne Stickland, Winterborne Whitechurch, Winterborne Zelston, Winterbourne Abbas, Winterbourne Steepleton, Witchampton, Woodlands, Woodsford, Wool, Wolland, Wootton Fitzpaine, Worth Matravers, Wraxall, Wynford Eagle,

Yetminster.

PART 5 GLOUCESTERSHIRE

Adlestrop, Alderley, Alderton, Aldsworth, Alkington, Alvington, Ampney Crucis, Ampney St Mary, Ampney St Peter, Andoversford, Arlingham, Ashleworth, Ashley, Aston Subedge, Avening, Awre, Ayleburton,

Badgeworth, Bagendon, Barnsley, Barrington, Batsford, Baunton, Berkeley, Beverstone, Bibury, Bisley with Lypiatt, Blaisdon, Bledington, Blockley, Boddington, Bourton on the Hill, Bourton on the Water, Boxwell with Leighterton, Brimpsfield, Broadwell, Bromsberrow, Brookthorpe with Whaddon, Buckland,

Chaceley, Chedworth, Cherington, Chipping Campden, Churcham, Clapton, Coaley, Coates, Coberley, Cold Aston, Colesbourne, Coln St Aldwyns, Coln St Dennis, Compton Abdale, Condicote, Corse, Cowley, Cranham, Cutsdean,

Daglingworth, Deerhurst, Didmarton, Donnington, Dowdeswell, Down Ampney, Down Hatherley, Driffield, Drybrook, Dumbleton, Duntisbourne Abbots, Duntisbourne Rouse, Dymock,

Eastington, Eastleach, Ebrington, Edgeworth, Elkstone, Elmore, Elmstone Hardwicke, English Bicknor, Evenlode,

Fairford, Farmington, Forthampton, Frampton on Severn, Fretherne with Saul, Frocester,

Gotherington, Great Rissington, Great Witcombe, Guiting Power,

Ham and Stone, Hamfallow, Hampnett, Hardwicke, Harescombe, Haresfield, Hartpury, Hasfield, Hatherop, Hawling, Hazelton, Hewelsfield, Highnam, Hillesley and Tresham, Hinton, Horsley, Huntley,

Icomb,

Kemble, Kempley, Kempsford, Kings Stanley, Kingscote, Kingswood,

Lechlade, Leigh, Leonard Stanley, Little Rissington, Littledean, Long Newnton, Longborough, Longhope, Longney, Lower Slaughter, Lydbrook,

Maisemore, Maiseyhampton, Maugersbury, Mickleton, Minsterworth, Miserden, Mitcheldean, Moreton Valence, Moreton in Marsh,

Naunton, Newland, Newnham, North Cerney, North Nibley, Northleach with Eastington, Norton, Notgrove, Nympsfield,

Oddington, Owlpen, Oxenhall, Oxenton, Ozelworth,

Painswick, Pauntley, Pitchcombe, Poole Keynes, Poulton, Prescott, Preston,

Quenington,

Redmarley D'Abitot, Rendcomb, Rodmarton, Ruardean, Rudford and Highleadon, Ruspidge,

Saintbury, Sandhurst, Sapperton, Sevenhampton, Sezincote, Sherborne, Shipton, Shipton Moyne, Shurdington, Siddington, Slimbridge, Snowshill, Somerford Keynes, Southam, South Cerney, Southrop, St Briavels, Standish, Stanton, Stanway, Staunton Coleford, Staunton, Staverton, Stinchcombe, Stoke Orchard, Stow on the Wold, Sudeley, Swell, Syde,

Taynton, Teddington, Temple Guiting, Tibberton, Tidenham, Tirley, Toddington, Todenham, Turkdean, Twigworth, Twyning,

Uckington, Uley, Upleadon, Upper Slaughter,

Walton Cardiff, Westbury on Severn, Westcote, Weston Subedge, Westonbirt with Lasborough, Wheatpieces, Whiteshill and Ruscombe, Whitminster, Whittington, Wick Rissington, Willersey, Windrush, Winson, Winstone, Withington, Woodchester, Woodmancote, Woolaston,

Yanworth.

Part 6 North Somerset

Abbotts Leigh,

Banwell, Barrow Gurney, Blagdon, Bleadon, Brockley, Burrington, Butcombe,

Churchill, Clapton-in-Gordano, Cleeve,

Dundry,

Flax Bourton,

Hutton,

Kenn, Kewstoke, Kingston Seymour,

Locking, Loxton,

Portbury, Puxton,

Tickenham,

Walton-in-Gordano, Weston-in-Gordano, Wick St Lawrence, Winford, Wraxhall, Wrington.

Part 7 Somerset

Abbas and Templecombe, Alford, Aller, Ansford, Ash, Ash Priors, Ashbrittle, Ashcott, Ashill, Ashwick, Axbridge,

Babcary, Badgworth, Baltonsborough, Barrington, Barton St David, Barwick, Batcombe, Bathealton, Bawdrip, Beckington, Beercrocombe, Berkley, Berrow, Bickenhall, Bicknoller, Binegar, Bishops Lydeard, Bradford on Tone, Bratton Seymour, Brean, Brent Knoll, Brewham, Bridgewater Without, Broadway, Brompton Ralph, Brompton Regis, Broomfield, Brushford, Bruton, Buckland Dinham, Buckland St Mary, Burnham Without, Burrowbridge, Burtle, Butleigh,

Cannington, Carhampton, Castle Cary, Catcott, Chaffcombe, Chapel Allerton, Charlton Horethorne, Charlton Mackrell, Charlton Musgrove, Cheddon Fitzpaine, Chedzoy, Chewton Mendip, Chilcompton, Chillington, Chilthorne Domer, Chilton Cantelo, Chilton Polden, Chilton Trinity, Chipstable, Chiselborough, Churchstanton, Clatworthy, Closworth, Coleford, Combe Florey, Combe St Nicholas, Compton Bishop, Compton Dundon, Compton Pauncefoot, Corfe, Corton Denham, Cossington, Cothelstone, Cranmore, Creech St Michael, Cricket St Thomas, Croscombe, Crowcombe, Cucklington, Cudworth, Curland, Curry Mallet, Curry Rivel, Cutcombe,

Dinnington, Ditcheat, Donyatt, Doulting, Dowlish Wake, Downhead, Drayton, Dulverton, Dunster, Durston,

East Brent, East Chinnock, East Huntspill, East Pennard, East Quantoxhead, Edington, Elm, Elworthy, Emborough, Enmore, Evercreech, Exford, Exmoor, Exton,

Fiddington, Fitzhead, Fivehead,

Goathurst, Godney, Greinton,

Halse, Hambridge and Westport, Hardington Mandeville, Haselbury Plucknett, Hatch Beauchamp, Hemington, Henstridge, High Ham, Hinton St George, Holcombe, Holford, Holton, Horsington, Horton, Huish Champflower, Huish Episcopi,

Ilchester, Ilton, Isle Abbotts, Isle Brewers,

Keinton Mandeville, Kilmersdon, Kilve, Kingsbury Episcopi, Kingsdon, Kingston St Mary, Kingstone, Kingweston, Knowle St Giles,

Lamyat, Langford Budville, Langport, Leigh on Mendip, Limington, Litton, Long Load, Long Sutton, Lopen, Lovington, Luccombe, Lullington, Luxborough, Lydeard St Lawrence, Lydford on Fosse, Lympsham, Lyng,

Maperton, Mark, Marston Magna, Meare, Mells, Merriott, Middlezoy, Milborne Port, Milton Clevedon, Milverton, Minehead Without, Misterton, Monksilver, Montacute, Moorlinch, Muchelney, Mudford,

Nether Stowey, Nettlecombe, North Barrow, North Cadbury, North Cheriton, North Curry, North Perrott, North Wootton, Norton Fitzwarren, Norton St Phillip, Norton Sub Hamdon, Nunney, Nynehead,

Oake, Oare, Odcombe, Old Cleeve, Orchard Portman, Othery, Otterford, Otterhampton, Over Stowey,

Pawlett, Pen Selwood, Pilton, Pitcombe, Pitminster, Pitney, Porlock, Priddy, Puckington, Puriton, Pylle,

Queen Camel,

Rimpton, Rode, Rodney Stoke, Ruishton,

Sampford Arundel, Sampford Brett, Seavington St Mary, Seavington St Michael, Selwood, Selworthy, Shapwick, Sharpham, Shepton Beachamp, Shepton Montague, Shipham, Skilgate, South Barrow, South Cadbury, South Petherton, Sparkford, Spaxton, St Cuthbert Out, Staple Fitzpaine, Staplegrove, Stawell, Stawley, Stockland Bristol, Stocklinch, Stogumber, Stogursey, Stoke St Gregory, Stoke St Mary, Stoke St Michael, Stoke Sub Hamdon, Stoke Trister, Ston Easton, Stratton on the Fosse, Stringston,

Tatworth and Forton, Tellisford, Thornfalcon, Thurloxton, Timberscombe, Tintinhull, Tolland, Treborough, Trudoxhill, Trull,

Upton, Upton Noble,

Walton, Wambrook, Wanstrow, Wayford, Weare, Wedmore, Wellington Without, Wembdon, West Bagborough, West Bradley, West Buckland, West Camel, West Chinnock, West Coker, West Crewkerne, West Hatch, West Huntspill, West Monkton, West Pennard, West Quantoxhead, Westbury, Westonzoyland, Whatley, Whitelackington, Whitestaunton, Williton, Winsford, Winsham, Witham Friary, Withycombe, Withypool, Wiveliscombe, Wookey, Woolavington, Wootton Courtenay,

Yarlington, Yeovilton.

PART 8 SOUTH GLOUCESTERSHIRE

Acton Turville, Alveston, Aust,
Badminton,
Charfield, Cold Ashton, Cromhall,
Doynton, Dyrham and Hinton,
Falfield,
Hawkesbury, Hill, Horton,
Iron Acton,
Little Sodbury,
Marshfield,
Oldbury-upon-Severn, Olveston,
Pilning and Severn Beach, Pucklechurch,
Rangeworthy, Rockhampton,
Tormarton, Tortworth, Tytherington,
Wick and Abson, Wickwar.

PART 9 WILTSHIRE

Aldbourne, Alderbury, Allcannings, Allington, Alton, Alvediston, Ansty, Ashton Keynes, Atworth, Avebury,

Barford St Martin, Baydon, Beechingstoke, Berwick Bassett, Berwick St James, Berwick St John, Berwick St Leonard, Biddestone, Bishopstone (in the district of Thamesdown),

Bishopstone (in the district of Salisbury), Bishopstrow, Blunsdon St Andrew, Bower Chalke, Box, Boyton, Bratton, Braydon, Bremhill, Brinkworth, Britford, Brixton Deverill, Broad Chalke, Broad Hinton, Broad Town, Brokenborough, Bromham, Broughton Gifford, Bulkington, Burbage, Burcombe Without, Buttermere,

Calne Without, Castle Combe, Castle Eaton, Chapmanslade, Charlton (in the district of Kennet), Charlton (in the district of North Wiltshire), Cherhill, Cheverell Magna, Cheverell Parva, Chicklade, Chilmark, Chilton Foliat, Chirton, Chiseldon, Chitterne, Cholderton, Christian Malford, Chute, Chute Forest, Clarendon Park, Clyffe Pypard, Codford, Colerne, Collingbourne Ducis, Collingbourne Kingston, Compton Bassett, Compton, Chamberlayne, Coombe Bissett, Corsley, Coulston, Crudwell,

Dauntsey, Dilton Marsh, Dinton, Donhead St Andrew, Donhead St Mary, Downton, Durnford,

East Kennett, East Knoyle, Easterton, Easton Royal, Easton Grey, Ebbesborne Wake, Edington, Enford, Erlestoke, Etchilhampton, Everleigh,

Figheldean, Firsdown, Fittleton, Fonthill Bishop, Fonthill Gifford, Fovant, Froxfield, Fyfield,

Grafton, Great Bedwyn, Great Hinton, Great Somerford, Great Wishford, Grimstead, Grittleton,

Ham, Hankerton, Hannington, Heddington, Heytesbury, Heywood, Hilmarton, Hindon, Holt, Horningsham, Huish, Hullavington,

Idmiston, Inglesham,

Keevil, Kilmington, Kingston Deverill, Kington Langley, Kington St Michael, Knook,

Lacock, Landford, Langley Burrell Without, Latton, Lea and Cleverton, Leigh, Liddington, Limpley Stoke, Little Bedwyn, Little Somerford, Longbridge Deverill, Luckington, Lydiard Millicent, Lydiard Tregoze,

Maiden Bradley with Yarnfield, Manningford, Marden, Market Lavington, Marston, Marston Maisey, Melksham Without, Mere, Mildenhall, Milston, Milton Lilbourne, Minety, Monkton Farleigh,

Netheravon, Nettleton, Newton Toney, North Bradley, North Newnton, North Wraxall, Norton, Norton Bavant,

Oaksey, Odstock, Ogbourne St Andrew, Ogbourne St George, Orcheston,

Patney, Pewsey, Pitton and Farley, Potterne, Poulshot, Preshute,

Quidhampton,

Ramsbury, Redlynch, Rowde, Rushall,

Savernake, Seagry, Sedgehill and Semley, Seend, Semington, Shalbourne, Sherrington, Sherston, Shrewton, Sopworth, South Marston, South Newton, South Wraxall, Southwick, Stanton Fitzwarren, Stanton St Bernard, Stanton St Quentin, Stapleford, Staverton, Steeple Ashton, Steeple Langford, Stert, Stockton, Stourton with Gasper, Stratford Toney, Sutton Benger, Sutton Mandeville, Sutton Veny, Swallowcliffe,

Teffont, Tidcombe and Fosbury, Tilshead, Tisbury, Tockenham, Tollard Royal,

Upavon, Upton Lovell, Upton Scudamore, Urchfont,

Wanborough, West Ashton, West Dean, West Knoyle, West Lavington, West Overton, West Tisbury, Westwood, Whiteparish, Wilcot, Wilsford, Wilsford cum Lake, Wingfield, Winsley, Winterbourne Bassett, Winterbourne, Winterbourne Monkton, Winterbourne Stoke, Winterslow, Woodborough, Woodford, Wootton Rivers, Worton, Wylye,

Yatton Keynell,

Zeals.

Regulation 3(b)

Schedule 4 Designated Protected Areas in the South West—By Maps

Part 1 Bath and North East Somerset

The parishes of—

Norton Radstock,

Peasedown St John.

The unparished area of the borough constituency of Bath.

Part 2 Cornwall

The parishes of—

Bodmin, Bude Stratton,
Callington, Camborne,
Falmouth,
Hayle,
Illogan,
Kenwyn,
Launceston, Liskeard, Looe,
Newquay,
Penzance,
Redruth,
Saltash, St Blaise, St Ives,
Wadebridge.

The unparished area bounded by the parishes of Treverbyn, St Blaise, Mevagissey, St Ewe and St Mewan.

Part 3 Devon

The parishes of—

Ashburton, Axminster,
Berry Pomeroy, Bideford, Bovey Tracey, Braunton, Broad Clyst, Budleigh Salterton,
Chudleigh, Cullompton,
Dartmouth, Dawlish,
Fremington,
Honiton,
Ilfracombe,
Kingskerswell, Kingsteignton,
Newton Abbot,
Ogwell, Ottery St Mary,
Salcombe, Sidmouth, South Molton,
Tavistock, Tawstock, Tiverton.

The unparished area bounded by the parishes of Lympstone, East Budleigh, Budleigh Salterton, Dawlish and Starcross.
The unparished area bounded by the parishes of Stokeinteignhead, Shaldon, Kingswear, Dittisham, Stoke Gabriel, Berry Pomeroy, Marldon, Kingskerswell and Coffinswell.

Part 4 Dorset

The parishes of—

Bothenhampton, Bradpole,
Chickerell, Colehill, Corfe Mullen,
Ferndown Town,
Gillingham,
Lytchett Minster and Upton,

St Leonards and St Ives,
Verwood.

PART 5 GLOUCESTERSHIRE

The parishes of—

Ashchurch Rural,
Cam, Cinderford, Cirencester,
Lydney,
Minchinhampton,
Newent,
Northway,
Rodborough,
Siddington,
Tetbury Upton,
Tewksbury Town,
West Dean, Winchcombe, Wotton under Edge.

PART 6 NORTH SOMERSET

The parishes of—

Backwell,
Congresbury,
Long Ashton,
Nailsea,
Winscombe and Sandford,
Yatton.

PART 7 SOMERSET

The parishes of—

Bishops Hull, Brympton,
Cheddar,
Durleigh,
East Coker,
Glastonbury,
Martock,
North Petherton,
Shepton Mallet, Somerton,
Wellington, Wincanton,
Yeovil Without.

PART 8 SOUTH GLOUCESTERSHIRE

The parishes of—

Almondsbury,
Bitton,
Dodington,
Siston, Sodbury,
Thornbury,
Westerleigh, Winterbourne.

PART 9 WILTSHIRE

The parishes of—

Amesbury,
Bishops Cannings, Bulford,
Chippenham Without, Corsham, Cricklade,
Haydon Wick, Highworth, Hilperton,
Laverstock, Lyneham,
Marlborough,
Netherhampton,
Purton,
Roundway,
St Paul Malmesbury Without,
Wroughton.
The area of North Tidworth (within the parish of Tidworth).

Regulation 4(a)

SCHEDULE 5 DESIGNATED PROTECTED AREAS IN THE NORTH WEST—ENTIRE PARISHES

PART 1 CHESHIRE EAST

Acton, Adlington, Agden, Alpraham, Arclid, Ashley, Aston by Budworth, Aston juxta Mondrum, Audlem, Austerson
Baddiley, Baddington, Barthomley, Basford, Batherton, Betchton, Bexton, Bickerton, Blakenhall, Bosley, Bradwall, Brereton, Bridgemere, Brindley, Broomhall, Buerton, Bulkeley, Bunbury, Burland,
Calveley, Checkley cum Wrinehill, Chelford, Cholmondeley, Cholmondeston, Chorley (formerly Macclesfield Rural District), Chorley (formerly Nantwich Rural District), Chorlton, Church Lawton, Church Minshull, Coole Pilate, Cranage, Crewe by Farndon, Crewe Green,
Dodcott cum Wilkesley, Doddington,
Eaton, Edleston, Egerton,
Faddiley,
Gawsworth, Goostrey, Great Warford,
Hankelow, Hassall, Hatherton, Haughton, Henbury, Henhull, High Legh, Hough, Hulme Walfield, Hunsterson, Hurleston,
Kettleshulme,
Lea, Leighton, Little Bollington, Little Warford, Lower Withington, Lyme Handley,
Macclesfield Forest and Wildboarclough, Marbury cum Quoisley, Marthall, Marton, Mere, Millington, Minshull Vernon, Mobberley, Moreton cum Alcumlow, Moston, Mottram St Andrew,
Nether Alderley, Newbold Astbury, Newhall, Norbury, North Rode,
Odd Rode, Ollerton, Over Alderley,
Peckforton, Peover Inferior, Peover Superior, Pickmere, Plumley, Poole, Pott Shrigley, Rainow, Ridley, Rostherne,
Siddington, Smallwood, Snelson, Somerford, Somerford Booths, Sound, Spurstow, Stapeley, Stoke, Sutton, Swettenham,
Tabley Inferior, Tabley Superior, Tatton, Toft, Twemlow,
Walgherton, Wardle, Warmingham, Weston, Wettenhall, Wincle, Wirswall, Woolstanwood, Worleston, Wrenbury cum Frith, Wybunbury.

PART 2 CHESHIRE WEST AND CHESTER

Acton Bridge, Agden, Aldersey, Aldford, Allostock, Alvanley, Anderton with Marbury, Antrobus, Ashton Hayes, Aston,

Backford, Barrow, Barton, Beeston, Bickley, Bostock, Bradley, Bridge Trafford, Broxton, Bruen Stapleford, Buerton, Burton, Burwardsley, Byley,

Caldecote, Capenhurst, Carden, Chidlow, Chorlton, Chorlton by Backford, Chowley, Church Shocklach, Churton by Aldford, Churton by Farndon, Churton Heath, Claverton, Clotton Hoofield, Clutton, Coddington, Comberbach, Cotton Abbotts, Cotton Edmunds, Croughton, Crowton, Cuddington,

Darnhall, Delamere, Dodleston, Duckington, Duddon, Dunham-on-the-Hill, Dutton,

Eaton, Eccleston, Edge, Edgerley, Elton,

Farndon, Foulk Stapleford,

Golborne Bellow, Golborne David, Grafton, Great Budworth, Guilden Sutton,

Hampton, Handley, Hapsford, Harthill, Hatton, Hockenhull, Hoole Village, Horton by Malpas, Horton-cum-Peel, Huntington, Huxley,

Iddinshall, Ince,

Kelsall, Kings Marsh, Kingsley,

Lach Dennis, Larkton, Lea by Backford, Lea Newbold, Ledsham, Little Budworth, Little Leigh, Little Stanney, Littleton, Lower Kinnerton,

Macefen, Malpas, Manley, Marlston-cum-Lache, Marston, Mickle Trafford, Mollington, Mouldsworth, Moulton

Nether Peover, Newton by Malpas, Newton-by-Tattenhall, Norley,

Oakmere, Oldcastle, Overton,

Picton, Poulton, Prior's Heys, Puddington, Pulford,

Rowton, Rushton,

Saighton, Shocklach Oviatt, Shotwick, Shotwick Park, Sproston, Stanthorne, Stockton, Stoke, Stretton, Sutton,

Tarporley, Tarvin, Tattenhall, Thornton-le-Moors, Threapwood, Tilston, Tilstone Fearnall, Tiverton, Tushingham cum Grindley,

Utkinton,

Waverton, Wervin, Whitegate and Marton, Whitley, Wigland, Willington, Wimbolds Trafford, Wimboldsley, Wincham, Woodbank, Wychough.

PART 3 CUMBRIA

Above Derwent, Aikton, Ainstable, Aldingham, Allhallows, Allonby, Alston Moor, Angerton, Appleby-in-Westmorland, Arlecdon and Frizington, Arnside, Arthuret, Asby, Askam and Ireleth, Askerton, Askham, Aspatria,

Bampton, Barbon, Barton, Bassenthwaite, Beaumont, Beetham, Bewaldeth and Snittlegarth, Bewcastle, Blawith and Subberthwaite, Blennerhasset and Torpenhow, Blindbothel, Blindcrake, Bolton, Boltons, Bootle, Borrowdale, Bothel and Threapland, Bowness, Bridekirk, Brigham, Bromfield, Brough, Brough Sowerby, Brougham, Broughton, Broughton East, Broughton Moor, Broughton West, Burgh by Sands, Burtholme, Burton in Kendal, Buttermere,

Caldbeck, Camerton, Carlatton, Cartmel Fell, Casterton, Castle Carrock, Castle Sowerby, Catterlen, Claife, Cliburn, Clifton, Colby, Colton, Coniston, Crackenthorpe, Crook, Crosby Garrett, Crosby Ravensworth, Crosscanonby, Crossthwaite and Lyth, Culgaith, Cummersdale, Cumrew, Cumwhitton,

Dacre, Dalston, Dean, Dearham, Dent, Distington, Docker, Drigg and Carleton, Dufton, Dundraw, Dunnerdale with Seathwaite,

Egton with Newland, Embleton, Ennerdale and Kinniside, Eskdale,

Farlam, Fawcett Forest, Firbank,

Garsdale, Gilcrux, Glassonby, Gosforth, Grayrigg, Great Clifton, Great Salkeld, Great Strickland, Greysouthen, Greystoke,

Haile, Hartley, Haverthwaite, Hawkshead, Hayton and Mealo, Hayton, Helbeck, Helsington, Hesket, Hethersgill, Heversham, Hincaster, Hoff, Holme Abbey, Holme, Holme East Waver, Holme Low, Holme St Cuthbert, Hugill, Hunsonby, Hutton, Hutton Roof,

Ireby and Uldale, Irthington, Irton with Santon,

Kaber, Kentmere, Killington, Kings Meaburn, Kingmoor, Kingwater, Kirkandrews, Kirk-bampton, Kirkbride, Kirkby Ireleth, Kirkby Lonsdale, Kirkby Stephen, Kirkby Thore, Kirklinton Middle, Kirkoswald,

Lakes, Lambrigg, Lamplugh, Langwathby, Lazonby, Levens, Lindal and Marton, Little Clifton, Little Strickland, Long Marton, Longsleddale, Lorton, Lowca, Lower Allithwaite, Lower Holker, Loweswater, Lowick, Lowside Quarter, Lowther, Lupton,

Mallerstang, Mansergh, Mansriggs, Martindale, Matterdale, Meathop and Ulpha, Mid-dleton, Midgeholme, Milburn, Millom Without, Milnthorpe, Moresby, Morland, Mun-caster, Mungrisdale, Murton, Musgrave,

Nateby, Natland, Nether Denton, Nether Staveley, Nether Wasdale, New Hutton, New-biggin, Newby, Nicholforest,

Old Hutton and Holmescales, Ormside, Orton (in the district of Carlisle), Orton (in the district of Eden), Osmotherley, Oughterside and Allerby, Ousby, Over Staveley,

Papcastle, Parton, Patterdale, Pennington, Plumbland, Ponsonby, Preston Patrick, Preston Richard,

Ravenstonedale, Rockcliffe,

Satterthwaite, Scaleby, Scalthwaiterigg, Seascale, Sebergham, Sedbergh, Sedgwick, Set-murthy, Shap, Shap Rural, Silloth-on-Solway, Skelsmergh, Skelton, Skelwith, Sleagill, Sockbridge and Tirril, Solport, Soulby, St Bees, St Bridget Beckermet, St Cuthbert Without, St Johns Castlerigg and Wythburn, Stainmore, Stainton, Stanwix Rural, Staple-ton, Staveley in Cartmel, Strickland Ketel, Strickland Roger,

Tebay, Temple Sowerby, Threlkeld, Thrimby, Thursby, Torver,

Ulpha, Ulverston, Underbarrow and Bradleyfield, Underskiddaw, Upper Allithwaite, Upper Denton, Urswick,

Waberthwaite, Waitby, Walton, Warcop, Waterhead, Waverton, Weddicar, Westlinton, Westnewton, Westward, Wetheral, Wharton, Whicham, Whinfell, Whitwell and Selside, Winscales, Winton, Witherslack, Woodside, Wythop,

Yanwath and Eamont Bridge.

PART 4 GREATER MANCHESTER

Dunham,
Massey,
Ringway,
Warburton, Worthington.

PART 5 HALTON

Daresbury,
Moore,
Preston Brook.

PART 6 LANCASHIRE

Aighton, Bailey and Chaigley, Altham, Anglezarke, Arkholme with Cawood,

Balderstone, Barley with Wheatley Booth, Barnacre with Bonds, Barton, Bashall Eaves, Bickerstaffe, Billington, Bispham, Blackco, Bleasdale, Bolton by Bowland, Borwick, Bowland Forest High, Bowland Forest Low, Bowland with Leagram, Bracewell and Brogden, Bretherton, Brindle, Broughton, Burrow with Burrow,

Cantsfield, Caton with Littledale, Catteral, Charnock Richard, Chatburn, Chipping, Claughton (in the district of Wyre), Claughton (in the district of Lancaster), Cliviger, Cockerham, Croston, Cuerdale, Cuerden,

Dalton, Dinckley, Downham, Down Holland, Dunnockshaw, Dutton,

Easington, Eccleshill, Ellel, Elswick,

Forton, Foulridge,

Gisburn, Gisburn Forest, Goldshaw Booth, Goosnarch, Great Altcar, Great Eccleston, Great Mitton, Greenhalgh with Thistleton, Gressingham, Grimsargh, Grindleton,

Haighton, Halsall, Halton with Aughton, Hambleton, Hapton, Heapey, Heath Charnock, Heaton with Oxcliffe, Heskin, Higham with West Close Booth, Hoghton, Hornby with Farleton, Horton, Hothersall, Hutton,
Ightenhill, Inskip with Sowerby, Ireby,
Kirkland,
Lathom, Leck, Little Hoole, Little Mitton, Little Eccleston with Larbreck, Longridge, Mawdesley, Mearley, Melling with Wrayton, Mellor, Middleton, Middop, Much Hoole, Myerscough and Bilsborrow,
Nateby, Nether Kellet, Nether Wyersdale, Newburgh, Newsholme, Newton, Newton with Clifton, North Turton,
Old Laund Booth, Osbaldeston, Out Rawcliffe, Over Kellet, Over Wyresdale, Ovrerton, Parbold, Paythorne, Pendleton, Pilling, Pleasington, Priest Hutton,
Quernmore,
Read, Ribby with Rea, Ribchester, Rimington, Rivington, Roeburndale, Roughlee Booth Rufford,
Sabden, Salesbury, Salterforth, Samlesbury, Sawley, Scarisbrick, Scotforth, Silverdale, Simonstone, Singleton, Slaidburn, Staining, Stalmine with Staynall,
Tatham, Thornley with Wheatley, Thurnham, Tockholes, Trawden Forest, Treales, Roseacre and Wharles, Tunstall, Twiston,
Ulnes Walton, Upper Rawcliffe with Tarnacre,
Waddington, Warton, Weeton with Preese, Wenninghton, West Bradford, Westby with Plumptons, Whalley, Wheelton, Whittingham, Whittington, Winmarleigh, Wiswell, Withnell, Woodplumpton, Worsthorne with Hurstwood, Worston, Wray with Botton, Wrightington,
Yate and Pickup Bank, Yealand Coyners, Yealand Redmayne.

PART 7 MERSEYSIDE

Bold,
Cronton,
Ince Blundell,
Sefton, Simonswood,
Tarbock.

PART 8 WARRINGTON

Croft, Cuerdley,
Hatton,
Rixton and Glazebrook,
Stretton,
Winwick.

Regulation 4(b)

SCHEDULE 6 DESIGNATED PROTECTED AREAS IN THE NORTH WEST—BY MAPS

PART 1 CHESHIRE EAST

The parishes of—

Bollington,
Haslington,
Prestbury,
Willaston, Wistaston.

The unparished area bounded by the parishes of Warmingham, Moston, Haslington, Crewe Green, Weston, Basford, Savington cum Gresty, Rope, Wistaston, Woolstanwood, Leighton and Minshull Vernon.

The unparished area bounded by the parishes of Mottram St Andrew, Alderly Edge, Chorley, Mobberley and Ringway and by the borough constituencies of Cheadle and Manchester Wythenshawe.

PART 2 CHESHIRE WEST AND CHESTER

The parishes of—

Appleton,
Culcheth and Glazebury,
Davenham,
Lostock Gralam, Lymm,
Walton, Winsford.

The unparished area of the county constituency of Ellesmere Port and Neston excluding the parishes of Ince, Elton, Hapsford, Thornton-le-Moors, Dunham-on-the-Hill, Wimbolds Trafford, Bridge Trafford, Stoke, Wervin, Picton, Mickle Trafford, Hoole Village, Crought, Caughall, Moston, Mollington, Saughall, Shotwick Park, Woodbank, Shotwick, Charlton-by-Beckford, Little Stanley, Backford, Lea-by-Backford, Capenhurst, Ledsham and Puddington.

PART 3 CUMBRIA

The parishes of—

Brampton,
Cleator Moor,
Dalton Town and Newton,
Egremont,
Maryport, Millom,
St John Beckermet,
Windermere, Workington.

The unparished area bounded by the parishes of Askram and Ireleth, Dalton Town with Newton and Aldingham.
The unparished area bounded by the parishes of Lazonby, Great Salkeld, Langwathby, Brougham, Yanwath and Eamont Bridge, Dacre, Catterlen and Hesket.
The unparished area bounded by the parishes of Parton, Moresby, Weddicar and St Bees.

PART 4 GREATER MANCHESTER

The parishes of—

Haigh, Heywood and Middleton.
Saddleworth,
Westhoughton.

The unparished area of the borough constituency of Bury North.
The unparished area of the county constituency of Littleborough and Saddleworth excluding the parishes of Saddleworth and Shaw and Crompton.
The unparished area of the county constituency of Rochdale.

PART 5 LANCASHIRE

The parishes of—

Anderton, Aughton,

Briercliffe, Brying with Warton, Burscough,
Cabus, Clayton-Le-Dale,
Euxton,
Farington, Freckleton,
Hesketh with Becconsall,
Lea, Longton,
Ramsgreave,
Tarleton,
Up Holland,
Whitworth.

The unparished area bounded by the parishes of Trawden Forest, Reedley Hallows, Old Laund Booth, Barrowford, Blacko, Foulridge, Salterforth; the borough constituency of Burnley; and the parishes of Thornton in Craven and Lothersdale in North Yorkshire.
The unparished area bounded by the parishes of Cliviger, Whitworth, North Turton, Yate and Pickup Bank, Hyndburn, Hapton, Dunnockshaw, Habergham Eaves; the borough constituency of Hyndburn; the parish of Todmorden in West Yorkshire; the county constituency of Heywood and Middleton and the borough constituency of Bury North in Greater Manchester.
The unparished area bounded by the parishes of Latham, Newburgh, Dalton, Up Holland, Bickerstaffe, Aughton, Scarisbrick and Burscough.
The unparished area bounded by the parishes of Cuerdale, Salmesbury, Hoghton, Brindle, Clayton-le-Woods, Cuerden, Farington, Penwortham; and the borough constituency of Preston.

PART 6 MERSEYSIDE

The parishes of—

Knowsley,
Melling,
Rainford,
Thornton.

The unparished area of the borough constituency of Crosby bounded by the parishes of Little Altcar, Ince Blundell, Thornton and Sefton and by the borough constituency of Bootle.
The unparished area of the county constituency of Wirral South.

PART 7 WARRINGTON

Burtonwood and Westbrook.

Regulation 5(a)

SCHEDULE 7 DESIGNATED PROTECTED AREAS IN THE EAST OF ENGLAND—ENTIRE PARISHES

PART 1 BEDFORD

Aspley Heath, Astwick,
Battlesden, Biddenham, Billington, Bletsoe, Blunham, Bolnhurst and Keysoe, Brogborough,
Campton and Chicksands, Cardington, Carlton and Chellington, Chalgrave, Clifton, Clophill, Colmworth, Cople,
Dean and Shelton, Dunton,

Eastcotts, Edworth, Eggington, Elstow, Eversholt, Everton, Eyeworth,
Felmersham, Flitton and Greenfield,
Gravenhurst, Great Barford,
Harlington, Harrold, Haynes, Heath and Reach, Henlow, Hockliffe, Houghton Conquest,
Hulcote and Salford, Husbourne Crawley, Hyde,
Kempston Rural, Kensworth, Knotting and Souldrop,
Lidlington, Little Barford, Little Staughton,
Maulden, Marston Moretaine, Melchbourne and Yielden, Meppershall, Millbrook, Milton
Bryan, Milton Ernest, Mogerhanger,
Northill,
Oakley, Odell, Old Warden,
Pavenham, Pertenhall, Podington, Potsgrove, Potton, Pulloxhill,
Ravensden, Renhold, Ridgmont, Riseley, Roxton,
Silsoe, Sharnbrook, Shefford, Shillington, Southill, Stagsden, Stanbridge, Staploe, Step-
pingley, Stevington, Stewartby, Stondon, Streatley, Studham, Sundon, Sutton, Swines-
head,
Tempsford, Thurleigh, Tilsworth, Tingrith, Totternhoe, Turvey,
Westoning, Whipsnade, Wilden, Willington, Wilshamstead, Woburn, Wrestlingworth and
Cockayne Hatley, Wymington.

Part 2 Cambridgeshire

Abbots Ripton, Abbotsley, Abington Pigotts, Ailsworth, Alconbury, Alconbury Weston,
Alwalton, Arrington, Ashley,
Babraham, Bainton, Balsham, Barham and Woolley, Barnack, Barrington, Bartlow, Bar-
ton, Bassingbourn cum Kneesworth, Benwick, Bluntisham, Borough Fen, Bottisham,
Bourn, Boxworth, Brington and Molesworth, Brinkley, Broughton, Buckden, Buckworth,
Burrough Green, Bury, Bythorn and Keyston,
Caldecote, Carlton, Castle Camps, Castor, Catworth, Caxton, Chesterton, Cheveley,
Childerley, Chippenham, Christchurch, Colne, Comberton, Connington (in the district of
South Cambridgeshire), Connington (in the district of Huntingdonshire), Coton, Coveney,
Covington, Croxton, Croydon,
Deeping Gate, Denton and Caldecote, Diddington, Doddington, Downham, Dry Drayton,
Dullingham, Duxford,
Earith, Easton, Ellington, Elsworth, Eltisley, Elton, Etton, Eye, Eynesbury Hardwicke,
Farcet, Fen Ditton, Fen Drayton, Fenstanton, Folksworth and Washingley, Fordham,
Fowlmere, Foxton,
Gamlingay, Glatton, Glinton, Grafham, Grantchester, Graveley, Great Abington, Great
and Little Chishill, Great Eversden, Great Gidding, Great Gransden, Great Paxton, Great
Staughton, Great Wilbarham, Guilden Morden,
Haddenham, Hail Weston, Hamerton and Steeple Gidding, Hardwick, Harlton, Harston,
Haslingfield, Hatley, Hauxton, Helpston, Hemingford Abbotts, Hemingford Grey, Hey-
don, Hildesham, Hilton, Hinxton, Holme, Holywell cum Needingworth, Horningsea,
Horseheath, Houghton and Wyton,
Ickleton, Isleham,
Kennett, Kimbolton, Kings Ripton, Kingston, Kirtling, Knapwell,
Landbeach, Leighton, Litlington, Little Abington, Little Eversden, Little Gidding, Little
Gransden, Little Shelford, Little Wilbraham, Lode, Lolworth, Longstanton, Longstowe,
Madingley, Manea, Marholm, Maxey, Meldreth, Mepal, Morborne,
Newborough, Newton (in the district of Fenland), Newton (in the district of South
Cambridgeshire), Northborough,
Oakington and Westwick, Offord Cluny and Offord D'Arcy, Old Hurst, Old Weston,
Orwell, Over,
Pampisford, Papworth Everard, Papworth St Agnes, Parson Drove, Peakirk, Perry, Pidley
cum Fenton,
Rampton, Reach,

Shepreth, Shingay cum Wendy, Shudy Camps, Sibson cum Stibbington, Snailwell, Southoe and Midloe, Southorpe, Spaldwick, St Martins Without, St Neots, Steeple Morden, Stetchworth, Stilton, Stow cum Quy, Stow Longa, Stretham, Sutton (in the district of East Cambridgeshire), Sutton (in the district of Peterborough) Swaffham Bulbeck, Swaffham Prior, Swavesey,

Tadlow, Teversham, The Stukeleys, Thetford, Thorney, Thornhaugh, Thriplow, Tilbrook, Toft, Toseland, Tydd St Giles,

Ufford, Upton and Coppingford, Upton, Upwood and the Raveleys,

Wansford, Warboys, Waresley cum Tetworth, Water Newton, Waterbeach, Wentworth, West Wickham, West Wratting, Westley Waterless, Weston Colville, Whaddon, Whittlesford, Wicken, Wilburton, Wimblington, Wimpole, Winwick, Wisbech St Mary, Wistow, Witcham, Witchford, Wittering, Wood Walton, Woodditton, Woodhurst, Wothorpe, Yelling.

PART 3 ESSEX

Abberton, Abbess Beauchamp and Berners Roding, Aldham, Alphamstone, Alresford, Althorne, Ardleigh, Arkesden, Ashdon, Asheldham, Ashen, Aythorpe Roding,

Bardfield Sailing, Barling Magna, Barnston, Beaumont cum Moze, Belchamp Otten, Belchamp St Paul, Belchamp Walter, Berden, Birch, Birchanger, Birdbrook, Black Notley, Blackmore, Bobbingworth, Borley, Boxted, Bradfield, Bradwell, Bradwell on Sea, Broxted, Bulmer, Bures Hamlet,

Canewdon, Castle Hedingham, Chappel, Chickney, Chignall, Chrishall, Clavering, Cold Norton, Colne Engaine, Copford, Cressing,

Debden, Dedham, Dengie, Doddinghurst,

East Donyland, East Hanningfield, East Mersea, Eight Ash Green, Elmdon, Elsenham, Epping Upland,

Fairstead, Farnham, Faulkbourne, Feering, Felsted, Finchingfield, Fingrinhoe, Fordham, Foulness, Foxearth, Frating, Fyfield,

Gestingthorpe, Goldhanger, Good Easter, Gosfield, Great and Little Leighs, Great and Little Wigborough, Great Bardfield, Great Bentley, Great Braxted, Great Bromley, Great Canfield, Great Chesterford, Great Easton, Great Hallingbury, Great Henny, Great Horkesley, Great Maplestead, Great Oakley, Great Saling, Great Sampford, Great Tey, Great Totham, Great Waltham, Great Yeldham, Greenstead Green and Halstead Rural,

Hadstock, Hatfield Broad Oak, Hatfield Heath, Hazeleigh, Hellions Bumpstead, Hempstead, Henham, High Easter, High Laver, High Ongar, High Roothing, Highwood,

Kelvedon, Kelvedon Hatch,

Lamarsh, Lambourne, Langenhoe, Langford, Langham, Langley, Latchingdon, Layer Breton, Layer Marney, Layer de la Haye, Leaden Roding, Lindsell, Liston, Little Baddow, Little Bardfield, Little Bentley, Little Braxted, Little Bromley, Little Burstead, Little Canfield, Little Chesterford, Little Clacton, Little Dunmow, Little Easton, Little Hallingbury, Little Henny, Little Horkesley, Little Laver, Little Maplestead, Little Oakley, Little Sampford, Little Totham, Little Waltham, Little Yeldham, Littlebury,

Magden Laver, Manuden, Margaret Roding, Margaretting, Marshbury, Matching, Messing cum Inworth, Middleton, Mistley, Moreton, Mount Bures, Mountnessing, Mundon,

Navestock, Newport, North Fambridge, North Weald Basset,

Ovington,

Paglesham, Panfield, Pebmarsh, Peldon, Pentlow, Pleshey, Purleigh,

Quendon and Rickling,

Radwinter, Ramsden Bellhouse, Ramsden Crays, Ramsey and Parkeston, Rawreth, Rayne, Rettendon, Ridgewell, Rivenhall, Roxwell, Roydon,

Salcott, Sandon, Shalford, Sheering, South Hanningfield, St Lawrence, St Osyth, Stambourne, Stambridge, Stanford Rivers, Stapleford Abbotts, Stapleford Tawney, Stebbing, Steeple Bumpstead, Steeple, Stisted, Stock, Stondon Massey, Stow Maries, Strethall, Sturmer, Sutton,

Takeley, Tendring, Terling, Thaxted, Theydon Bois, Theydon Garnon, Theydon Mount, Thorrington, Thorpe le Soken, Tilbury Juxta Clare, Tillingham, Tilty, Tollesbury, Tolleshunt d'Arcy, Tolleshunt Knight, Tolleshunt Major, Toppesfield, Twinstead,
Ugley, Ulting,
Virley,
Wakes Colne, Weeley, Wenden Lofts, Wendens Ambo, West Hanningfield, Wethersfield, White Colne, White Notley, White Roothing, Wicken Bonhunt, Wickham Bishops, Wickham St Paul, Widdington, Willingale, Wimbish, Wix, Woodham Ferrers & Bicknare, Woodham Mortimer, Woodham Walter, Wormingford, Wrabnes.

Part 4 Hertfordshire

Albury, Aldbury, Anstey, Ardeley, Ashwell, Aspenden, Aston, Ayot St Lawrence, Ayot St Peter,
Barkway, Barley, Bayford, Bengeo Rural, Benington, Bramfield, Braughing, Brent Pelham, Brickendon Liberty, Buckland, Bygrave,
Caldecote, Chipperfield, Clothall, Codicote, Cottered,
Datchworth,
Eastwick, Essendon,
Flamstead, Flaunden, Furneux Pelham,
Gilston, Graveley, Great Amwell, Great Gaddesden, Great Munden,
Harpenden Rural, Hertford Health, Hertingfordbury, Hexton, High Wych, Hinxworth, Holwell, Hormead, Hunsdon,
Ickleford,
Kelshall, Kimpton, Kings Walden,
Langley, Lilley, Little Berkhamsted, Little Gaddesden, Little Hadham, Little Munden, Markyate, Meesden, Much Hadham,
Nettleden with Potten End, Newnham, Nuthampstead,
Offley,
Pirton, Preston,
Radwell, Reed, Ridge, Rushden,
Sacombe, Sandon, Sarratt, Shenley, St Pauls Walden, Standon, Stapleford, Stocking Pelham,
Tewin, Therfield, Thorley, Thundridge, Tring Rural,
Walkern, Wallington, Ware Rural, Watton at Stone, Westmill, Weston, Widford, Wiggington Wyddial, Wymondley.

Part 5 Norfolk

Acle, Alburgh, Alby with Thwaite, Aldborough, Aldeby, Alderford, Alpington, Anmer, Antingham, Ashby St Mary, Ashby with Oby, Ashill, Ashmanhaugh, Ashwellthorpe, Aslacton, Attlebridge, Aylmerton,
Baconsthorpe, Bacton, Bagthorpe with Barmer, Banham, Barford, Barnham Broom, Barsham, Barton Bendish, Barton Turf, Barwick, Bawburgh, Bawdeswell, Bawsey, Beachamwell, Bedingham, Beeston Regis, Beeston St Andrew, Beeston with Bittering, Beetley, Beighton, Belaugh, Bergh Apton, Besthorpe, Billingford, Binham, Bintree, Bircham, Bixley, Blakeney, Blickling, Blo' Norton, Blofield, Bodham, Booton, Boughton, Bracon Ash, Bradenham, Bramerton, Brampton, Brancaster, Brandiston, Bressingham, Brettenham, Bridgham, Briningham, Brinton, Brisley, Briston, Brockdish, Brooke, Broome, Brumstead, Bunwell, Burgh and Tuttington, Burgh Castle, Burgh St Peter, Burnham Market, Burnham Norton, Burnham Overy, Burnham Thorpe, Burston and Shimpling, Buxton with Lammas, Bylaugh,
Caistor St Edmund, Cantley, Carbrooke, Carleton Rode, Carlton St Peter, Castle Acre, Castle Rising, Caston, Catfield, Cawston, Chedgrave, Choseley, Claxton, Clenchwarton, Cley Next the Sea, Cockley Cley, Colby, Colkirk, Colney, Coltishall, Congham, Corpusty, Cranwich, Cranworth, Crimplesham, Cringleford, Crostwick, Croxton,

Denton, Denver, Deopham, Dickleburgh and Rushall, Didlington, Dilham, Ditchingham, Docking, Downham West, Dunton,

Earsham, East Beckham, East Carleton, East Rudham, East Ruston, East Tuddenham, East Walton, East Winch, Easton, Edgefield, Ellingham, Elsing, Erpingham,

Felbrigg, Felmingham, Felthorpe, Feltwell, Field Dalling, Filby, Fincham, Fleggburgh, Flitcham with Appleton, Florden, Fordham, Forncett, Foulden, Foulsham, Foxley, Framingham Pigot, Fransham, Freethorpe, Frettenham, Fring, Fritton and St Olaves, Fulmodeston,

Garboldisham, Garvestone, Gateley, Gayton, Geldeston, Gillingham, Gimingham, Gissing, Gooderstone, Great and Little Plumstead, Great Cressingham, Great Dunham, Great Ellingham, Great Massingham, Great Melton, Great Moulton, Great Snoring, Great Witchingham, Gresham, Gressenhall, Grimston, Griston, Guestwick, Guist, Gunthorpe,

Haddiscoe, Hainford, Hales, Halvergate, Hanworth, Happisburgh, Hardingham, Harling, Harpley, Haveringland, Heckingham, Hedenham, Helhoughton, Hellington, Hemblington, Hempnall, Hempstead, Hempton, Hevingham, Heydon, Hickling, High Kelling, Hilborough, Hilgay, Hillington, Hindolveston, Hindringham, Hingham, Hockering, Hockham, Hockwold cum Wilton, Hoe, Holkham, Holme Hale, Holme next the Sea, Holverston, Holt, Honing, Honingham, Horning, Horningtoft, Horsey, Horsford, Horsham St Faith and Newton St Faith, Horstead with Stanninghall, Houghton, Howe,

Ickburgh, Ingham, Ingoldisthorpe, Ingworth, Itteringham,

Kelling, Kempstone, Kenninghall, Keswick, Ketteringham, Kettlestone, Kilverstone, Kimberley, Kirby Bedon, Kirby Cane, Kirstead, Knapton,

Langham, Langley with Hardley, Lessingham, Letheringsett with Glandford, Lexham, Leziate, Lingwood and Burlingham, Litcham, Little Barningham, Little Cressingham, Little Dunham, Little Ellingham, Little Massingham, Little Melton, Little Snoring, Little Witchingham, Loddon, Long Stratton, Longham, Ludham, Lynford, Lyng,

Marham, Marlingford, Marsham, Marshland St James, Martham, Matlask, Mattishall, Mautby, Melton Constable, Merton, Methwold, Middleton, Mileham, Moreley, Morning Thorpe, Morston, Morton on the Hill, Mulbarton, Mundesley, Mundford, Mundham,

Narborough, Narford, Neatishead, Necton, Needham, New Buckenham, Newton by Castle Acre, Newton Flotman, Nordelph, North Creake, North Elmham, North Lopham, North Pickenham, North Tuddenham, North Wootton, Northwold, Norton Subcourse,

Old Buckenham, Old Hunstanton, Ormesby St Michael, Ormesby St Margaret with Scatby, Oulton, Outwell, Overstrand, Ovington, Oxborough,

Paston, Pentney, Plumstead, Postwick, Potter Heigham, Pudding Norton, Pulham Market, Pulham St Mary,

Quidenham,

Rackheath, Raveningham, Raynham, Reedham, Reepham, Repps with Bastwick, Riddlesworth, Ringland, Ringstead, Rockland St Mary, Rocklands, Rollesby, Roudham, Rougham, Roughton, Roydon (in the Kings Lynn and West Norfolk district), Runcton Holme, Runhall, Runton, Ryburgh, Ryston,

Saham Toney, Salhouse, Sall, Salthouse, Sandringham, Saxlingham Nethergate, Scarning, Scole, Scottow, Scoulton, Sea Palling, Sedgeford, Seething, Shelfanger, Shelton, Shernborne, Shipdham, Shotesham, Shouldham, Shouldham Thorpe, Shropham, Sidestrand, Sisland, Skeyton, Sloley, Smallburgh, Snetterton, Snettisham, Somerton, South Acre, South Creake, South Lopham, South Pickenham, South Walsham, Southery, Southrepps, Sparham, Sporle with Palgrave, Stalham, Stanfield, Stanford, Stanhoe, Starston, Stibbard, Stiffkey, Stockton, Stody, Stoke Ferry, Stoke Holy Cross, Stokesby with Herringby, Stow Bardolph, Stow Bedon, Stradsett, Stratton Strawless, Strumpshaw, Sturston, Suffield, Surlingham, Sustead, Sutton, Swafield, Swainsthorpe, Swannington, Swanton Abbott, Swanton Morley, Swanton Novers, Swardeston, Syderstone,

Tacolneston, Tasburgh, Tattersett, Terrington St Clement, Terrington St John, Tharston, Themelthorpe, Thompson, Thornage, Thornham, Thorpe Market, Thurlton, Thurne, Thurning, Thursford, Thurton, Thwaite, Tibenham, Tilney All Saints, Tilney St Lawrence, Titchwell, Tittleshall, Tivetshall St Margaret, Tivetshall St Mary, Toft Monks, Topcroft, Tottenhill, Tottington, Trimingham, Trowse With Newton, Trunch, Tunstead, Twyford, Upper Sheringham, Upton with Fishley, Upwell,

Wacton, Walpole, Walpole Cross Keys, Walpole Highway, Walsingham, Warham, Watlington, Weasenham All Saints, Weasenham St Peter, Weeting with Broomhill, Wellingham, Wells next the Sea, Welney, Wendling, Wereham, West Acre, West Beckham, West Caister, West Dereham, West Rudham, West Walton, West Winch, Weston Longville, Westwick, Weybourne, Wheatacre, Whinburgh, Whissonsett, Wicklewood, Wickmere, Wiggenhall St Germans, Wiggenhall St Mary Magdalen, Wighton, Wimbotsham, Winfarthing, Winterton on Sea, Witton, Wiveton, Wood Dalling, Wood Norton, Woodbastwick, Woodton, Wormegay, Worstead, Wortwell, Wramplingham, Wreningham, Wretham, Wretton,
Yaxham, Yelverton.

PART 6 SUFFOLK

Acton, Akenham, Aldeburgh, Alderton, Aldham, Aldringham cum Thorpe, All Saints and St Nicholas South Elmham, Alpheton, Ampton, Arwarton, Ashbocking, Ashfield cum Thorpe, Aspall, Assington, Athelington,
Bacton, Badingham, Badley, Badwell Ash, Bardwell, Barham, Barking, Barnardiston, Barnby, Barnham, Barningham, Barrow, Barsham, Barton Mills, Battisford, Bawdsey, Baylham, Bedfield, Bedingfield, Belstead, Benacre, Benhall, Bentley, Beyton, Bildeston, Blaxhall, Blundeston, Blyford, Blythburgh, Botesdale, Boulge, Boxford, Boxted, Boyton, Bradfield Comburst with Stanningfield, Bradfield St Clare, Bradfield St George, Braiseworth, Bramfield, Bramford, Brampton with Stoven, Brandeston, Brantham, Bredfield, Brent Eleigh, Brettenham, Brightwell, Brockley, Brome and Oakley, Bromeswell, Bruisyard, Brundish, Bucklesham, Bures St Mary, Burgate, Burgh, Burstall, Butley, Buxhall, Campsey Ash, Capel St Andrew, Cavendish, Cavenham, Charsfield, Chattisham, Chedburgh, Chediston, Chelmodiston, Chelsworth, Chevington, Chillesford, Chilton, Clare, Claydon, Clopton, Cockfield, Coddenham, Combs, Coney Weston, Cookley, Copdock, Corton, Cotton, Covehithe, Cowlinge, Cransford, Cratfield, Creeting St Mary, Creeting St Peter or West Creeting, Cretingham, Crowfield, Culford, Culpho,
Dalham, Dallinghoo, Darsham, Debach, Debenham, Denham (in the district of mid Suffolk), Denham (in the district of St Edmundsbury), Dennington, Denston, Depden, Drinkstone, Dunwich,
Earl Soham, East Bergholt, Easton, Edwardstone, Ellough, Elmsett, Elmswell, Elveden, Eriswell, Euston, Eye, Eyke,
Fakenham Magna, Falkenham, Farnham, Felsham, Finningham, Flempton, Flixton (in the district of Waveney, Lothingland Ward), Flixton (in the district of Waveney, South Elmham Ward), Flowton, Fornham St Genevieve, Fornham St Martin, Foxhall, Framlingham, Framsden, Freckenham, Fressingfield, Freston, Friston, Frostenden,
Gazeley, Gedding, Gedgrave, Gipping, Gisleham, Gislingham, Glemsford, Gosbeck, Great Ashfield, Great Barton, Great Bealings, Great Blakenham, Great Bradley, Great Bricett, Great Finborough, Great Glemham, Great Livermere, Great Thurlow, Great Waldingfield, Great Whelnetham, Great Wratting, Groton, Grundisburgh,
Hacheston, Hargrave, Harkstead, Harleston, Hartest, Hasketon, Haughley, Hawkedon, Hawstead, Helmingham, Hemingstone, Hemley, Hengrave, Henley, Henstead with Hulver Street, Hepworth, Herringswell, Hessett, Heveningham, Higham (in the district of Babergh), Higham (in the district of Forest Heath), Hinderclay, Hintlesham, Hitcham, Holbrook, Hollesley, Holton, Holton St Mary, Honington, Hoo, Hopton, Horham, Horringer, Hoxne, Hundon, Hunston, Huntingfield,
Icklingham, Ickworth, Iken, Ingham, Ixworth, Ixworth Thorpe,
Kedington, Kelsale Cum Carlton, Kentford, Kenton, Kersey, Kettlebaston, Kettleburgh, Kirton, Knettishall, Knodishall,
Lackford, Langham, Lavenham, Lawshall, Laxfield, Layham, Leavenheath, Letheringham, Levington, Lidgate, Lindsey, Linstead Magna, Linstead Parva, Little Bealings, Little Blakenham, Little Bradley, Little Cornard, Little Finborough, Little Glemham, Little Livermere, Little Thurlow, Little Waldingfield, Little Whelnetham, Little Wratting, Lound,

Market Weston, Marlesford, Mellis, Mendham, Mendlesham, Metfield, Mettingham, Mickfield, Middleton, Milden, Monewden, Monk Soham, Monks Eleigh, Moulton, Mutford,

Nacton, Nayland with Wissington, Nedging with Naughton, Nettleshead, Newbourne, Newton, North Cove, Norton, Nowton,

Occold, Offton, Old Newton with Dagworth, Onehouse, Orford, Otley, Ouseden,

Pakenham, Palgrave, Parham, Peasenhall, Pettaugh, Pettistree, Playford, Polstead, Poslingford, Preston St Mary, Purdis Farm,

Ramsholt, Rattlesden, Raydon, Reydon, Red Lodge, Rede, Redgrave, Redisham, Redlingfield, Rendham, Rendlesham, Rickinghall Inferior, Rickinghall Superior, Ringsfield, Ringshall, Risby, Rishangles, Rumburgh, Rushbrooke with Rougham, Rushmere,

Santon Downham, Sapiston, Saxmundham, Saxtead, Semer, Shadingfield, Shelland, Shelly, Shimpling, Shipmeadow, Shotley, Shottisham, Sibton, Snape, Somerleyton, Ashby and Herringfleet, Somersham, Somerton, Sotherton, Sotterley, South Cove, Southolt, Spexhall, St Andrew Ilketshall, St Cross South Elmham, St James South Elmham, St John Ilketshall, St Lawrence Ilketshall, St Margaret Ilketshall, St Margaret South Elmham, St Mary South Elmham Otherwise Homersfield, St Michael South Elmham, St Peter South Elmham, Stansfield, Stanstead, Stanton, Sternfield, Stoke Ash, Stoke By Clare, Stoke By Nayland, Stoneham Aspal, Stoneham Earl, Stoneham Parva, Stowlangtoft, Stowupland, Stradbroke, Stradishall, Stratford St Andrew, Stratford St Mary, Stratton Hall, Stuston, Stutton, Sudbourne, Sutton, Swefling, Swilland, Syleham,

Tannington, Tattingstone, The Saxhams, Theberton, Thelnetham, Thorington, Thorndon, Thornham Magna, Thornham Parva, Thorpe Morieux, Thrandeston, Thurston, Thwaite, Timworth, Tostock, Troston, Tuddenham St Martin, Tunstall,

Ubbeston, Ufford, Uggeshall,

Walberswick, Waldringfield, Walpole, Walsham Le Willows, Wangford, Wangford with Henham, Wantisden, Washbrook, Wattisfield, Wattisham, Wenham Magna, Wenham Parva, Wenhaston with Mells Hamlet, West Stow, Westerfield, Westhall, Westhorpe, Westleton, Westley, Weston, Wetherden, Wetheringsett cum Brockford, Weybread, Whatfield, Whepstead, Wherstead, Whitton, Wickham Market, Wickham Skeith, Wickhambrook, Wilby, Willingham St Mary, Willisham, Wingfield, Winston, Wissett, Withersfield, Witnesham, Wixoe, Woolpit, Woolverston, Wordwell, Worlington, Worlingworth, Wortham, Wrentham, Wyverstone,

Yaxley, Yoxford.

Regulation 5(b)

Schedule 8 Designated Protected Areas in the East of England—By Maps

Part 1 Bedford

The parishes of—

Caddington and Slip End, Cranfield,
Houghton Regis,
Langford,
Sandy,
Toddington.

Part 2 Cambridgeshire

The parishes of—

Elm, Ely,
Leverington,
March,

Ramsey,
Soham,
Whittlesey.

The unparished area of Stanground North bounded by the parish of Thorney, the parish of Whittlesey in the District of Fenland and the unparished area of the city of Peterborough.

PART 3 ESSEX

The parishes of—

Ashingdon,
Elmstead,
Frinton and Walton,
Ingatestone and Fryerning,
Marks Tey,
Nazeing,
Ongar,
Saffron Walden, Southminster, Stansted Mountfitchet, Stanway,
Waltham Abbey, Writtle.

The unparished area of the county constituency of Billericay.

The unparished area bounded by the parishes of Gosfield, Sisted, Cressing, Black Notley, Felsted, Rayne, Panfield, Shalford and Wethersfield.

The unparished area of the county constituency of Brentwood and Ongar excluding the parishes of Matching, Abbess Beauchamp & Berners Roding, High Laver, Little Laver, Magdalen Laver, Moreton, Fyfield Willingdale, Bobbingworth, Ongar, High Ongar, Theydon Garnon, Theydon Mount, Stapleford Rowney, Stanford Rivers, Lambourne, Stapleford Abbots, Navestock, Kelvedon Hatch, Standon Massey, Blackmore, Ingatestone & Fryerning, Doddinghurst and Mountnessing.

The unparished area bounded by the parishes of Runwell, Rettendon, Hullbridge, Hockley, Hawkwell, Rochford, the borough constituency of Southend West, the borough constituency of Castle Point, the borough constituency of Basildon and the county constituency of Billericay.

The unparished area of the borough constituency of Thurrock.

PART 4 HERTFORDSHIRE

The parishes of—

Abbots Langley, Aldenham,
Hatfield,
Ippollitts,
Knebworth,
Northaw and Cuffley, Northchurch,
St Michael, St Stephen,
Tring,
Wheathampstead.

The unparished area bounded by the parishes of Ridge, North Mymms, Northaw and Cuffley, the London borough of Enfield and the London Borough of Barnet.

The unparished area bounded by the parishes of Chorley Wood, Sarratt, Croxley Green and Watford Rural, the borough constituency of Watford, the London Borough of Hillingdon and the parishes of Chalfont St Peter and Denham in the county of Buckinghamshire.

PART 5 NORFOLK

The parishes of—

Belton with Browston,
East Dereham, Emneth,
Hopton on Sea,
North Runcton, Northrepps,
Redenhall with Harleston, Roydon (in the district of South Norfolk),
Sculthorpe,
Wymondham.

PART 6 SUFFOLK

The parishes of—

Fornham All Saints,
Lakenheath, Leiston,
Mildenhall,
Oulton,
Sproughton.

The unparished area bounded by the parish of Moulton and the parishes of Fordham, Snailwell, Cheveley, Wooditton and Burwell in Cambridgeshire.

Regulation 6(a)

SCHEDULE 9 DESIGNATED PROTECTED AREAS IN THE NORTH EAST—ENTIRE PARISHES

PART 1 DURHAM

Archdeacon Newton,
Barforth, Barmpton, Barningham, Bearpark, Bishop Middleham, Bishopton, Bolam, Boldron, Bournmoor, Bowes, Bradbury and the Isle, Brafferton, Brancepeth, Brignall,
Castle Eden, Cleatlam, Coatham Mundeville, Cockfield, Cornforth, Cornsay, Cotherstone, Coxhoe, Croxdale and Hett,
Denton,
Easington Village, East and West Newbiggin, Edmonbyers, Edmondsley, Eggleston, Eggleston Abbey, Esh, Etherley, Evenwood and Barony,
Fishburn, Forest and Frith,
Gainford, Gilmonby, Great Burdon, Great Stainton, Greencroft,
Hamsterley, Haswell, Hawthorn, Headlam, Healeyfield, Hedleyhope, Heighington, High Coniscliffe, Hilton, Holwick, Hope, Houghton le Side, Hunderthwaite, Hustanworth, Hutton Henry, Hutton Magna,
Ingleton,
Kelloe, Killerby,
Langley, Langleydale and Shotton, Langton, Lartington, Little Lumley, Little Stainton, Low Coniscliffe and Merrybent, Low Dinsdale, Lunedale, Lynesack and Softley,
Mickleton, Middleton in Teesdale, Middleton St George Middridge, Monk Heselden, Mordon, Morton Palms, Morton Tinmouth, Muggleswick,
Neasham, Nesbitt, Newbiggin,
Ovington,
Piercebridge, Pittington,
Raby with Keverstone, Rokeby, Romaldkirk,
Sadeberge, Satley, Scargill, Seaton with Slingley, Shadforth, Sheraton with Hulam, Sherburn, Shincliffe, Shotton, Sockburn, South Bedburn, South Hetton, Staindrop, Stanhope, Streatlam and Stainton, Summerhouse,

Thornley, Tow Law, Trimdon Foundry,
Wackerfield, Walworth, West Rainton, Westwick, Whessoe, Whitton Gilbert, Whorlton,
Windlestone, Winston, Wolsingham, Woodland, Wycliffe with Thorpe.

Part 2 Hartlepool

Brierton,
Claxton,
Dalton Piercy,
Elwick,
Greatham,
Hart,
Newton Bewley.

Part 3 Middlesbrough

Stainton and Thornton.

Part 4 Northumberland

Acklington, Acomb, Adderstone with Lucker, Akeld, Allendale, Alnham, Alnmouth,
Alwinton, Ancroft,
Bamburgh, Bardon Mill, Bavington, Beadnell, Belford, Bellingham, Belsay, Bewick,
Biddlestone, Birtley, Blanchland, Bowsden, Branxton, Brinkburn, Broomhaugh and Rid-
ing, Broomley and Stocksfield, Bywell,
Callaly, Capheaton, Carham, Cartington, Chatton, Chillingham, Chollerton, Coanwood,
Cornhill on Tweed, Corsenside, Craster, Cresswell,
Denwick, Doddington, Duddo,
Earle, Easington, East Chevington, Edlingham, Eglingham, Ellingham, Ellington, Elsdon,
Embleton, Ewart,
Falstone, Featherstone, Felton, Ford,
Glanton, Greenhead, Greystead,
Harbottle, Hartburn, Hartleyburn, Hauxley, Haydon, Healey, Hebron, Heddon on the Wall,
Hedgeley, Hedley, Henshaw, Hepple, Hepscott, Hesleyhurst, Hexhamshire, Hexhamshire
Low Quarter, Hollinghill, Holy Island, Horncliffe, Horsley, Humshaugh,
Ilderton, Ingram,
Kielder, Kilham, Kirknewton, Kirkwhelpington, Knaresdale with Kirkhaugh, Kyloe,
Lesbury, Lilburn, Longframlington, Longhirst, Longhorsley, Longhoughton, Lowick,
Lynemouth,
Matfen, Meldon, Melkridge, Middleton, Milfield, Mitford,
Netherton, Netherwitton, Newbrough, Newton by the Sea, Newton on the Moor, Norham,
North Sunderland, Nunnykirk,
Otterburn, Ovington,
Plenmeller with Whitfield,
Rennington, Rochester, Roddam, Rothbury, Rothley,
Sandhoe, Shilbottle, Shoreswood, Shotley Low Quarter, Simonburn, Slaley, Snitter, Stam-
fordham, Stannington,
Tarset, Thirlwall, Thirston, Thropton, Togston, Tritlington,
Ulgham,
Wall, Wallington Demesne, Warden, Wark, West Allen, West Chevington, Whalton,
Whittingham, Whittington, Whitton and Tosson, Widdrington, Widdrington Station and
Stobswood, Wooler, Wylam.

Part 5 Redcar and Cleveland

Lockwood.

PART 6 STOCKTON-ON-TEES

Aislaby,
Carlton, Castlelevington,
Elton,
Grindon,
Hilton,
Ingleby Barwick,
Kirklevington,
Longnewton,
Maltby,
Newsham,
Redmarshall,
Stillington and Whitton,
Wolviston.

PART 7 TYNE AND WEAR

Burdon,
Dinnington,
Warden Law.

Regulation 6(b)

SCHEDULE 10 DESIGNATED PROTECTED AREAS IN THE NORTH EAST—BY MAPS

PART 1 DURHAM

The parishes of—

Brandon and Byshottles,
Cassop cum Quarrington,
Dalton le Dale,
Great Lumley,
Hurworth,
Kimblesworth and Plawsworth,
Lanchester,
Marwood,
Pelton,
Sedgefield, Shildon, Spennymoor, Startforth,
Trimdon,
Urpeth,
Waldridge.

The unparished area bounded by the parishes of Spennymoor, Windlestone, Shildon, Etherley, Evenwood and Barony and the borough constituency of North West Durham.
The unparished area bounded by the county constituency of North Durham, the borough constituency of Blaydon, and by the parishes of Greencroft, Lanchester and Healeyfield, and the parish of Shotley Low Quarter Northumberland County Council.
The unparished area bounded by the parishes of Urpeth, Edmondsley, the county constituency of North West Durham and the borough constituency of Blaydon.
The unparished area bounded by the county constituency of Bishop Auckland and the parishes of Wolsingham, Hedleythorpe, Brandon and Byshottles, Brancepeth and Spennymore.

PART 2 HARTLEPOOL

The unparished area of the borough constituency of Hartlepool.

PART 3 NORTHUMBERLAND

The parishes of—

> Hexham,
> Ord,
> Ponteland, Prudhoe,
> Warkworth.

The unparished area of the borough constituency of Blyth Valley.
The unparished area of the county constituency of Wansbeck excluding the parishes of
Longhurst, Pegswood, Hepscott, Morpeth, Mitford and Hebron.

PART 4 REDCAR AND CLEVELAND

The parishes of—

> Guisborough,
> Loftus,
> Skelton and Brotton.

The unparished area of the borough constituency of Redcar.

PART 5 TYNE AND WEAR

The parishes of—

> Hetton,
> Lamesley,
> Woolsington.

The unparished area of the borough constituency of Blaydon excluding the parishes of
Lamesley.
The unparished area of Birtley.

Regulation 7(a)

SCHEDULE 11 DESIGNATED PROTECTED AREAS IN THE SOUTH EAST—ENTIRE PARISHES

PART 1 BUCKINGHAMSHIRE

Addington, Adstock, Akeley, Ashendon, Ashley Green, Aston Abbotts, Aston Sandford,
Astwood,
Barton Hartshorn, Beachampton, Biddlesden, Bierton with Broughton, Bledlow cum
Saunderton, Boarstall, Bow Brickhill, Bradenham, Brill, Buckland,
Castlethorpe, Charndon, Chartridge, Chearsley, Cheddington, Chenies, Chetwode, Chi-
cheley, Chilton, Cholesbury cum St Leonards, Clifton Reynes, Cold Brayfield, Coleshill,
Creslow, Cublington, Cuddington,
Dinton with Ford and Upton, Dorney, Dorton, Drayton Beauchamp, Draton Parslow,
Dunton,
East Claydon, Edgcott, Edlesborough, Ellesborough, Emberton,
Fawley, Fleet Marston, Foscott, Fulmer,
Gawcott with Lenborough, Gayhurst, Granborough, Great and Little Hampden, Great and
Little Kimble, Great Brickhill, Great Horwood, Grendon Underwood,
Halton, Hambleden, Hanslope, Hardmead, Hardwick, Haversham cum Little Linford,
Hedgerley, Hedsor, Hillesden, Hoggeston, Hogshaw, Hugheden, Hulcott,

Ibstone, Ickford, Ivinghoe,

Kingsey, Kingswood,

Lacy Green, Lane End, Lathbury, Latimer, Lavendon, Leckhampstead, Lillingstone-Dayrell with Luffield Abbey, Lillingstone-Lovell, Little Brickhill, Little Horwood, Little Marlow, Long Crendon, Longwick cum Ilmer, Lower Winchendon, Ludgershall,

Maids Moreton, Marsh Gibbon, Marsworth, Medmenham, Mentmore, Middle Claydon, Moulsoe, Mursley,

Nash, Newton Blossomville, Newton Longville, North Crawley, North Marston,

Oakley, Oving,

Padbury, Piddington and Wheeler End, Pitchcott, Pitstone, Poundon, Preston Bissett, Quainton, Quarrendon,

Radclive cum Chackmore, Radnage, Ravenstone,

Seer Green, Shabbington, Shalstone, Sherington, Slapton, Soulbury, Steeple Claydon, Stewkley, Stoke Goldington, Stoke Hammond, Stone with Bishopstone and Hartwell, Stowe, Swanbourne,

Taplow, The Lee, Thorton, Thornborough, Tingewick, Turville, Turweston, Twyford, Upper Winchendon,

Waddesdon, Warrington, Water Stratford, Weedon, West Wycombe, Westbury, Westcott, Weston Turville, Weston Underwood, Wexham, Whaddon, Whitchurch, Wing, Wingrave with Rowsham, Woodham, Worminghall, Wotton Underwood.

The unparished area bounded by the parishes of Olney, Emberton, Sherrington, Lathbury, Gayhurst, Stoke Goldington, Ravenstone and Weston Underwood.

PART 2 EAST SUSSEX

Alciston, Alfriston, Arlington, Ashburnham,

Barcombe, Beckley, Beddingham, Berwick, Bodiam, Brede, Brightling, Burwash, Buxted,

Camber, Catsfield, Chailey, Chalvington with Ripe, Chiddingly, Crowhurst, Cuckmere Valley,

Dallington, Danehill, Ditchling,

East Chillington, East Dean and Friston, East Guldeford, East Hoathly, Etchingham, Ewhurst,

Falmer, Fairlight, Firle, Fletching, Framfield, Frant,

Glynde, Guestling,

Hadlow Down, Hamsey, Hartfield, Hellingly, Herstmonceux, Hooe, Horam, Hurst Green,

Icklesham, Iden, Iford, Isfield,

Kingston Near Lewes,

Laughton, Little Horsted, Long Man,

Maresfield, Mayfield, Mountfield,

Newick, Ninfield, Northiam,

Peasmarsh, Penhurst, Pett, Pevensey, Piddinghoe, Playden, Plumpton,

Ringmer, Rodmell, Rotherfield, Rye Foreign,

Salehurst, Sedlescombe, Selmeston, South Heighton, Southease, St Ann (Without), St John (Without), Streat,

Tarring Neville, Ticehurst,

Udimore,

Wadhurst, Warbleton, Wartling, Westfield, Westham, Westmeston, Whatlington, Withyam, Wivelsfield.

PART 3 HAMPSHIRE

Ampfield, Amport, Appleshaw, Ashford Hill with Headley, Ashley, Ashmansworth, Ashurst and Colbury, Awbridge,

Barton Stacey, Baughurst, Beaulieu, Beauworth, Bentley, Bentworth, Bighton, Binsted, Bishops Sutton, Boarhunt, Boldre, Bossington, Bradley, Braishfield, Bramdean, Bramley,

Bramshaw, Bramshill, Breamore, Brockenhurst, Broughton, Buckholt, Bullington, Burghclere, Buriton, Burley,

Candovers, Chawton, Cheriton, Chilbolton, Chilcomb, Cliddesden, Colden Common, Colemore and Priors Dean, Compton and Shawford, Copythorne, Corhampton and Meonstoke, Crawley, Crondall, Crookham Village, Curdridge,

Damerham, Deane, Denmead, Denny Lodge, Dogmersfield, Droxford, Dummer, Durley,

East Boldre, East Dean, East Tisted, East Tytherley, East Woodhay, Eastmeon, Ecchinswell and Sydmonton, Ellingham, Harbridge and Ibsley, Ellisfield, Eversley, Exbury and Lepe, Exton,

Faccombe, Farleigh Wallop, Farringdon, Four Marks, Frenchmoor, Froxfield, Froyle, Fyfield,

Goodworth Clatford, Grately, Grayshott, Greatham, Greywell,

Hale, Hambledon, Hannington, Hartley Wespall, Hawkley, Heckfield, Herriard, Highclere, Houghton, Hursley, Hurstbourne Priors, Hurstbourne Tarrant, Hyde,

Itchen Stoke and Ovington,

Kilmiston, Kimpton, Kings Somborne, Kingsley,

Langrish, Lasham, Laverstoke, Leckford, Lindford, Linkenholt, Litchfield and Woodcott, Little Somborne, Lockerley, Long Sutton, Longparish, Longstock, Lyndhurst,

Mapledurwell and Up Nately, Martin, Mattingley, Medstead, Melchet Park and Plaitford, Micheldever, Michelmersh, Minstead, Monk Sherborne, Monxton, Mortimer West End, Mottisfont,

Nether Wallop, Netley Marsh, Newnham, Newton Valence, Newtown, North Waltham, Northington, Nutley,

Odiham, Old Alresford, Otterbourne, Over Wallop, Owlesbury,

Penton Grafton, Penton Mewsey, Popham, Preston Candover,

Quarley,

Rockbourne, Romsey Extra, Ropley, Rotherwick, Rowlands Castle,

Sandleheath, Selborne, Shalden, Shedfield, Sherborne St John, Sherfield English, Sherfield on Loddon, Shipton Bellinger, Silchester, Smannell, Soberton, Sopley, South Warnborough, South Wonston, Southwick and Widley, Sparsholt, St Mary Bourne, Steep, Steventon, Stockbridge, Stratfield Saye, Stratfield Turgis, Stroud, Swanmore, Sway,

Tangley, Thruxton, Tichborne, Tunworth, Twyford,

Upham, Upper Clatford, Upton Grey,

Vernhams Dean,

Warnford, West Tisted, West Tytherley, Westmeon, Weston Corbett, Weston Patrick, Wherwell, Whitsbury, Wickham, Wield, Winchfield, Winslade, Wonston, Woodgreen, Wootton St Lawrence, Worldham.

Part 4 Isle of Wight

Arreton,
Brightstone,
Calbourne, Chale,
Gatcombe, Godshill, Gurnard,
Newchurch, Niton and Whitwell,
Rookley,
Shalfleet, Shorwell, St Helens,
Wroxall,
Yarmouth.

Part 5 Kent

Acol, Acrise, Addington, Adisham, Aldington, Alkham, Allhallows, Appledore, Ash, Badlesmere, Barham, Bean, Bekesbourne with Patrixbourne, Benenden, Bethersden, Bicknor, Bidborough, Biddenden, Bilsington, Birling, Bishopsbourne, Bobbing, Bonnington, Borden, Borough Green, Boughton Aluph, Boughton in the Blean, Boughton Malherbe, Boughton Monchelsea, Boxley, Brabourne, Brasted, Bredgar, Bredhurst,

Brenchley, Brenzett, Bridge, Brook, Brookland, Broomfield, Buckland, Norton and Stone, Burham, Burmarsh,

Capel, Capel le Fern, Challock, Charing, Chart Sutton, Chartham, Chiddingstone, Chilham, Chislet, Cliffe, Cobham, Cooling, Cowden, Crockenhill, Crundale, Cuxton,

Denton with Wootton, Detling, Doddington, Dunkirk,

East Farleigh, East Peckham, East Sutton, Eastchurch, Eastling, Eastry, Eastwell, Egerton, Elham, Elmsted, Eynsford, Eythorne,

Farningham, Fawkham, Fordwich, Frinsted, Frittenden,

Godmersham, Goodnestone, Goudhurst, Graveney with Goodenstone, Great Chart with Singleton, Guston,

Hackington, Halling, Halstead, Harrietsham, Hartlip, Hastingleigh, Headcorn, Hernhill, Hever, Higham, High Halden, High Halstow, Hoath, Hollingbourne, Horsmonden, Horton Kirby & South Darenth, Hothfield, Hougham Without, Hucking, Hunton,

Ickham and Well, Ightham, Isle of Grain, Ivychurch, Iwade,

Kenardington, Kingsnorth, Kingston, Knockholt,

Lamberhurst, Langdon, Langley, Leaveland, Leeds, Leigh, Lenham, Leybourne, Leysdown, Linton, Little Chart, Littlebourne, Lower Halstow, Lower Hardres, Luddenham, Luddesdown, Lydden, Lyminge, Lympne, Lynsted,

Manston, Marden, Meopham, Mereworth, Mersham, Milstead and Kingsdown, Molash, Monks Horton, Monkton,

Nettlestead, Newchurch, Newenden, Newington (in the district of Shepway), Newington (in the district of Swale) Newnham, Nonington, Northbourne,

Oare, Offham, Old Romney, Orlestone, Ospringe, Otham, Otterden,

Paddlesworth, Penshurst, Petham, Platt, Plaxtol, Pluckley, Postling, Preston,

Ringwould with Kingsdown, Ripple, Rodmersham, Rolvenden, Ruckinge, Ryarsh,

Saltwood, Sandhurst, Sarre, Seal, Sellindge, Selling, Sevenoaks Weald, Sevington, Shadoxhurst, Sheldwich, Shepherdswell with Coldred, Shipbourne, Sholden, Shoreham, Shorne, Smarden, Smeeth, Snargate, Southfleet, St Margarets at Cliffe, St Mary Hoo, St Nicholas at Wade, Stalisfield, Stanford, Stansted, Staple, Stelling Minnis, Stockbury, Stoke, Stone cum Ebony, Stourmouth, Stowting, Sundridge, Sutton, Sutton Valence, Swingfield,

Teston, Throwley, Thurnham, Tilmanstone, Tonge, Trottiscliffe,

Ulcombe, Upchurch, Upper Hardres,

Waltham, Warden, Warehorne, Wateringbury, West Farleigh, West Malling, West Peckham, Westbere, Westwell, Wichling, Wickhambreaux, Wingham, Wittersham, Womenswold, Woodchurch, Woodnesborough, Wormshill, Worth, Wouldham, Wrotham, Yalding.

PART 6 OXFORDSHIRE

Adderbury, Adwell, Alvescot, Ambrosden, Appleford, Appleton with Eaton, Ardington, Ardley, Arncott, Ascott under Wychwood, Ashbury, Asthal, Aston Rowant, Aston Tirrold, Aston Upthorpe, Aston, Cote, Shifford and Chimney,

Bampton, Barford St John and St Michael, Baulking, Beckley and Stowood, Begbroke, Benson, Berinsfield, Berrick Salome, Besselsleigh, Bix and Assendon, Black Bourton, Blackthorn, Bladon, Blenheim, Bletchingdon, Blewbury, Bloxham, Bodicote, Bourton (in the district of the Vale of the White Horse), Bourton (in the district of Cherwell), Brightwell, Baldwin, Brightwell cum Sotwell, Britwell Salome, Brize Norton, Broadwell, Broughton, Bruern, Buckland, Bucknell, Burford, Buscot,

Cassington, Caversfield, Chadlington, Chalgrove, Charlbury, Charlton on Otmoor, Charney Bassett, Chastleton, Checkendon, Chesterton, Childrey, Chilson, Chilton, Cholsey, Churchill, Clanfield, Claydon with Clattercot, Clifton Hampden, Coleshill, Combe, Compton Beauchamp, Cornbury and Wychwood, Cornwell, Cottisford, Crawley, Cropredy, Crowell, Crowmarsh, Cuddesdon and Denton, Culham, Curbridge, Cuxham with Easington,

Deddington, Denchworth, Dorchester, Drayton (in the district of the Vale of the White Horse), Drayton St Leonard, Ducklington, Duns Tew,

East Challow, East Hagbourne, East Hanney, East Hendred, Eaton Hastings, Elsfield, Enstone, Epwell, Ewelme, Eye and Dunsden, Eynsham,

Fawler, Fencott and Murcott, Fernham, Fifield, Filkins and Broughton Poggs, Finmere, Finstock, Forest Hill with Shotover, Freeland, Frilford, Fringford, Fritwell, Fulbrook, Fyfield and Tubney,

Garford, Garsington, Glympton, Godington, Goosey, Goring Heath, Grafton and Radcot, Great Coxwell, Great Haseley, Great Milton, Great Tew,

Hailey, Hampton Gay and Poyle, Hanborough, Hanwell, Hardwick with Tusmore, Hardwick with Yelford, Harpsden, Harwell, Hatford, Hethe, Heythrop, Highmoor, Hinton Waldrist, Holton, Holwell, Hook Norton, Horley, Hornton, Horspath, Horton cum Studley,

Idbury, Ipsden, Islip,

Kelmscott, Kencot, Kiddington with Asterleigh, Kidmore End, Kingham, Kingston Bagpuize with Southmoor, Kingston Lisle, Kirtlington,

Langford, Launton, Leafield, Letcombe Bassett, Letcombe Regis, Lew, Lewknor, Little Coxwell, Little Faringdon, Little Milton, Little Tew, Little Wittenham, Littleworth, Lockinge, Long Wittenham, Longcot, Longworth, Lower Heyford, Lyford, Lyneham,

Mapledurham, Marcham, Marsh Baldon, Merton, Middle Aston, Middleton Stoney, Milcombe, Milton (in the district of the Vale of the White Horse), Milton (in the district of Cherwell), Milton under Wychwood, Minster Lovell, Mixbury, Mollington, Moulsford,

Nettlebed, Newington, Newton Purcell with Shelswell, Noke, North Aston, North Leigh, North Moreton, North Newington, Northmoor, Nuffield, Nuneham Courtenay,

Oddington, Over Norton,

Piddington, Pishill with Stonor, Prescote, Pusey, Pyrton,

Radley, Ramsden, Rollright, Rotherfield Greys, Rotherfield Peppard, Rousham,

Salford, Sandford St Martin, Sandford on Thames, Sarsden, Shellingford, Shenington with Alkerton, Shilton, Shiplake, Shipton on Cherwell and Thrupp, Shipton under Wychwood, Shirburn, Shutford, Sibford Ferris, Sibford Gower, Somerton, Souldern, South Hinksey, South Leigh, South Moreton, South Newington, South Stoke, Sparsholt, Spelsbury, St Helen Without, Stadhampton, Standlake, Stanford in the Vale, Stanton Harcourt, Stanton St John, Steeple Aston, Steeple Barton, Steventon, Stoke Lyne, Stoke Row, Stoke Talmage, Stonesfield, Stratton Audley, Sunningwell, Sutton Courtenay, Swalcliffe, Swerford, Swinbrook and Widford, Swyncombe, Sydenham,

Tackley, Tadmarton, Taynton, Tetsworth, Tiddington and Albury, Toot Baldon, Towersey,

Uffington, Upper Heyford, Upton.

Warborough, Wardington, Watchfield, Waterperry, Waterstock, Watlington, Wendlebury, West Challow, West Hagbourne, West Hanney, West Hendred, Westcot Barton, Weston on the Green, Westwell, Wheatfield, Whitchurch, Wigginton, Woodcote, Woodeaton, Woodstock, Woolstone, Wootton (in the district of the Vale of the White Horse), Wootton (in the district of West Oxfordshire), Worton, Wroxton, Wytham,

Yarnton.

Part 7 Surrey

Abinger, Albury, Alfold,

Betchworth, Bletchingley, Bramley, Brockham, Buckland, Busbridge,

Capel, Charlwood, Chelsham and Farleigh, Chiddingfold, Compton, Crowhurst, Dockenfield, Dunsfold,

East Clandon, Effingham, Elstead, Ewhurst,

Felbridge, Frensham,

Godstone,

Hambledon, Hascombe, Headley, Holmwood, Horne,

Leigh, Limpsfield, Lingfield,

Mickleham,

Newdigate, Normandy, Nutfield,

Ockham, Ockley,
Peper Harrow, Pirbright, Puttenham,
Ripley,
Seale and Sands, Shackleford, Shalford, Shere, St. Martha,
Tandridge, Tatsfield, Thursley, Tilford, Titsey,
Wanborough, West Clandon, Wisley, Wonersh, Wotton.

Part 8 West Berkshire

Aldermaston, Aldworth, Arborfield and Newland, Ashampstead,
Barkham, Basildon, Beech Hill, Beedon, Beenham, Bisham, Boxford, Bradfield, Brightwalton, Brimpton, Bucklebury,
Catmore, Chaddleworth, Charvil, Chieveley, Cold Ash, Combe, Compton, Cookham,
East Garston, East Ilsley, Enborne, Englefield, Eton,
Farnborough, Fawley, Frilsham,
Great Shefford,
Hampstead Marshall, Hampstead Norreys, Hermitage, Horton, Hurley,
Inkpen,
Kintbury,
Lamboarn, Leckhampstead,
Midgeham,
Old Windsor,
Padworth, Pangbourne, Peasemore,
Remenham, Ruscombe,
Shottesbrooke, St. Nicholas Hurst, Stanford Dingley, Stratfield-Mortimer, Streatley, Sulham, Sulhamstead, Swallowfield,
Tidmarsh,
Ufton Nervet,
Waltham St. Lawrence, Warfield, Wasing, Welford, West Ilsley, West Woodhay, White Waltham, Winterbourne, Wokefield, Woolhampton, Wraysbury,
Yattendon.

Part 9 West Sussex

Albourne, Aldingbourne, Amberley, Appledram, Ardingly, Arundel, Ashurst,
Balcombe, Barlavington, Bepton, Bignor, Birdham, Bolney, Bosham, Boxgrove, Broadbridge Heath, Burpham, Bury,
Chidham, Clapham, Climping, Cocking, Coldwaltham, Colgate, Compton, Coombes, Cowfold, Cuckfield, Cuckfield Rural,
Duncton,
Earnley, Eartham, Easeborne, East Dean, East Lavington, Ebernoe, Elsted and Treyford,
Fernhurst, Findon, Fittleworth, Fishbourne, Ford, Fulking, Funtington,
Graffam,
Harting, Heyshott, Horsted Keynes, Houghton, Hunston,
Itchingfield,
Kirdford,
Linch, Linchmere, Lodsworth, Lower Beeding, Loxwood, Lurgashall, Lyminster,
Madehurst, Marden, Milland,
Newtimber, North Mundham, Northchapel, Nuthurst,
Oving,
Parham, Patching, Petworth, Plaistow, Poling, Poynings, Pyecombe,
Rogate, Rudgwick, Rusper,
Shermanbury, Shipley, Sidlesham, Singleton, Slaugham, Slindon, Slinfold, South Stoke, Steadham with Iping, Stopham, Stoughton, Sutton,
Tangmere, Tillington, Trotton with Chithurst, Turners Hill, Twineham,

Upwaltham,
Walberton, Warnham, Warningcamp, West Chiltington, West Dean, West Grinstead, West Hoathly, West Itchenor, West Lavington, West Thorney, Westbourne, Westhampnett, Wisborough Green, Wiston, Woodmancote, Woolbeding.

Regulation 7(b)

Schedule 12 Designated Protected Areas in the South East—By Maps

Part 1 Buckinghamshire

The parishes of—

Amersham, Aston Clinton,
Beaconsfield, Bow Brickhill,
Chesham,
Edlesborough,
Great Marlow, Great Missenden,
Haddenham,
Little Missenden,
Penn,
Stoke Poges, Stokenchurch,
Wendover.

The unparished area bounded by the parishes of Castlethorpe, Haversham-cum-Little Linford, Stantonbury, Bradwell Abbey, Shenley Church End, Whaddon and Beachampton and the parishes of Deanshanger, Old Stratford and Cosgrove in Northamptonshire.

Part 2 East Sussex

The parishes of—

Battle,
Forest Row,
Hailsham, Heathfield and Waldron,
Polegate,
Ringmer,
Telscombe,
Willingdon and Jevington.

The unparished area bounded by the parishes of Newhaven, South Heighton, Alfriston and Cuckmere Valley.

Part 3 Hampshire

The parishes of—

Abbotts Ann, Alton,
Bishops Waltham, Bramshott and Liphook, Bransgore,
Chilworth, Clanfield,
Fair Oak and Horton Heath, Fawley, Fordingbridge,
Hartley Wintney, Headbourne Worthy, Headley, Hook, Hordle, Horndean, Hythe and Dibden,
Itchen Valley,
Kings Worthy,
Liss, Littleton and Harestock, Lymington and Pennington,
Milford on Sea,

New Milton, Nursling and Rownhams,
Oakley, Overton,
Pamber, Petersfield,
Ringwood,
Totton and Eling,
Wellow, Whitchurch, Whitehill.

The unparished area bounded by the parishes of Smannell, St. Mary Bourne, Longparish, Goodworth Clatford, Upper Clatford, Abbotts Ann, Monxton, Penton Mewsey, Charlton and Tangley.

Part 4 Isle of Wight

The parishes of—

Bembridge, Brading,
Freshwater,
Shanklin,
Totland,
Ventnor.

The unparished area bounded by the parishes of Wootton Bridge, Nettlestone & Seaview, Brading, Newchurch, Arreton, Gatcombe, Shorwell, Brighstone, Calbourne, Gurnard and Cowes.

Part 5 Kent

The parishes of—

Ash Cum Ridley, Aylesford, Aylesham,
Chestfield, Chevening, Cranbrook,
Darenth, Dunton Green,
Edenbridge,
Frindsbury Extra,
Hadlow, Harbledown, Hawkhurst, Hawkinge, Hildenborough, Hoo St Werburgh,
Hythe,
Lydd,
Manston, Minster,
Queenborough,
Sandwich, Speldhurst, St Cosmus and St Damian in the Blean, St Mary in the Marsh,
Sturry, Sutton at Hone and Hawley, Swanley,
Tenterden, Teynham, Tunstall,
West Kingsdown, Westerham, Whitfield, Wye with Hinxhill.

The unparished area bounded by the parishes of Ringwould with Kingsdown, Ripple, Sutton, Northbourne and Sholden.
The unparished area bounded by the parishes of St Nicholas at Wade, Chislet, Hoath, Sturry, Hackington and Chestfield.
The unparished area bounded by the parishes of Chestfield, St Cosmus and St Damian in the Blean, Dunkirk, Hernhill, Graveney with Goodnestone and Leysdown.

Part 6 Oxfordshire

The parishes of—

Chinnor, Cumnor,
Drayton (in the district of Cherwell),
Gosford and Water Eaton,
Thame.

PART 7 SURREY

The parishes of—

> Artington,
> Burstow,
> Chobham, Cranleigh,
> Salfords and Sidlow,
> West Horsley, Witley, Worplesdon.

The unparished area of the county constituency of Mole Valley excluding the parishes of Headley, Mickleham, Bickland, Betchworth, Leigh, Charlwood, Newdigate, Capel, Holmwood, Ockley, Wotton and Abinger.

The unparished area bounded by the parishes of Chelsham and Fairleigh, Oxted, Tandridge, Godstone, Bletchingley, the borough constituency of Reigate and the London borough of Croydon.

The unparished area of the county constituency of Woking excluding the parishes of Byfleet, Pirbright, Normandy and Ash.

PART 8 WEST BERKSHIRE

The parishes of—

> Bray, Burghfield,
> Greenham,
> Hungerford,
> Shaw cum Donnington, Shinfield, Speen, Sulhamstead,
> Thatcham, Theale,
> Wargrave, Winkfield, Wokingham Without.

PART 9 WEST SUSSEX

The parishes of—

> Ashington,
> Billingshurst, Bramber,
> Clayton,
> Donnington,
> East Grinstead,
> Henfield, Hurstpierpoint,
> Lavant, Lindfield Rural,
> Pagham, Pulborough,
> Selsey, Southwater, Storrington,
> Thakeham,
> Upper Beeding,
> Washington, West Wittering.

Regulation 8(a)

SCHEDULE 13 DESIGNATED PROTECTED AREAS IN THE EAST MIDLANDS—ENTIRE PARISHES

PART 1 DERBYSHIRE

Abney and Abney Grange, Aldercar and Langley Mill, Alderwasley, Aldwark, Alkmorton, Ash, Ashford in the Water, Ashleyhay, Ashover, Aston, Aston upon Trent, Atlow, Ault Hucknall,
Bakewell, Ballidon, Bamford, Barlborough, Barlow, Barrow upon Trent, Barton Blount, Baslow and Bubnell, Bearwardcote, Beeley, Biggin, Birchover, Blackwell, Blackwell in

the Peak, Bonsall, Boylestone, Brackenfield, Bradbourne, Bradley, Bradwell, Brailsford, Brampton, Brassington, Breadsall, Bretby, Brough and Shatton, Brushfield, Burnaston, Buxworth and Brownside,

Calke, Callow, Calow, Calver, Carsington, Castle Gresley, Castleton, Catton, Cauldwell, Charlesworth, Chatsworth, Chelmorton, Chinley, Chisworth, Church Broughton, Clifton and Compton, Coton in the Elms, Crich, Cromford, Cubley, Curbar,

Dalbury Lees, Denby, Derwent, Dethick Lea and Holloway, Doveridge, Drakelow, Draycott and Church Wilne,

Eaton and Alsop, Edale, Edensor, Edlaston and Wyaston, Eggington, Elton, Elvaston, Etwall, Eyam,

Fenny Bentley, Findern, Flagg, Foolow, Foremark, Foston and Scropton, Froggatt,

Glapwell, Grassmoor Hasland & Winsick, Gratton, Great Hucklow, Great Longstone, Green Fairfield, Grindleford, Grindlow,

Harthill, Hartington Middle Quarter, Hartington Nether Quarter, Hartington Town Quarter, Hartington Upper Quarter, Hartshone, Hathersage, Hassop, Hatton, Hayfield, Hazelwood, Hazelbadge, Heath and Holmewood, Highlow, Hilton, Hognaston, Holbrook, Hollington, Holmesfield, Holymoorside and Walton, Hoon, Hope, Hope Woodlands, Hopton, Hopwell, Horsley, Horsley Woodhouse, Hulland, Hulland Ward, Hungry Bentley,

Ible, Idridgehay and Alton, Ingleby, Ironville, Ivonbrook Grange,

Kedlesston, Killamarsh, King Sterndale, Kirk Ireton, Kirk Langley, Kniveton,

Lea Hall, Linton, Little Eaton, Little Hucklow, Little Longstone, Litton, Longford, Lullington,

Mackworth, Mapleton, Mapperley, Marston Montgomery, Marstone on Dove, Matlock Bath, Mercaston, Middleton, Middleton and Smerrill, Monyash, Morley, Morton,

Nether Haddon, Netherseal, Newton Grange, Newton Solney, Norbury and Roston, Northwood and Tinkersley,

Offcote and Underwood, Offerton, Osleston and Thurvaston, Osmaston, Outseats, Over Haddon, Overseal,

Parwich, Peak Forest, Pentrich, Pilsley (in the district of the Derbyshire Dales), Pilsley (in the district of North East Derbyshire), Pleaseley,

Quarndon,

Radbourne, Ravensdale Park, Repton, Risley, Rodsley, Rosliston, Rowland, Rowsley,

Shardlow and Great Wilne, Sheldon, Shipley, Shirland and Higham, Shirley, Shottle and Postern, Smalley, Smisby, Snelston, Somersal Herbert, South Darley, South Wingfield, Stanley, Stanton, Stanton by Bridge, Stanton by Dale, Stenson Fields, Stoney Middleton, Stretton, Sudbury, Sutton cum Duckmartonton, Sutton on the Hill, Swarkestone,

Taddington, Tansley, Temple Normanton, Thornhill, Thorpe, Ticknall, Tideswell, Tintwistle, Tissington, Trusley, Tupton, Turnditch, Twyford and Stenson,

Unstone,

Walton upon Trent, Wardlow, Wessington, West Hallam, Weston Underwood, Weston upon Trent, Wheston, Willington, Windley, Winster, Woodville, Wormhill,

Yeaveley, Yeldersley, Youlgreave.

PART 2 LEICESTERSHIRE

Ab Kettleby, Allexton, Appleby Magna, Arnesby, Ashby Woulds, Ashfordby, Ashby Magna, Ashby Parva, Aswell, Aston Flamville, Ayston,

Bagworth, Bardon, Barkby, Barkby Thorpe, Barlestone, Barleythorpe, Barrow, Barrowden, Beaumont Chase, Beeby, Belton, Belton in Rutland, Belvoir, Billesdon, Bisbrooke, Bittesby, Bitteswell, Blaby, Blaston, Bottesford, Braunston in Rutland, Breedon on the Hill, Bringhurst, Brooke, Broughton and Old Dalby, Bruntingthorpe, Buckminster, Burley, Burton and Dalby, Burton on the Wolds, Burton Overy,

Cadeby, Caldecott, Carlton, Carlton Curlieu, Catthorpe, Charley, Chilcote, Clawson, Hose and Harby, Claybrooke Magna, Claybrooke Parva, Clipsham, Cold Newton, Coleorton, Cossington, Cotes, Cotesbach, Cottesmore, Cranoe, Croft, Croxton Kerrial,

Drayton, Dunton Bassett,

East Langton, East Norton, Eaton, Edith Weston, Egleton, Elmesthorpe, Empingham, Essendine, Exton,

Foxton, Freeby, Frisby, Frisby on the Wreake, Frolesworth,

Gaddesby, Garthorpe, Gaulby, Gilmorton, Glaston, Glooston, Goadby, Great Casterton, Great Easton, Greetham, Grimston, Gumley, Gunthorpe,

Hallaton, Hambleton, Hathern, Heather, Higham on the Hill, Hoby with Rotherby, Horn, Horninghold, Hoton, Houghton on the Hill, Huncote, Hungarton, Husbands Bosworth, Illston on the Hill, Isley cum Langley,

Ketton, Keyham, Kibworth Harcourt, Kilby, Kimcote and Walton, Kings Norton, Kirkby Bellars, Knaptoft, Knossington and Cold Overton,

Langham, Laughton, Launde, Leicester Forest West, Leighfield, Leire, Little Casterton, Little Stretton, Lockington-Hemington, Loddington, Long Whatton, Lowesby, Lubbes-thorpe, Lubenham, Lyddington, Lyndon,

Manton, Marefield, Market Bosworth, Market Overton, Martinsthorpe, Medbourne, Mis-terton, Morcott, Mowsley,

Nailstone, Nevill Holt, Newton Linford, Normanton, Normanton le Heath, North Kil-worth, North Luffenham, Noseley,

Oakthorpe and Donisthorpe, Osbaston, Osgathorpe, Owston and Newbold,

Packington, Peatling Magna, Peatling Parva, Peckleton, Pickworth, Pilton, Potters Mar-ston, Preston, Prestwold,

Ratcliffe on the Wreake, Ravenstone with Snibstone, Rearsby, Redmile, Ridlington, Rolleston, Ryhall,

Saddington, Sapcote, Scalford, Scraptoft, Seagrave, Seaton, Shackerstone, Shangton, Sharnford, Shawell, Shearsby, Sheepy, Skeffington, Slawston, Smeeton Westerby, Snar-estone, Somerby, South Croxton, South Kilworth, South Luffenham, Sproxton, Stanton under Bardon, Stathern, Staunton Harold, Stokerston, Stoke Dry, Stoke Golding, Stonton Wyville, Stoughton, Stretton, Stretton en le Field, Stretton Magna, Sutton Cheney, Swan-nington, Swepstone, Swinsford, Swithland,

Teigh, Theddingworth, Thisleton, Thorpe by Water, Thorpe Langton, Thussington, Thur-caston and Cropston, Thurlaston, Tickencote, Tilton, Tinwell, Tixover, Tugby and Key-thorpe, Tur Langton, Twycross, Twyford and Thorpe,

Ullesthorpe, Ulverscroft,

Waltham, Walton on the Wolds, Wanlip, Wardley, Welham, West Langton, Westrill and Starmore, Whatborough, Whissendine, Whitwell, Wigston Parva, Willough by Waterleys, Wing, Wistow, Withcote, Witherley, Woodhouse, Worthington, Wymeswold, Wymond-ham.

PART 3 LINCOLNSHIRE

Aby with Greenfield, Addlethorpe, Aisthorpe, Alford, Algarkirk, Allington, Alvingham, Amber Hill, Ancaster, Anderby, Anwick, Apley, Asgarby and Howell, Ashby de Launde & Bloxholm, Ashby with Scremby, Aslackby and Laughton, Asterby, Aswarby and Swarby, Aswardby, Aubourn Haddington and South Hykeham, Aunsby and Dembleby, Authorpe,

Bardney, Barholm and Stow, Barkston, Barlings, Barrowby, Bassingham, Baston, Baum-ber, Beckingham, Beesby with Saleby, Belchford, Belleau, Belton with Manthorpe, Benington, Benniworth, Bicker, Bigby, Billingborough, Billinghay, Bilsby, Binbrook, Bishop Norton, Bitchfield and Bassingthorpe, Blankney, Blyborough, Blyton, Boling-broke, Boothby Graffoe, Boothby Pagnell, Braceborough with Wilsthorpe, Braceby and Sapperton, Brackenborough with Little Grimsby, Brampton, Brant Broughton and Strag-glethorpe, Bratoft, Brattleby, Brauncewell, Brinkhill, Broadholme, Brocklesby, Brox-holme, Bucknall, Bullington, Burgh le Marsh, Burgh on Bain, Burton, Burton Coggles, Burton Pedwardine, Burwell, Buslingthorpe, Butterwick,

Cabourne, Caenby, Caistor, Calcethorpe with Kelstern, Cammeringham, Candlesby with Gunby, Canwick, Careby Aunby and Holywell, Carlby, Carlton Scroop, Carlton le

Moorland, Carrington, Castle Bytham, Caythorpe, Chapel St Leonards, Cherry Willingham, Claxby (in the district of West Lindsey), Claxby (in the district of East Lindsey), Claxby with Moorby, Claypole, Claythorpe, Cold Hanworth, Coleby, Colsterworth, Coningsby, Conisholme, Corby Glen, Corringham, Counthorpe and Creeton, Covenham St Bartholomew, Covenham St Mary, Cowbit, Cranwell and Byard's Leap, Croft, Crowland, Culverthorpe and Kelby, Cumberworth,

Dalby, Deeping St Nicholas, Denton, Digby, Doddington and Whisby, Dogdyke, Donington, Donington on Bain, Dorrington, Dowsby, Dunholme, Dunsby,

Eagle and Swinethorpe, East Barkwith, East Ferry, East Keal, East Kirkby, East Stockwith, Easton, Eastville, Edenham, Edlington with Wispington, Elkington, Ewerby and Evedon,

Faldingworth, Farlesthorpe, Fenton (in the district of West Lindsey), Fenton (in the district of South Kesteven), Fillingham, Firsby, Fiskerton, Folkingham, Fosdyke, Foston, Fotherby, Frampton, Freiston, Friesthorpe, Friskney, Frithville and Westville, Fulbeck, Fulletby, Fulnetby, Fulstow,

Gate Burton, Gautby, Gayton le Marsh, Gayton le Wold, Gedney, Gedney Hill, Glentham, Glentworth, Goltho, Gosberton, Goulceby, Grainsby, Grainthorpe, Grange de Lings, Grasby, Grayingham, Great Carlton, Great Gonerby, Great Hale, Great Limber, Great Ponton, Great Steeping, Great Sturton, Greatford, Greetham with Somersby, Greetwell, Grimoldby, Gunby with Stainby,

Hackthorn, Haconby, Hagworthingham, Hainton, Hallington, Haltham, Halton Holegate, Hameringham, Hannah cum Hagnaby, Hardwick, Harlaxton, Harmston, Harpswell, Harrington, Hatton, Haugh, Haugham, Haydor, Heapham, Heckington, Helpringham, Hemingby, Hemswell, High Toynton, Hogsthorpe, Holland Fen with Brothertoft, Holton cum Beckering, Holton le Moor, Honington, Horbling, Horsington, Hough on the Hill, Hougham, Hundleby, Huttoft,

Ingham, Ingoldmells, Ingoldsby, Irby in the Marsh, Irnham,

Keddington, Keelby, Kettlethorpe, Kexby, Kirkby la Thorpe, Kirkby on Bain, Kirkby Underwood, Kirmond le Mire, Kirton, Knaith,

Langriville, Langtoft, Langton by Spilsby, Langton by Wragby, Langton, Laughton, Leadenham, Leasingham, Legbourne, Legsby, Lenton, Lenton Keisby and Osgodby, Leverton, Linwood, Lissington, Little Bytham, Little Carlton, Little Cawthorpe, Little Hale, Little Ponton and Stroxton, Little Steeping, Little Sutton, Long Bennington, Low Toynton, Ludborough, Ludford, Lusby with Winceby, Lutton,

Maidenwell, Maltby le Marsh, Manby, Mareham le Fen, Mareham on the Hill, Markby, Market Rasen, Market Stainton, Marsh Chapel, Marston, Martin, Marton, Mavis Enderby, Metheringham, Middle Rasen, Midville, Minting, Morton (in the district of South Kesteven), Moulton, Muckton, Mumby,

Navenby, Nettleton, New Leake, Newball, Newton and Haceby, Newton on Trent, Nocton, Normanby by Spital, Normanby le Wold, Normanton, North Carlton, North Coates, North Cockerington, North Kelsey, North Kyme, North Ormsby, North Rauceby, North Scarle, North Somercotes, North Thoresby, North Willingham, North Witham, Northorpe, Norton Disney,

Old Leake, Old Somerby, Orby, Osbournby, Osgodby, Owersby, Owmby,

Partney, Pickworth, Pilham, Pointon and Sempringham, Potter Hanworth,

Quadring,

Raithby, Raithby cum Maltby, Ranby, Rand, Reepham, Reston, Revesby, Riby, Rigsby with Ailby, Rippingale, Riseholme, Ropsley and Humby, Rothwell, Roughton, Rowston, Roxholm,

Saltfleetby, Sausthorpe, Saxby, Saxilby with Ingleby, Scamblesby, Scampton, Scopwick, Scothern, Scotter, Scotton, Scredington, Scrivelsby, Searby cum Owmby, Sedgebrook, Sibsey, Silk Willoughby, Sixhills, Skendleby, Skidbrooke with Saltfleet Haven, Skillington, Snarford, Snelland, Snitterby, Somerby, Sotby, South Carlton, South Cockerington, South Kelsey, South Kyme, South Ormsby cum Ketsby, South Rauceby, South Somercotes, South Thoresby, South Willingham, South Witham, Spilsby, Spridlington, Springthorpe, Stainfield, Stainton by Langworth, Stainton le Vale, Stapleford, Stenigot, Stewton,

Stickford, Stickney, Stixwould and Woodhall, Stoke Rochford, Stow, Strubby with Wood-thorpe, Stubton, Sturton by Stow, Sudbrooke, Surfleet, Sutterton, Sutton Bridge, Sutton St Edmond, Sutton St James, Swaby, Swallow, Swaton, Swayfield, Swinderby, Swineshead, Swinhope, Swinstead, Syston,

Tallington, Tathwell, Tattershall, Tattershall Thorpe, Tealby, Temple Bruer with Temple High Grange, Tetford, Tetney, Theddlethorpe All Saints, Theddlethorpe St Helen, Thimbleby, Thonock, Thoresway, Thorganby, Thorton le Fen, Thorpe in the Fallows, Thorpe on the Hill, Thorpe St Peter, Threekingham, Thurlby (in the district of North Kesteven), Thurlby (in the district of South Kesteven), Timberland, Toft Newton, Toft with Lound & Manthorpe, Torksey, Toynton All Saints, Toynton St Peter, Tumby, Tupholme, Tydd St Mary,

Uffington, Ulceby with Fordington, Upton, Utterby,

Waddingham, Waddington, Waddingworth, Wainfleet All Saints, Wainfleet St Mary, Waithe, Walcot Near Folkingham, Walcott, Walesby, Walkerith, Walmsgate, Welbourn, Welby, Well, Wellingore, Welton, Welton le Marsh, Welton le Wold, West Ashby, West Barkwith, West Deeping, West Fen, West Firsby, West Keal, West Rasen, West Torrington, Westborough and Dry Doddington, Weston, Whaplode, Wickenby, Wigtoft, Wildmore, Wildsworth, Willingham, Willoughby with Sloothby, Willoughton, Wilsford, Witham on the Hill, Withcall, Withern with Stain, Wood Enderby, Woodhall Spa, Woolsthorpe, Wragby, Wrangle, Wyberton, Wyham cum Cadeby, Wycliffe cum Hungerton, Yarburgh.

Part 4 Northamptonshire

Abthorpe, Adstone, Aldwincle, Althorp, Apethorpe, Arthingworth, Ashby St Ledgers, Ashley, Ashton (in the district of East Northamptonshire), Ashton (in the district of South Northamptonshire), Aston le Walls, Aynho,

Badby, Barby, Barnwell, Benefield, Blakesley, Blatherwycke, Blisworth, Boddington, Boughton, Bozeat, Bradden, Brafield on the Green, Brampton Ash, Braunston, Braybrooke, Brigstock, Brington, Brockhall, Broughton, Bugbrooke, Bulwick, Byfield,

Canons Ashby, Castle Ashby, Catesby, Chacombe, Charwelton, Chelveston cum Caldecott, Chipping Warden, Church with Chapel Brampton, Clay Coton, Clipston, Clopton, Cogenhoe and Whiston, Cold Ashby, Cold Higham, Collingtree, Collyweston, Cosgrove, Cotterstock, Cottesbrooke, Cottingham, Courteenhall, Cranford, Cransley, Creaton, Crick, Croughton, Culworth,

Deanshanger, Deene, Deenethorpe, Denford, Denton, Dingley, Dodford, Draughton, Duddington with Fineshade,

East Carlton, East Farndon, East Haddon, Easton Maudit, Easton Neston, Easton on the Hill, Ecton, Edgcote, Elkington, Evenley, Everdon, Eydon,

Farthinghoe, Farthingstone, Fawsley, Flore, Fotheringhay,

Gayton, Geddington, Glapthorn, Grafton Regis, Grafton Underwood, Great Addington, Great Doddington, Great Harrowden, Great Houghton, Great Oxendon, Greatworth, Greens Norton, Grendon, Gretton, Guilsborough,

Hackleton, Hannington, Hardwick, Hargrave, Harlestone, Harpole, Harrington, Harringworth, Hartwell, Haselbech, Hellidon, Helmdon, Hemington, Hinton in the Hedges, Holcot, Holdenby, Hollowell,

Isham, Islip,

Kelmarsh, Kilsby, Kings Cliffe, King's Sutton, Kislingbury,

Lamport, Laxton, Lilbourne, Lilford cum Wigsthorpe, Litchborough, Little Addington, Little Harrowden, Little Houghton, Loddington, Lowick, Luddington, Lutton,

Maidford, Maidwell, Marston St Lawrence, Marston Trussell, Mears Ashby, Middleton, Milton Malsor, Moreton Pinkney,

Naseby, Nassington, Nether Heyford, Newbottle, Newnham, Newton Bromswold, Newton, Norton,

Old, Old Stratford, Orlingbury, Orton, Overstone,

Pattishall, Paulerspury, Pilton, Pitsford, Polebrook, Potterspury, Preston Capes, Pytchley,

Quinton,

Radstone, Ravensthorpe, Ringstead, Roade, Rockingham, Rothersthorpe, Rushton, Scaldwell, Shutlanger, Sibbertoft, Silverstone, Slapton, Southwick, Spratton, Stanford, Stanion, Staverton, Stoke Albany, Stoke Bruerne, Stoke Doyle, Stowe Nine Churches, Strixton, Sudborough, Sulby, Sulgrave, Sutton Bassett, Syresham, Sywell,

Tansor, Thenford, Thornby, Thorpe Achurch, Thorpe Malsor, Thorpe Mandeville, Thurning, Tiffield, Twywell,

Upper Heyford,

Wadenhoe, Wakerley, Walgrave, Wappenham, Warkton, Warkworth, Warmington, Watford, Weedon Bec, Weekley, Weldon, Welford, Welton, West Haddon, Weston and Weedon, Weston by Welland, Whilton, Whitfield, Whittlebury, Wicken, Wilbarston, Wilby, Winwick, Wollaston, Woodend, Woodford, Woodford cum Membris, Woodnewton, Yardley Gobion, Yardley Hastings, Yarwell, Yelvertoft.

PART 5 NOTTINGHAMSHIRE

Alverton, Annesley, Askham, Aslockton, Averham, Awsworth,

Babworth, Barnby in the Willows, Barnby Moor, Barton in Fabis, Bathley, Beckingham, Besthorpe, Bestwood St Albans, Bevercotes, Bilsthorpe, Bleasby, Blyth, Bole, Bothamsall, Bradmore, Brinsley, Bunny, Broadholme,

Car Colston, Carburton, Carlton on Trent, Caunton, Caythorpe, Clarborough, Clayworth, Clipston, Clipstone, Coddington, Collingham, Colston Bassett, Cossall, Costock, Cotham, Cottam, Cromwell, Cropwell Bishop, Cropwell Butler, Cuckney,

Darlton, Dunham on Trent,

Eakring, East Bridgeford, East Drayton, East Markham, East Stoke, Eaton, Edingley, Egmanton, Elkesley, Elston, Elton, Epperstone, Everton,

Farndon, Farnsfield, Felley, Fiskerton cum Morton, Flawborough, Fledborough, Flintham,

Gamston (in the district of Bassetlaw), Gamston (in the district of Rushcliffe), Girton, Gonalston, Gotham, Granby, Grassthorpe, Gringley on the Hill, Grove, Gunthorpe,

Halam, Halloughton, Harby, Haughton, Hawksworth, Hawton, Hayton, Headon cum Upton, Hickling, Hockerton, Hodsock, Holbeck, Holme, Holme Pierrepont, Hoveringham,

Kelham, Kersall, Kilvington, Kingstoon on Soar, Kinoulton, Kirklington, Kirton, Kneesall, Kneeton,

Lambley, Laneham, Langar cum Barnstone, Langford, Laxton and Moorhouse, Linby, Lindhurst, Lound, Lowdham,

Maplebeck, Marnham, Mattersey, Meering, Misson, Misterton,

Nether Langwith, Newstead, Normanton on Soar, Normanton on the Wolds, Normanton on Trent, North Clifton, North Leverton with Habblesthorpe, North Muskham, North Wheatley, Norton, Norwell,

Ompton, Orston, Ossington, Owthorpe, Oxton,

Papplewick, Perlethorpe cum Budby, Plumtree,

Ragnall, Rampton, Ranskill, Ratcliffe on Soar, Rempstone, Rhodesia, Rolleston, Rufford,

Saundby, Saxondale, Scaftworth, Scarrington, Screveton, Scrooby, Shelford and Newton, Shelton, Shireoaks, Sibthorpe, South Clifton, South Leverton, South Muskham, South Scarle, South Wheatley, Spalford, Stanford on Soar, Staunton, Staythorpe, Stoke Bardolph, Stokeham, Strelley, Sturton le Steeple, Styrrup with Oldcotes, Sutton Bonington, Sutton, Sutton on Trent, Syerston,

Thorney, Thoroton, Thorpe, Thorpe in the Glebe, Thrumpton, Thurgarton, Tithby, Tollerton, Torworth, Treswell, Trowell, Tuxford,

Upper Broughton, Upton,

Walesby, Walkeringham, Wallingwells, Welbeck, Wellow, West Burton, West Drayton, West Leake, West Markham, West Stockwith, Weston, Whatton, Widmerpool, Wigsley, Willoughby on the Wolds, Winkburn, Winthorpe, Wiseton, Wiverton Hall, Woodborough, Wysall.

Regulation 8(b)

SCHEDULE 14 DESIGNATED PROTECTED AREAS IN THE EAST MIDLANDS—BY MAPS

PART 1 DERBYSHIRE

The parishes of—

Belper,
Chapel en le Frith,
Dale Abbey, Darley Dale,
Eckington, Elmton,
Kilburn,
Matlock Town, Melbourne,
New Mills,
Ocbrook, Old Bolsover,
Ripley,
Scarcliffe, Staveley,
Whaley Bridge, Whitwell, Wirksworth.

The unparished area bounded by the parishes of Chapel en le Frith, Wormhill, Green Fairfield, King Sterndale and Hartington Upper Quarter.
The unparished area bounded by the parishes of Tintwhistle, Charlesworth and by the county constituency of Stalybridge and Hyde in Greater Manchester.

PART 2 LEICESTERSHIRE

The parishes of—

Ashby de la Zouch,
Desford,
Markfield,
Narborough,
Rothley.

The unparished area bounded by the parishes of Cotes, Prestwold, Burton on the Wolds, Walton on the Wolds, Quordon, Woodhouse, Charley, Shepshed, Hathern; and the parishes of Normanton on Soar and Stanford on Soar in Nottinghamshire.
The unparished area bounded by the parishes of Thorpe Langton, Weston by Welland, Sutton Bassett, Lubenham, Foxton and East Langton; and the parishes of Dingley, Braybrooke, Great Oxenden, East Farndon in Northamptonshire.
The unparished area bounded by the parishes of Thurlaston, Potters Marston, Elmesthorpe, Burbage, Higham on the Hill, Stoke Golding, Peckleton; and the county constituency of Nuneaton.
The unparished area bounded by the parishes of Belton, Charley, Bardon, Markfield, Stanton-under-Bardon, Ibstock, Ravenstone with Snibstone, Swannington and Osgathorpe.

PART 3 LINCOLNSHIRE

The parishes of—

Bourne, Branston and Mere,
Coningsby,
Fishtoft, Fleet,
Holbeach

Londonthorpe and Harrowby Without,
Mablethorpe and Sutton, Morton (in the district of West Lindsey),
Pinchbeck,
Sleaford,
Welton.

PART 4 NORTHAMPTONSHIRE

The parishes of—

Irchester,
Middleton Cheney,
Raunds,
Titchmarsh, Towcester,
Upton.

PART 5 NOTTINGHAMSHIRE

The parishes of—

Bulcote,
Greasley,
Hayton,
Selston, Southwell, Stanton on the Wolds,
Warsop.

The unparished area bounded by the parishes of Hayton, Clarborough, North Leverton with Habblesthorpe, South Leverton, Grove, Eaton, Babworth and Sutton.
The unparished area bounded by the parishes of Carlton in Lindrick, Barnby Moor, Babworth, Elkesley, Perlethorpe cum Budby, Carbuton, Welbeck, Shireoaks, Rhodesia; the parishes of Woodsets, North and South Anston in South Yorkshire; and the parish of Whitwell in Derbyshire.
The unparished area in the county constituency of Ashfield excluding the parishes of Annesley, Felley, Selston, Brinsley and Eastwood.

Regulation 9(a)

SCHEDULE 15 DESIGNATED PROTECTED AREAS IN YORKSHIRE AND THE HUMBER—ENTIRE
PARISHES

PART 1 EAST RIDING OF YORKSHIRE

Airmyn, Aldbrough, Allerthorpe, Asselby, Atwick,
Bainton, Barmby Moor, Barmby on the Marsh, Barmston, Beeford, Bempton, Beswick, Bewholme, Bielby, Bilton, Bishop Burton, Bishop Wilton, Blacktoft, Boynton, Brandesburton, Brantingham, Broomfleet, Bubwith, Bugthorpe, Burstwick, Burton Agnes, Burton Constable, Burton Fleming, Burton Pidsea,
Carnaby, Catton, Catwick, Cherry Burton, Coniston, Cottam, Cottingwith,
Dalton Holme,
Easington, East Garton, Eastrington, Ellerby, Ellerker, Ellerton, Elstronwick, Etton, Everingham,
Fangfoss, Fimber, Flamborough, Foggathorpe, Foston, Fridaythorpe, Full Sutton,
Garton, Gilberdyke, Goodmanham, Goole Fields, Gowdall, Grindale,
Halsham, Harpham, Hatfield, Hayton, Hollym, Holme upon Spalding Moor, Holmpton, Hook, Hotham, Huggate, Humbleton, Hutton Cranswick,
Kelk, Keyingham, Kilham, Kilpin, Kirby Underdale, Kirkburn,

Langtoft, Laxton, Leconfield, Leven, Lockington, Londesborough, Lund,
Mappleton, Melbourne, Middleton, Millington,
Nafferton, Newbald, Newport, Newton on Derwent, North Cave, North Dalton, North Frodingham, Nunburnholme,
Ottringham,
Patrington, Paull, Pollington, Preston,
Rawcliffe, Reedness, Rimswell, Rise, Riston, Roos, Routh, Rowley, Rudston,
Sancton, Seaton, Seaton Ross, Shipton Thorpe, Sigglesthorne, Skeffling, Skerne and Wansford, Skidby, Skipsea, Skirlaugh, Skirpenbeck, Sledmere, Snaith and Cowick, South Cliffe, Spaldington, Sproatley, Stamford Bridge, Sunk Island, Sutton upon Derwent, Swine, Swinefleet,
Thorngumbald, Thornton, Thwing, Tibthorpe, Tickton, Twin Rivers,
Ulrome,
Walkington, Warter, Watton, Wawne, Welton, Welwick, Wetwang, Wilberfoss, Withernwick, Wold Newton (split between the District of Cleethorpes and the District of East Yorkshire), Wressle,
Yapham.

Part 2 North East Lincolnshire

Ashby cum Fenby, Aylesby,
Barnoldby le Beck, Beelsby, Bradley, Brigsley,
East Ravendale,
Habrough, Hatcliffe, Hawerby cum Beesby, Healing,
Irby,
Stallingborough,
West Ravendale, Wold Newton (split between Cleethorpes District and East Yorkshire District).

Part 3 North Lincolnshire

Alkborough, Amcotts, Appleby, Aylesby,
Barnetby le Wold, Barrow upon Humber, Bonby, Burringham, Burton upon Stather,
Cadney, Crowle, Croxton,
East Butterwick, East Halton, Eastoft, Elsham, Epworth,
Flixborough,
Garthorpe and Fockerby, Goxhill, Gunness,
Haxey, Hibaldstow, Holme, Horkstow,
Keadby with Althorpe, Kirmington, Kirton in Lindsey,
Luddington and Haldenby,
Manton, Melton Ross, Messingham,
New Holland, North Killingholme,
Owston Ferry,
Redbourne, Roxby cum Risby,
Saxby all Saints, Scawby, South Ferriby, South Killingholme,
Thornton Curtis,
Ulceby,
West Butterwick, West Halton, Whitton, Winteringham, Wootton, Worlaby, Wrawby, Wroot.

Part 4 North Yorkshire

Acaster Malbis, Acaster Selby, Acklam, Ainderby Mires with Holtby, Ainderby Quernhow, Ainderby Steeple, Airton, Aiskew, Aislaby (in the district of Scarborough), Aislaby (in the district of Ryedale), Akebar, Aldborough, Aldfield, Aldwark, Allerston, Allerton Mauleverer with Hopperton, Alne, Amotherby, Ampleforth, Angram Grange, Appleton East and West, Appleton Roebuck, Appleton Wiske, Appleton Le Moors, Appleton Le

Street with Easthorpe, Appletreewick, Arkendale, Arkengarthdale, Arncliffe, Arrathorne, Asenby, Aske, Askham Bryan, Askham Richard, Askrigg, Askwith, Austwick, Aysgarth, Azerley,

Bagby, Bainbridge, Baldersby, Balk, Balne, Bank Newton, Barden (in the district of Richmondshire), Barden (in the district of Craven), Barkston Ash, Barlow, Barnby, Barton, Barton le Street, Barton le Willows, Barugh (Great and Little), Beadlam, Beal, Beamsley, Bedale, Bellerby, Beningbrough, Bentham, Bewerley, Biggin, Bilbrough, Bilsdale Midcable, Bilton in Ainsty with Bickerton, Birdforth, Birdsall, Birkby, Birkin, Birstwith, Bishop Monkton, Bishop Thornton, Bishopdale, Blubberhouses, Boltby, Bolton Abbey, Bolton Percy, Bolton on Swale, Bordley, Boroughbridge, Borrowby (in the district of Hambleton), Borrowby (in the district of Scarborough), Bradleys Both, Brafferton, Brandsby cum Stearsby, Bransdale, Brawby, Brearton, Bridge Hewick, Brompton (in the district of Scarborough), Brompton (in the district of Hambleton), Brompton on Swale, Brotherton, Brough with St Giles, Broughton (in the district of Ryedale), Broughton (in the district of Craven), Broxa cum Troutsdale, Buckden, Bulmer, Burn, Burneston, Burniston, Burnsall, Burrill with Cowling, Burton cum Walden, Burton in Lonsdale, Burton Leonard, Burton Salmon, Burton on Yore, Burythorpe, Buttercrambe with Bossall, Byland with Wass, Byram cum Sutton,

Caldbergh with East Scrafton, Caldwell, Calton, Camblesforth, Carleton, Carlton (in the district of Hambleton), Carlton (in the district of Selby), Carlton Highdale, Carlton Husthwaite, Carlton Miniott, Carlton Town, Carperby cum Thoresby, Carthorpe, Castle Bolton with East and West Bolton, Castley, Cattal, Catterick, Catton, Cawood, Cawton, Cayton, Chapel Haddlesey, Church Fenton, Clapham Cum Newby, Claxton, Cleasby, Cliffe (in the district of Richmond shire), Cliffe (in the district of Selby), Clifton on Yore, Clint, Cloughton, Colburn, Cold Kirby, Colsterdale, Colton, Commondale, Coneysthorpe, Coneythorpe and Clareton, Coniston Cold, Conistone with Kilnsey, Cononley, Constable Burton, Copgrove, Copmanthorpe, Copt Hewick, Cotcliffe, Coulton, Coverham with Agglethorpe, Cowesby, Cowling, Coxwold, Cracoe, Crakehall, Crambe, Crathorne, Crayke, Cridling Stubbs, Croft on Tees, Cropton, Crosby, Cundall with Leckby,

Dacre, Dalby cum Skewsby, Dalton (in the district of Richmondshire), Dalton (in the district of Hambleton), Dalton on Tees, Danby, Danby Wiske and Lazenby, Darncome cum Langdale End, Deighton (in the district of Hambleton), Deighton (in the district of Selby), Denton, Dishforth, Downholme, Draughton, Drax, Dunsforths,

Earswick, Easby (in the district of Richmondshire), Easby (in the district of Hambleton), Easingwold, East Ayton, East Cowton, East Harlsey, East Hauxwell, East Layton, East Rounton, East Tanfield, East Witton, Eavestone, Ebberston and Yedingham, Edstone, Eggborough, Egton, Eldmire with Crakehill, Ellenthorpe, Ellerbeck, Ellerby, Ellerton Abbey, Ellerton on Swale, Ellingstring, Ellington High and Low, Elslack, Elvington, Embsay with Eastby, Eppleby, Eryholme, Escrick, Eshton, Eskdaleside cum Ugglebarnby, Exelby, Leeming and Newton,

Faceby, Fadmoor, Fairburn, Farlington, Farndale East, Farndale West, Farnham, Farnhill, Farnley, Fawdington, Fearby, Felixkirk, Felliscliffe, Ferrensby, Fewston, Finghall, Firby, Flasby with Winterburn, Flawith, Flaxby, Flaxton, Folkton, Follifoot, Forcett and Carkin, Foston, Fountains Earth, Foxholes, Fryton, Fulford, Fylingdales,

Ganton, Gargrave, Garriston, Gate Helmsley, Gateforth, Gatenby, Gayles, Giggleswick, Gillamoor, Gilling East, Gilling with Hartforth and Sedbury, Girsby, Givendale, Glaisdale, Glusburn, Goathland, Goldsborough, Grantley, Grassington, Great and Little Broughton, Great Busby, Great Langton, Great Ouseburn, Great Ribston with Walshford, Great Smeaton, Great Timble, Green Hammerton, Grewelthorpe, Grimston, Grimstone, Grinton, Gristhorpe, Grosmont,

Habton, Hackforth, Hackness, Halton East, Halton Gill, Halton West, Hambleton, Hampsthwaite, Hanlith, Harmby, Harome, Hartlington, Hartoft, Harton, Hartwith cum Winsley, Harwood Dale, Haverah Park, Hawes, Hawkswick, Hawnby, Hawsker cum Stainsacre, Hazelwood with Storiths, Healaugh, Healey, Hebden, Heck, Hellifield, Helmsley, Helperby, Hemingborough, Henderskelfe, Hensall, Heslerton, Hessay, Hetton, High Abbotside, High and Low Bishopside, High Worsall, Hillam, Hinderwell, Hipswell, Hirst Courtney, Holme, Holtby, Hood Grange, Hornby (in the district of Richmondshire),

Hornby (in the district of Hambleton), Horton in Ribblesdale, Hovingham, Howe, How-grave, Howsham, Huby, Huddleston with Newthorpe, Hudswell, Humberton, Hunsingore, Hunton, Husthwaite, Hutton Bonville, Hutton Buscel, Hutton Conyers, Hutton Hang, Hutton Mulgrave, Hutton Rudby, Hutton Le Hole, Hutton Sessay, Huttons Ambo, Ilton cum Pott, Ingleby Arncliffe, Ingleby Greenhow, Ingleton, Irton,

Kearby with Netherby, Kelfield, Kellington, Kepwick, Kettlewell with Starbotton, Kexby, Kilburn High and Low, Kildale, Kildwick, Killerby, Killinghall, Kiplin, Kirby Grindal-ythe, Kirby Hall, Kirby Hill (in the district of Richmondshire), Kirby Hill (in the district of Harrogate), Kirby Knowle, Kirby Misperton, Kirby Sigston, Kirby Wiske, Kirk Deighton, Kirk Hammerton, Kirk Smeaton, Kirkby, Kirkby Fleetham with Fencote, Kirkby Malham, Kirkby Malzeard, Kirkby Overblow, Kirkby Wharfe with North Milford, Kirkbymoorside, Kirklington cum Upsland, Knayton with Brawith,

Landmoth cum Catto, Langcliffe, Langthorne, Langthorpe, Langton, Lastingham, Lav-erton, Lawkland, Lands common to the Parishes of Fylingdales and Hawsker cum Stainsacre, Lead, Leake, Leathley, Leavening, Lebberston, Levisham, Leyburn, Lillings Ambo, Lindley, Lindrick with Studley Royal and Fountains, Linton, Linton on Ouse, Little Ayton, Little Busby, Little Fenton, Little Langton, Little Ouseburn, Little Ribston, Little Smeaton (in the district of Hambleton), Little Smeaton (in the district of Selby), Little Timble, Littlethorpe, Litton, Lockton, Long Drax, Long Marston, Long Preston, Lothersdale, Low Abbotside, Low Worsall, Luttons, Lythe,

Malham, Malham Moor, Manfield, Marishes, Markingfield Hall, Markington with Wal-lerthwaite, Marrick, Marske, Marton, Marton cum Grafton, Marton cum Moxby, Marton Le Moor, Martons Both, Masham, Maunby, Melbecks, Melmerby (in the district of Richmondshire), Melmerby (in the district of Harrogate), Melsonby, Menwith with Dar-ley, Mickleby, Middleham, Middleton (in the district of Ryedale), Middleton (in the district of Harrogate), Middleton Quernhow, Middleton Tyas, Middleton on Leven, Milby, Monk Fryston, Moor Monkton, Morton on Swale, Moulton, Muker, Muston, Myton on Swale,

Naburn, Nappa, Nawton, Newfield with Langbar, Nether Poppleton, Nether Silton, New Forest, Newall with Clifton, Newbiggin, Newburgh, Newby, Newby Wiske, Newby with Mulwith, Newholme cum Dunsley, Newland, Newsham, Newsham with Breckenbrough, Newton, Newton Kyme cum Toulston, Newton Morrell, Newton Mulgrave, Newton Le Willows, Newton on Ouse, Nidd, Normanby, North Cowton, North Deighton, North Duffield, North Kilvington, North Otterington, North Rigton, North Stainley with Sle-ningford, Norton Conyers, Norton Le Clay, Norwood, Nun Monkton, Nunnington,

Old Byland and Scawton, Oldstead, Osgodby, Osmotherley, Oswaldkirk, Otterburn, Oul-ston, Over Dinsdale, Over Silton, Overton, Oxton,

Pannal, Patrick Brompton, Pickhill with Roxby, Picton, Plompton, Pockley, Potto, Preston under Scar,

Rainton with Newby, Rand Grange, Raskelf, Rathmell, Ravensworth, Redmire, Reeth Fremington & Healaugh, Reighton, Riccal, Rievaulx, Rillington, Ripley, Ripon, Roecliffe, Rookwith, Rosedale East Side, Rosedale West Side, Roxby, Rudby, Rufforth, Rylstone, Ryther cum Ossendyke,

Salton, Sand Hutton (in the district of Ryedale), Sandhutton (in the district of Hambleton), Sawley, Saxton with Scarthingwell, Scackleton, Scagglethorpe, Scampston, Scorton, Scosthrop, Scotton (in the district of Richmondshire), Scotton (in the district of Harro-gate), Scrayingham, Scruton, Seamer (in the district of Scarborough), Seamer (in the district of Hambleton), Sessay, Settrington, Sexhow, Sharow, Sherburn, Sherburn in Elmet, Sheriff Hutton, Shipton, Sicklinghall, Silpho, Sinderby, Sinnington, Skeeby, Skeld-ing, Skelton (in the district of Ryedale), Skelton (in the district of Harrogate), Skipton on Swale, Skipwith, Skutterskelfe, Slingsby, Snaiton, Snape with Thorp, Sneaton, South Cowton, South Holme, South Kilvington, South Milford, South Otterington, South Stain-ley with Cayton, Sowerby Under Cotcliffe, Spaunton, Spennithorne, Spofforth with Stockeld, Sproxton, Stainburn, Stainforth, Stainton, Stainton Dale, Stanwick St John, Stapleton (in the district of Richmondshire), Stapleton (in the district of Selby), Staveley, Steeton, Stillingfleet, Stillington, Stirton with Thorlby, St Martins, Stockton on the Forest, Stonebeck Down, Stonebeck Up, Stonegrave, Studley Roger, Suffield cum Everley,

Sutton, Sutton on the Forest, Sutton under Whitestonecliffe, Sutton with Howgrave, Swainby with Allerthorpe, Swinden, Swinton, Swinton with Warthermarske,
Temple Hirst, Terrington, Theakston, Thimbleby, Thirkleby High and Low with Osgodby, Thirlby, Thirn, Thixendale, Tholthorpe, Thoralby, Thorganby, Thormanby, Thornbrough, Thornthwaite with Padside, Thornton Bridge, Thornton in Craven, Thornton in Lonsdale, Thornton Rust, Thornton Steward, Thornton Watlass, Thornton Le Beans, Thornton Le Clay, Thornton Le Dale, Thornton Le Moor, Thornton Le Street, Thornton on the Hill, Thornville, Thorpe Bassett, Thorpe, Thorpe Underwoods, Thorpe Willoughby, Threshfield, Thrintoft, Thruscross, Tockwith, Tollerton, Topcliffe, Towthorpe, Towton, Tunstall,
Uckerby, Ugthorpe, Ulleskelf, Upper Helmsley, Upper Poppleton, Upsall,
Walburn, Walden Stubbs, Walkingham Hill with Occaney, Warlaby, Warsill, Warthill, Wath, Weaverthorpe, Weeton, Welburn (Amotherby Ward in the district of Ryedale), Welburn (Kirkbymoorside Ward in the district of Ryedale), Welbury, Well, Wensley, West Ayton, West Haddlesey, West Harlsey, West Hauxwell, West Layton, West Rounton, West Scrafton, West Tanfield, West Witton, Westerdale, Weston, Westow, Westwick, Wharram, Whashton, Wheldrake, Whenby, Whitley, Whitwell, Whitwell on the Hill, Whixley, Whorlton, Wig glesworth, Wighill, Wildon Grange, Willerby, Wilstrop, Wilton, Winksley, Winton Stank and Hallikeld, Wintringham, Wistow, Wombleton, Womersley, Wrelton, Wykeham,
Yafforth, Yearsley, Youlton.

PART 5 SOUTH YORKSHIRE

Auckley, Austerfield,
Barnburgh, Bawtry, Billingley, Blaxton, Braithwell, Burghwallis,
Cadeby, Cantley, Cawthorne, Clayton with Frickley, Conisbrough Parks,
Denaby, Dunford,
Edenthorpe,
Fenwick, Finningley, Firbeck, Fishlake,
Gildingwells, Great Houghton, Gunthwaite and Ingbirchworth,
Hampole, Harthill with Woodall, Hickleton, High Hoyland, High Melton, Hooton Levitt, Hooton Pagnell, Hooton Roberts, Hunshelf,
Kirk Bramwith,
Langsett, Letwell, Little Houghton, Loversall,
Marr, Moss Norton,
Owston, Oxspring,
Ravenfield,
Shafton, Silkstone, Stainborough, Stainton, Stensall with Towthorpe Sykehouse,
Tankersley, Thorpe in Balne, Thorpe Salvin, Thurgoland, Todwick, Treeton,
Ulley,
Wadworth, Wentworth, Woodsetts, Wortley.

PART 6 WEST YORKSHIRE

Aberford, Addingham, Austhorpe,
Badsworth, Bardsey cum Rigton, Barwick in Elmet and Scholes, Blackshaw, Bramham cum Oglethorpe,
Carlton, Chevet, Clifford, Collingham, Crofton, Cullingworth,
Darrington, Denholme,
East Hardwick, East Keswick, Erringden,
Great and Little Preston,
Havercroft with Cold Hiendley, Heptonstall, Hessle and Hill Top, Huntwick with Foulby and Nostell,
Ledsham, Ledston, Lotherton cum Aberford,
Micklefield,

Newland with Woodhouse Moor, Notton,
Oxenhope,
Parlington, Pool,
Ripponden, Ryhill,
Scarcroft, Sharlston, Sitlington, South Hiendley, Steeton with Eastburn, Sturton Grange,
Thorner, Thorpe Audlin,
Wadsworth, Walton (in the district of Leeds), Walton (in the district of Wakefield), Warmfield cum Heath, West Bretton, West Hardwick, Wintersett, Woolley, Wothersome.

The unparished area of the borough of Pudsey excluding the settlements of Guisely and Yeadon, and the unparished area of the county constituency of Elmet, bounded by the county consituency of Pontefract and Castleford, the county constituency of Normanton and the parishes of Swillingon, Great and Little Preston, Austhorpe, Barwick in Elmet and Scholes, Parlington, Sturton Grange and Ledston excluding the settlements of Garforth, Great Preston and Kippax.

Regulation 9(b)

SCHEDULE 16 DESIGNATED PROTECTED AREAS IN YORKSHIRE AND THE HUMBER—BY MAPS

PART 1 EAST RIDING OF YORKSHIRE

The parishes of—

> Howden,
> Pocklington,
> South Cave,
> Woodmansey.

PART 2 NORTH LINCOLNSHIRE

The parish of Bottesford.

PART 3 NORTH YORKSHIRE

The parishes of—

> Barlby, Brayton,
> Dunnington,
> Filey,
> Great Ayton,
> Hunmanby, Huntington,
> Malton, Murton,
> Newby and Scalby, Northallerton, Norton on Derwent,
> Pickering,
> Scriven, Selby, Settle, Stutton with Hazlewood,
> Thirsk,
> Whitby.

The unparished area bounded by the parishes of Nida, Brearton, Scotton, Knaresborough, Plompton, Follifoot, Spofforth with Stockfield, Kirkby Overblow, North Rigton, Pannal and Killinghall.

PART 4 SOUTH YORKSHIRE

The parishes of—

Adwick Upon Dearne,
Bradfield, Brampton Bierlow, Brierley, Brodsworth,
Dinnington St John's,
Edlington,
North and South Anston,
Penistone,
Stocksbridge,
Thurcroft,
Whiston.

PART 5 WEST YORKSHIRE

The parishes of—

Ackworth, Arthington,
Denby Dale,
Featherstone,
Harewood, Hebden Royd,
Kirkburton,
North Elmsall,
Swillington.

The unparished area of the county constituency of Keighly excluding the parishes of Seeton with Eastburn, Silsden, Addingham, Ilkley and Oxenhope.

The unparished area of the borough constituency of Leeds North East excluding the parish of Harewood.

The unparished area of the county constituency of Normanton excluding the parishes of Normanton, Newland with Woodhouse Moor, Warmfield cum Heath and Sharlston.

APPENDIX 2Z

The Tribunal Procedure (Upper Tribunal) (Lands Chamber) Rules 2010

(SI 2010/2600)

1228Z *After consulting in accordance with paragraph 28(1) of Schedule 5 to the Tribunals, Courts and Enforcement Act 2007, the Tribunal Procedure Committee has made the following Rules in exercise of the power conferred by sections 10(3), 16(9), 22 and 29(3) and (4) of, and Schedule 5 to, that Act, section 84(3A) of the Law of Property Act 1925 and section 2(5) of the Rights of Light Act 1959. The Lord Chancellor has allowed the Rules in accordance with paragraph 28(3) of Schedule 5 to the Tribunals, Courts and Enforcement Act 2007.*

PART 1

INTRODUCTION

Citation, commencement, application and interpretation

1.—(1) These Rules may be cited as the Tribunal Procedure (Upper Tribunal) (Lands Chamber) Rules 2010 and come into force on 29th November 2010.

(2) These Rules apply to proceedings before the Lands Chamber of the Upper Tribunal.

(3) In these Rules—

"the 1949 Act" means the Lands Tribunal Act 1949;

"the 1961 Act" means the Land Compensation Act 1961;

"the 2007 Act" means the Tribunals, Courts and Enforcement Act 2007;

"appellant" means a person who sends or delivers a notice of appeal to the Tribunal and any person added or substituted as an appellant under rule 9 (addition, substitution and removal of parties);

"applicant" means a person who makes an application to the Tribunal and includes a person who—

(a) makes an application under section 84 of the Law of Property Act 1925;

(b) makes an application under section 2 of the Rights of Light Act 1959;

(c) applies for permission to appeal;

(d) in judicial review proceedings transferred to the Tribunal, was a claimant in the proceedings immediately before they were transferred; or

(e) is added or substituted as an applicant under rule 9 (addition, substitution and removal of parties);

"claimant" means a party to a reference sent or delivered under Part 5 (references) who is not a respondent authority, acquiring authority or compensating authority or has been added or substituted as a claimant under rule 9 (addition, substitution and removal of parties);

"hearing" means an oral hearing and includes a hearing conducted in whole or in part by video link, telephone or other means of instantaneous two-way electronic communication;

"objector" means a person who gives to the Tribunal notice of objection to an application under section 84 of the Law of Property Act 1925;

"party" means—

(a) an appellant;

(b) an applicant;

(c) a claimant;

(d) a respondent authority, an acquiring authority or a compensating authority in a reference made under Part 5 (references);

(e) an objector;

(f) a respondent; or

(g) in a case transferred to the Tribunal, any person who was a party to the proceedings immediately before the transfer or who has been added or substituted as a party under rule 9 (addition, substitution and removal of parties);

"practice direction" means a direction given under section 23 of the 2007 Act;

"respondent" means—

(a) in an application for permission to appeal or in an appeal against a decision of a tribunal, any person other than the applicant or the appellant who was a party in the proceedings before that tribunal and who—

(i) was present or represented at the hearing before that tribunal; or

(ii) where the proceedings were determined without a hearing, made representations in writing to that tribunal, unless the person has ceased to be a respondent under rule 25(2) (respondent's notice);

(b) a person added or substituted as a respondent under rule 9 (addition, substitution and removal of parties); and

(c) in a reference made under Part 5 (references) by consent, any person other than the claimant;

"Tribunal" means the Lands Chamber of the Upper Tribunal.

Overriding objective and parties' obligation to co-operate with the Tribunal

2.—(1) The overriding objective of these Rules is to enable the Tribunal to deal with cases fairly and justly.

(2) Dealing with a case fairly and justly includes—

(a) dealing with the case in ways which are proportionate to the importance of the case, the complexity of the issues, the anticipated costs and the resources of the parties;

(b) avoiding unnecessary formality and seeking flexibility in the proceedings;

(c) ensuring, so far as practicable, that the parties are able to participate fully in the proceedings;

(d) using any special expertise of the Tribunal effectively; and

(e) avoiding delay, so far as compatible with proper consideration of the issues.

(3) The Tribunal must seek to give effect to the overriding objective when it—

(a) exercises any power under these Rules; or

(b) interprets any rule or practice direction.

(4) Parties must—

(a) help the Tribunal to further the overriding objective; and

(b) co-operate with the Tribunal generally.

Alternative dispute resolution and arbitration

3.—(1) The Tribunal should seek, where appropriate—

(a) to bring to the attention of the parties the availability of any appropriate alternative procedure for the resolution of the dispute; and

(b) if the parties wish and provided that it is compatible with the overriding objective, to facilitate the use of the procedure.

(2) Except where rule 30 (references by consent: application of the Arbitration Act 1996) applies, Part 1 of the Arbitration Act 1996 does not apply to proceedings before the Tribunal.

PART 2

GENERAL POWERS AND PROVISIONS

Delegation to staff

4.—(1) Staff appointed under section 40(1) of the 2007 Act (tribunal staff and services) may, with the approval of the Senior President of Tribunals, carry out functions of a judicial nature permitted or required to be done by the Tribunal.

(2) The approval referred to at paragraph (1) may apply generally to the carrying out of specified functions by members of staff of a specified description in specified circumstances.

(3) Within 14 days after the date on which the Tribunal sends notice of a decision made by a member of staff under paragraph (1) to a party, that party may apply in writing to the Tribunal for that decision to be considered afresh by a judge.

Case management powers

5.—(1) Subject to the provisions of the 2007 Act and any other enactment, the Tribunal may regulate its own procedure.

(2) The Tribunal may give a direction in relation to the conduct or disposal of proceedings at any time, including a direction amending, suspending or setting aside an earlier direction.

(3) In particular, and without restricting the general powers in paragraphs (1) and (2), the Tribunal may—

(a) extend or shorten the time for complying with any rule or practice direction and order an extension even if the application for an extension is not made until after the time limit has expired;

(b) consolidate or hear together two or more sets of proceedings or parts of proceedings raising common issues, or treat a case as a lead case;

(c) permit or require a party to amend a document;

(d) permit or require a party or another person to provide documents, information, evidence submissions to the Tribunal or a party;

(e) deal with an issue in the proceedings as a separate or preliminary issue;

(f) hold a hearing to consider any matter, including a case management issue;

(g) decide the form of any hearing;

(h) adjourn or postpone a hearing;

(i) require a party to produce a bundle for a hearing;

(j) stay proceedings;

(k) transfer proceedings to another court or tribunal if that other court or tribunal has jurisdiction in relation to the proceedings and—

(i) because of a change of circumstances since the proceedings were started, the Tribunal no longer has jurisdiction in relation to the proceedings; or

(ii) the Tribunal considers that the other court or tribunal is a more appropriate forum for the determination of the case;

(l) suspend the effect of its own decision pending an appeal or review of that decision;

(m) in an appeal, or an application for permission to appeal, against the decision of another tribunal, suspend the effect of that decision pending the determination of the application for permission to appeal, and any appeal; or

(n) require any person, body or other tribunal whose decision is the subject of proceedings before the Tribunal to provide reasons for the decision, or other information or documents in relation to the decision or any proceedings before that person, body or tribunal.

Procedure for applying for and giving directions

6.—(1) The Tribunal may give a direction on the application of one or more of the parties or on its own initiative.

(2) An application for a direction may be made—

(a) by sending or delivering a written application to the Tribunal; or

(b) orally during the course of a hearing.

(3) An application for a direction must include the reason for making that application.

(4) If a written application for a direction is made with the consent of every party, it must be accompanied by consents signed by or on behalf of each party.

(5) If a written application for a direction is not made with the consent of every party the applicant must provide—

(a) a copy of the proposed application to every other party before it is made; and

(b) confirmation to the Tribunal that the other parties have been notified that any objection they wish to make to the application must be provided in accordance with paragraph (6).

(6) A party who wishes to object to an application for a direction must within 10 days of being sent a copy of the application, send written notice of the objection to the Tribunal and the applicant.

(7) Unless the Tribunal considers that there is good reason not to do so, the Tribunal must send written notice of any direction to every party and to any other person affected by the direction.

(8) If a party or any other person sent notice of the direction under paragraph (7) wishes to challenge a direction which the Tribunal has given, they may do so by applying for another direction which amends, suspends or sets aside the first direction.

Failure to comply with rules etc.

7.—(1) An irregularity resulting from a failure to comply with any requirement in these Rules, a practice direction or a direction, does not of itself render void the proceedings or any step taken in the proceedings.

(2) If any party has failed to comply with a requirement in these Rules, a practice direction or a direction, the Tribunal may, on the application of any party or on its own initiative, take such action as it considers just, which may include—

(a) waiving the requirement;

(b) requiring the failure to be remedied;

(c) exercising its power under section 25 of the 2007 Act (supplementary powers of the Tribunal); or

(d) exercising its power under rule 8 (striking out a party's case).

(3) A party will automatically be barred from taking further part in the proceedings or part of the proceedings if that party has failed to comply with a direction that stated that failure by that party to comply with the direction would lead to such a barring of that party.

(4) If a party has been barred under paragraph (3), that party may apply to the Tribunal for the lifting of the bar.

(5) An application made under paragraph (4) must be made in writing and received by the Tribunal within 14 days after the date on which the Tribunal sent notification of the bar to the parties.

(6) If a party has been barred from taking further part in proceedings under this rule and that bar has not been lifted, the Tribunal need not consider any response or other submission made by that party, and may summarily determine any or all issues against that party.

Striking out a party's case

8.—(1) The proceedings, or the appropriate part of them, will automatically be struck out if the appellant, applicant or claimant has failed to comply with a direction that stated that failure by that party to comply with the direction would lead to the striking out of the proceedings or that part of them.

(2) The Tribunal must strike out the whole or a part of the proceedings if the Tribunal—

(a) does not have jurisdiction in relation to the proceedings or that part of them; and

(b) does not exercise its power under rule 5(3)(k)(i) (transfer to another court or tribunal) in relation to the proceedings or that part of them.

(3) The Tribunal may strike out the whole or a part of the proceedings if—

(a) a party to the proceedings has failed to comply with a direction which stated that failure by that party to comply with the direction could lead to the striking out of the proceedings or part of them;

(b) the appellant, applicant or claimant has failed to co-operate with the Tribunal to such an extent that the Tribunal cannot deal with the proceedings fairly and justly; or

(c) the Tribunal considers there is no reasonable prospect of the case of the appellant, applicant or claimant, or part of it, succeeding.

(4) The Tribunal may not strike out the whole or a part of the proceedings under paragraph (2) or (3)(b) or (c) without first giving the appellant, applicant or claimant an opportunity to make representations in relation to the proposed striking out.

(5) If the proceedings have been struck out under paragraph (1) or (3)(a), the appellant, applicant or claimant may apply for the proceedings, or part of them, to be reinstated.

(6) An application made under paragraph (5) must be made in writing and received by the Tribunal within 14 days after the date on which the Tribunal sent notification of the striking out to the appellant, applicant or claimant.

Addition, substitution and removal of parties

9.—(1) The Tribunal may give a direction adding, substituting or removing a party in any proceedings.

(2) If the Tribunal gives a direction under paragraph (1) it may give such consequential directions as it considers appropriate.

(3) A person who is not a party may apply to the Tribunal to be added or substituted as a party.

(4) If a person who is entitled to be a party to proceedings by virtue of another enactment applies to be added as a party, and the conditions (if any) applicable to that entitlement have been satisfied, the Tribunal must give a direction adding that person as a party.

Orders for costs

10.—(1) The Tribunal may make an order for costs on an application or on its own initiative.

(2) A person making an application for an order for costs—

(a) must send or deliver a written application to the Tribunal and to the person against whom it is proposed that the order be made; and

(b) may send or deliver with the application a schedule of the costs claimed in sufficient detail to allow summary assessment of such costs by the Tribunal.

(3) An application for an order for costs may be made at any time during the proceedings but may not be made later than 14 days after the date on which—

(a) the Tribunal sends a decision notice recording the decision which finally disposes of all issues in the proceedings;

(b) the Tribunal sends notice of consent to a withdrawal under rule 20 (withdrawal) which ends the proceedings; or

(c) notice of withdrawal is sent to the Tribunal with the consent of all parties.

(4) The Tribunal may not make an order for costs against a person (the "paying person") without first giving that person an opportunity to make representations.

(5) The amount of costs to be paid under an order under this rule may be determined by—

(a) summary assessment by the Tribunal;

(b) agreement of a specified sum by the paying person and the person entitled to receive the costs (the "receiving person"); or

(c) detailed assessment of the whole or a specified part of the costs incurred by the receiving person on the standard basis or, if specified in the costs order, on the indemnity basis by the Tribunal or, if it so directs, on application to the Senior Courts Costs Office or a county court; and the Civil Procedure Rules 1998 shall apply, with necessary modifications, to that application and assessment as if the proceedings in the Tribunal had been proceedings in a court to which the Civil Procedure Rules 1998 apply.

(6) The Tribunal may order a party to pay to another party costs of an amount equal to the whole or part of any fee paid (which has not been remitted by the Lord Chancellor under the Upper Tribunal (Lands Chamber) Fees Order 2009) in the proceedings by that other party that is not otherwise included in an award of costs.

(7) In an appeal against the decision of a leasehold valuation tribunal, the Tribunal may not make an order for costs except—

(a) under section 29(4) of the 2007 Act (wasted costs);
(b) under paragraph (6); or
(c) if the Tribunal considers that the party ordered to pay costs has acted unreasonably in bringing, defending or conducting the proceedings.

(8) The amount that may be awarded under paragraph (7)(c), disregarding any amount that may be awarded under paragraph (6), must not exceed £500.

Representatives

11.—(1) A party may appoint a representative (whether a legal representative or not) to represent that party in the proceedings.

(2) If a party appoints a representative, that party (or the representative if the representative is legal representative) must send or deliver to the Tribunal and to each other party to the proceedings written notice of the representative's name and address.

(3) Anything permitted or required to be done by a party under these Rules, a practice direction or a direction may be done by the representative of that party, except signing a witness statement.

(4) A person who receives notice of the appointment of a representative—

(a) must provide to the representative any document which is required to be provided to the represented party, and need not provide that document to the represented party; and
(b) may assume that the representative is and remains authorised as such until they receive written notification that this is not so from the representative or the represented party.

(5) At a hearing a party may be accompanied by another person whose name and address has not been notified under paragraph (2) but who, with the permission of the Tribunal, may act as a representative or otherwise assist in presenting the party's case at the hearing.

(6) Paragraphs (2) to (4) do not apply to a person who accompanies a party under paragraph (5).

(7) In this rule "legal representative" means a person who, for the purposes of the Legal Services Act 2007, is an authorised person in relation to an activity which constitutes the exercise of a right of audience or the conduct of litigation within the meaning of that Act.

Calculating time

12.—(1) An act required by these Rules, a practice direction or a direction to be done on or by a particular day must be done by 5 pm on that day.

(2) If the time specified by these Rules, a practice direction or a direction for doing any act ends on a day other than a working day, the act is done in time if it is done on the next working day.

(3) In this Rule "working day" means any day except a Saturday or Sunday, Christmas Day, Good Friday or a bank holiday under section 1 of the Banking and Financial Dealings Act 1971.

Sending and delivery of documents

13.—(1) Any document to be provided to the Tribunal under these Rules, a practice direction or a direction must be—

(a) sent by pre-paid post or by document exchange, or delivered by hand, to the address of the office of the Tribunal;
(b) sent by fax to the fax number of the office of the Tribunal; or
(c) sent or delivered by such other method as the Tribunal may permit or direct.

(2) Subject to paragraph (3), if a party provides a fax number, email address or other details for the electronic transmission of documents to them, that party must accept delivery of documents by the relevant method.

(3) If a party informs the Tribunal and all other parties that a particular form of communication, other than pre-paid post or delivery by hand, should not be used to provide documents to that party, that form of communication must not be so used.

(4) If the Tribunal or a party sends a document to a party or the Tribunal by email or any other electronic means of communication, the recipient may request that the sender provide a hard copy of the document to the recipient. The recipient must make such a request as soon as reasonably practicable after receiving the document electronically.

(5) The Tribunal and each party may assume that the address provided by a party or its representative is and remains the address to which documents should be sent or delivered until it receives written notification to the contrary.

Waiver or alternative method of service

14. The Tribunal may waive a requirement under these Rules to send or deliver a notice or other document to a person or may make an order for service by an alternative method (whether by advertisement in a newspaper or otherwise) as the Tribunal may think fit—

(a) if that person cannot be found after all diligent enquiries have been made;
(b) if that person has died and has no personal representative; or
(c) if for any other reason a notice or other document cannot readily be sent or delivered to that person in accordance with these Rules.

Use of documents and information

15. The Tribunal may make an order prohibiting the disclosure or publication
of—

(a) specified documents or information relating to the proceedings; or

(b) any matter likely to lead members of the public to identify any person
whom the Tribunal considers should not be identified.

Evidence and submissions

16.—(1) Without restriction on the general powers in rule 5(1) and (2) (case
management powers), the Tribunal may give directions as to—

(a) issues on which it requires evidence or submissions;

(b) the nature of the evidence or submissions it requires;

(c) whether the parties are permitted to provide expert evidence, and if so
whether the parties must jointly appoint a single expert to provide such
evidence;

(d) any limit on the number of witnesses whose evidence a party may put
forward, whether in relation to a particular issue or generally;

(e) the manner in which any evidence or submissions are to be provided,
which may include a direction for them to be given—
(i) orally at a hearing; or
(ii) by written submission or witness statement; and

(f) the time by which any evidence or submissions are to be provided.

(2) The Tribunal may—

(a) admit evidence whether or not—
(i) the evidence would be admissible in a civil trial in England or
Wales; or
(ii) the evidence was available to a previous decision maker; or

(b) exclude evidence that would otherwise be admissible where—
(i) the evidence was not provided within the time allowed by a
direction or a practice direction;
(ii) the evidence was otherwise provided in a manner that did not
comply with a direction or a practice direction; or
(iii) it would otherwise be unfair to admit the evidence.

(3) The Tribunal may consent to a witness giving, or require any witness to
give, evidence on oath, and may administer an oath for that purpose.

(4) A witness statement must contain the words "I believe that the facts stated
in this witness statement are true", and be signed by the person who makes it.

(5) Where a witness who has made a witness statement is called to give oral
evidence, their witness statement shall stand as their evidence in chief unless the
Tribunal directs otherwise, but the witness may with the permission of the Tribunal—

(a) amplify the witness statement they have made; and

(b) give evidence in relation to new matters which have arisen since the witness statement was provided to the other parties.

Expert evidence

17.—(1) It is the duty of an expert to help the Tribunal on matters within the expert's expertise and this duty overrides any obligation to the person from whom the expert has received instructions or by whom the expert is paid.

(2) Subject to paragraph (3), no party may call more than one expert witness without the permission of the Tribunal.

(3) In proceedings relating to mineral valuations or business disturbance, no party may call more than two expert witnesses without the permission of the Tribunal.

(4) Expert evidence is to be given in a written report unless the Tribunal directs otherwise.

(5) A written report of an expert must—

(a) contain a statement that the expert understands the duty in paragraph (1) and has complied with it,
(b) contain the words "I believe that the facts stated in this report are true and that the opinions expressed are correct",
(c) comply with the requirements of any practice direction as regards its form and contents, and
(d) be signed by the expert.

Summoning of witnesses and orders to answer questions or produce documents

18.—(1) On the application of a party or on its own initiative, the Tribunal may—

(a) by summons, require any person to attend as a witness at a hearing at the time and place specified in the summons; and
(b) order any person to answer any questions or produce any documents in that person's possession or control which relate to any issue in the proceedings.

(2) A summons under paragraph (1)(a) must—

(a) give the person required to attend 14 days' notice of the hearing or such shorter period as the Tribunal may direct; and
(b) where the person is not a party, make provision for the person's necessary expenses of attendance to be paid, and state who is to pay them.

(3) No person may be compelled to give any evidence or produce any document that the person could not be compelled to give or produce on a trial of an action in a court of law.

(4) A person who receives a summons or order may apply to the Tribunal for it to be varied or set aside if they did not have an opportunity to object to it before it was made or issued.

(5) A person making an application under paragraph (4) must do so as soon as reasonably practicable after receiving notice of the summons or order.

(6) A summons or order under this rule must—

    (a) state that the person on whom the requirement is imposed may apply to the Tribunal to vary or set aside the summons or order, if they did not have an opportunity to object to it before it was made or issued; and

    (b) state the consequences of failure to comply with the summons or order.

Site inspections

19.—(1) Subject to paragraph (2), the Tribunal may, with the consent of the occupier, enter and inspect—

    (a) the land or property that is the subject of the proceedings; and

    (b) as far as practicable, any other land or property relevant to the proceedings to which the attention of the Tribunal is drawn.

(2) If the Tribunal proposes to enter any premises under paragraph (1) it must—

    (a) give reasonable notice to the occupier of the premises; and

    (b) give notice to the parties of the proposed inspection.

Withdrawal

20.—(1) Subject to paragraph (2), a party may give notice of the withdrawal of its case, or any part of it—

    (a) at any time before a hearing to consider the final disposal of the proceedings (or, if the Tribunal disposes of the proceedings without a hearing, before that final disposal), by sending or delivering to the Tribunal and all other parties a written notice of withdrawal; or

    (b) orally at a hearing.

(2) Notice of withdrawal will not take effect unless the Tribunal consents to the withdrawal.

(3) The requirement in paragraph (2) does not apply to—

    (a) an application for permission to appeal; or

    (b) a notice of withdrawal to which all the parties to the proceedings consent.

(4) A party which has withdrawn its case or part of it may apply to the Tribunal for the case to be reinstated.

(5) An application under paragraph (4) must be made in writing and be received by the Tribunal within 1 month after—

(a) the date on which the Tribunal received the notice under paragraph (1)(a); or
(b) the date of the hearing at which the case (or part of it) was withdrawn orally under paragraph (1)(b).

PART 3

APPLICATIONS FOR PERMISSION TO APPEAL

Application to the Tribunal for permission to appeal

21.—(1) Where permission to appeal to the Tribunal against the decision of another tribunal is required, a person may apply to the Tribunal for permission to appeal to the Tribunal against such a decision only if—

(a) they have made an application for permission to appeal to the tribunal which made the decision challenged; and
(b) that application has been refused or has not been admitted.

(2) An application for permission to appeal must be made in writing and received by the Tribunal no later than 14 days after the date on which the tribunal that made the decision under challenge sent notice of its refusal of permission to appeal or refusal to admit the application for permission to appeal to the applicant.

(3) The application must be signed and dated and must state—

(a) the name and address of the applicant and, if represented,—
  (i) the name and address of the applicant's representative; and
  (ii) the professional capacity, if any, in which the applicant's representative acts;
(b) an address where documents for the applicant may be sent or delivered;
(c) details (including the full reference) of the decision challenged;
(d) the grounds of appeal on which the applicant relies;
(e) the name and address of each respondent; and
(f) whether the applicant wants the application to be dealt with at a hearing.

(4) The applicant must provide with the application—

(a) a copy of—
  (i) any written record of the decision being challenged;
  (ii) any separate written statement of reasons for that decision;

      (iii) the notice of refusal of permission to appeal or refusal to admit the application for permission to appeal from the other tribunal; and

      (iv) any other document relied on in the application to the Tribunal; and

  (b) the fee payable to the Tribunal.

(5) If the applicant provides the application to the Tribunal later than the time required by paragraph (2) or by an extension of time allowed under rule 5(3)(a) (power to extend time)—

  (a) the application must include a request for an extension of time and the reason why the application was not provided in time; and

  (b) unless the Tribunal extends time for the application under rule 5(3)(a) (power to extend time), the Tribunal must not admit the application.

(6) If the tribunal that made the decision under challenge refused to admit the applicant's application for permission to appeal because the application for such permission or for a written statement of reasons was not made in time—

  (a) the application to the Tribunal must include the reason why the application to the other tribunal for permission to appeal or for a written statement of reasons, as the case may be, was not made in time; and

  (b) the Tribunal must only admit the application if the Tribunal considers that it is in the interests of justice for it to do so.

(7) The applicant must send or deliver to the Tribunal with the application for permission sufficient copies of the application and accompanying documents for service on the respondent.

(8) Unless it decides to dismiss the application without representations from the respondent, the Tribunal must send or deliver a copy of the application and accompanying documents to the respondent, and must specify a time limit within which any representations relating to the application must be made.

Respondent's representations in relation to permission to appeal

22.—(1) A respondent who wishes to make representations in relation to the application—

  (a) must do so in writing within the time limit specified under rule 21(8);

  (b) may include an application for permission to cross-appeal if the applicant is granted permission to appeal;

  (c) must at the same time send a copy of the representations and any application to all the other parties and inform the Tribunal in writing that this has occurred; and

  (d) must state whether the respondent wants the application to be dealt with at a hearing.

(2) An application for permission to cross-appeal under paragraph (1)(b) must state the grounds on which the application is made and must include a copy of any document relied on in the application.

Decision in relation to permission to appeal

23.—(1) The Tribunal may give permission to appeal with such limitations or conditions as the Tribunal thinks fit.

(2) If the Tribunal refuses permission to appeal, it must send written notice of the refusal and of the reasons for the refusal to the applicant.

(3) If the Tribunal gives permission to appeal—

(a) the Tribunal must send written notice of the permission, and of the reasons for any limitations or conditions on such permission, to each party;

(b) subject to any direction by the Tribunal, the application for permission to appeal stands as the notice of appeal; and

(c) the Tribunal may, with the consent of the parties, determine the appeal without further representations.

(4) In this rule, references to appeals include cross-appeals where appropriate.

PART 4

APPEALS

Notice of appeal

24.—(1) This rule applies—

(a) if another tribunal has given permission for a party to appeal to the Tribunal;

(b) if permission to appeal against the decision of another tribunal is not required; or

(c) subject to any other direction by the Tribunal, if the Tribunal has given permission to appeal and has given a direction that the application for permission to appeal does not stand as the notice of appeal.

(2) Unless some other time limit is prescribed by or under another enactment, the appellant must provide a notice of appeal to the Tribunal so that it is received within 1 month after—

(a) the date that the tribunal that gave permission to appeal sent notice of such permission to the appellant; or

(b) the date on which the notice of decision to which the appeal relates was sent to the appellant, if permission to appeal is not required.

(3) The notice of appeal must be signed and dated and must include the information listed in rule 21(3) (content of the application for permission to appeal).

(4) If another tribunal has given permission to appeal, or if permission is not required, the appellant must provide with the notice of appeal—

    (a) a copy of—
        (i) any written record of the decision being challenged;
        (ii) any separate written statement of reasons for that decision;
        (iii) any notice of permission to appeal; and
        (iv) if the appeal is against the decision of the Valuation Tribunal for England or [*a valuation tribunal in Wales*] **the Valuation Tribunal for Wales**[3], a copy of the proposal or determination that was the subject of the appeal to that tribunal; and
    (b) the fee payable to the Tribunal.

(5) If the appellant provides the notice of appeal to the Tribunal later than the time required by paragraph (2)—

    (a) the notice of appeal must include a request for an extension of time and the reasons why the notice was not provided in time; and
    (b) unless the Tribunal extends time for the notice of appeal under rule 5(3)(a) (power to extend time) the Tribunal must not admit the notice of appeal.

(6) The appellant must send or deliver to the Tribunal with the notice of appeal sufficient copies of the notice and accompanying documents for each respondent.

(7) When the Tribunal receives the notice of appeal it must send a copy of the notice and any accompanying documents to each respondent.

Respondent's notice

25.—(1) A respondent may provide a respondent's notice to an appeal.

(2) A respondent shall, unless given permission to cross-appeal, cease to be a respondent if no respondent's notice is provided within the time specified in paragraph (3) or such further time as may be allowed under rule 5(3)(a) (power to extend time).

(3) Any respondent's notice must be in writing and must be sent or delivered to the Tribunal and the appellant so that it is received no later than 1 month after the date on which the Tribunal sent—

    (a) notice that it had given permission to appeal to the respondent; or
    (b) a copy of the notice of appeal to the respondent.

---

[3] Words substituted by SI 2012/500, r. 6 with effect from April 6, 2012.

(4) The respondent's notice must be signed and dated and must state—

(a) the name and address of the respondent and, if represented,—
    (i) the name and address of the respondent's representative; and
    (ii) the professional capacity, if any, in which the respondent's representative acts;
(b) an address where documents for the respondent may be sent or delivered;
(c) the grounds on which the respondent relies in opposing the appeal or in support of a cross-appeal; and
(d) whether the respondent wants the case to be dealt with at a hearing.

(5) If the respondent provides a respondent's notice to the Tribunal later than the time required by paragraph (2), the notice must include a request for an extension of time and the reasons why the notice was not provided in time.

(6) If, in any proceedings, the Tribunal receives a respondent's notice from more than one respondent, it must send a copy of each notice received to each of the other respondents.

Appellant's reply

26.—(1) Subject to any direction given by the Tribunal, the appellant may provide a reply to any respondent's notice provided under rule 25 (respondent's notice).

(2) Any reply provided under paragraph (1) must be in writing and must be sent or delivered to the Tribunal and every respondent so that it is received within 1 month after the date on which the relevant respondent sent the respondent's notice to the appellant.

PART 5

REFERENCES

Application of Part 5

27. Part 5 applies to any proceedings allocated to the Tribunal except—

(a) an application for permission to appeal, or an appeal, against the decision of another tribunal;
(b) an application to which Part 6 (applications under section 84 of the Law of Property Act 1925) or Part 7 (applications under section 2 of the Rights of Light Act 1959) applies;
(c) proceedings to which Part 8 (proceedings, including judicial review proceedings, transferred to the Tribunal) applies.

Notice of reference

28.—(1) Proceedings to which this Part applies must be started by way of reference made by sending or delivering to the Tribunal a notice of reference.

(2) The parties to the proceedings are the person making the reference and any person named as a party in the notice of reference.

(3) The notice of reference must be signed and dated and must state—

(a) the name and address of the person making the reference and, if represented,—
   (i) the name and address of that person's representative; and
   (ii) the professional capacity, if any, in which the person's representative acts;

(b) an address where documents for the person making the reference may be sent or delivered;

(c) the address or description of the land to which the reference relates;

(d) the name and address of every other person with an interest in the land;

(e) the nature of the interest in the land of the person making the reference and that of any other person named in the notice;

(f) the statutory provision under which the reference is made (unless the reference is a reference by consent under section 1(5) of the 1949 Act);

(g) if the reference is made by a claimant for compensation or other monetary award, the amount claimed, an explanation of how that amount is calculated and a summary of the reasons for making that claim;

(h) the matter on which the person making the reference seeks the determination of the Tribunal and a summary of the reasons for seeking that determination; and

(i) whether the person making the reference wants the reference to be determined without a hearing.

(4) The person making the reference must provide with the notice of reference—

(a) a copy of the order or other documents in consequence of which the reference is made including any agreement conferring jurisdiction on the Tribunal;

(b) if the reference relates to compensation payable on the compulsory acquisition of land, a copy of any—
   (i) notice to treat that has been served;
   (ii) notice of entry that has been served; and
   (iii) notice of claim and amendments to it delivered to the acquiring authority in pursuance of section 4 of the 1961 Act; and

(c) the fee payable to the Tribunal.

(5) The person making the reference must provide with the notice of reference sufficient copies for every other person named as a party in the notice of reference, of—

(a) the notice of reference; and
(b) the documents listed in paragraph (4).

(6) A notice of reference in relation to compensation payable on the compulsory acquisition of land may not be sent or delivered to the Tribunal earlier than 1 month after the date of service or deemed service under section 7 of the Compulsory Purchase (Vesting Declarations) Act 1981of the notice to treat, or, if no such notice is served or deemed in accordance with any enactment to be served, of the notice of claim.

(7) The notice of reference must be sent or delivered so that it is received by the Tribunal within 1 month of—

(a) the date of service of a counter-notice, where the reference is made under section 153(1) of the Town and Country Planning Act 1990;
(b) the date of issue of notice of the decision or findings to which the reference relates, where the reference is made under regulation 7(1) or 12(3) of the Town and Country Planning (Compensation and Certificates) Regulations 1974;
(c) the date of the Secretary of State's determination, where the reference is made under regulation 15(1) of the Town and Country Planning (Compensation and Certificates) Regulations 1974.

(8) When the Tribunal receives a reference, it must send copies of the notice and the accompanying documents to the persons named in the notice.

(d) the date of issue of the certificate, where the reference is made under section 18(1) of the 1961 Act.[4]

Response to notice of reference

29.—(1) A person to whom the Tribunal sends a copy of the notice of reference must, within 1 month of the Tribunal sending the notice, send or deliver to the Tribunal and the party who made the reference a response to the notice of reference.

(2) The response to the notice of reference must be signed and dated and must

---

[4] Added by SI 2012/500, r. 6 with effect from April 6, 2012

state whether the person making the response intends to take part in the proceedings and, if so, must—

(a) state their name and address and, if represented,—
   (i) the name and address of their representative; and
   (ii) the professional capacity, if any, in which the representative acts;
(b) provide an address where documents for the person making the response may be sent or delivered;
(c) provide a summary of the contentions of the person making the response in relation to the reference;
(d) if the person making the response is a claimant and the claim is for compensation or a monetary award, the amount claimed, an explanation of how that amount is calculated and a summary of the reasons for making that claim; and
(e) whether the person making the response wants the reference to be determined without a hearing.

(3) After receipt of a response to a notice of reference the Tribunal must direct either—

(a) that the person who made the reference and any person making a response must, within such period as is stated in the direction, send or deliver to the Tribunal and each other party a statement of case that complies with the requirements of any practice direction; or
(b) that the notice of reference and any response to a notice of reference shall stand as the statement of case of the party that gave the notice or made the response.

References by consent: application of the Arbitration Act 1996

30. If the reference is by consent under section 1(5) of the 1949 Act and the parties have not agreed otherwise, the following provisions of the Arbitration Act 1996 apply to the proceedings—

(a) section 8 (whether agreement discharged by death of a party):
(b) section 9 (stay of legal proceedings);
(c) section 10 (reference of interpleader issue to arbitration);
(d) section 12 (power of court to extend time for beginning arbitral proceedings, etc.);
(e) section 23 (revocation of arbitrator's authority);
(f) section 49 (interest);
(g) section 57 (correction of award or additional award) in so far as it relates to costs and so that the reference to "award" includes a reference to any decision of the Tribunal;
(h) section 60 (agreement to pay costs in any event); and
(i) section 66 (enforcement of the award).

PART 6

APPLICATIONS UNDER SECTION 84 OF THE LAW OF PROPERTY ACT 1925
(DISCHARGE OR MODIFICATION OF RESTRICTIVE COVENANTS AFFECTING LAND)

[Omitted]

PART 7

APPLICATIONS UNDER SECTION 2 OF THE RIGHTS OF LIGHT ACT 1959

[Omitted]

PART 8

PROCEEDINGS, INCLUDING JUDICIAL REVIEW PROCEEDINGS, TRANSFERRED TO THE
TRIBUNAL

Proceedings transferred to the Tribunal

45. When proceedings, including judicial review proceedings, are transferred
to the Tribunal, the Tribunal—

  (a) must notify each party in writing that the proceeding have been trans-
        ferred to the Tribunal; and
  (b) must give directions as to the future conduct of the proceedings.

PART 9

HEARINGS

Decision with or without a hearing

46.—(1) Subject to paragraph (2), the Tribunal may make any decision
without a hearing.

(2) The Tribunal must have regard to any view expressed by a party when
deciding whether to hold a hearing to consider any matter, and the form of any
such hearing.

Notice of hearings

47.—(1) The Tribunal must give each party reasonable notice of the time and
place of any hearing and any change to the time and place of the hearing.

(2) The period of notice under paragraph (1) must be at least 14 days except that the Tribunal may give shorter notice—

(a) with the parties' consent; or

(b) in urgent or exceptional cases.

Public and private hearings

48.—(1) Subject to the following paragraphs, all hearings must be held in public.

(2) Subject to paragraph (6), each party is entitled to attend a hearing.

(3) Except in a compulsory purchase compensation reference, the Tribunal may give a direction that a hearing, or part of it, is to be held in private.

(4) If the Tribunal is acting as an arbitrator in a reference by consent under section 1(5) of the 1949 Act, any hearing must be held in private unless the parties agree otherwise.

(5) Where a hearing, or part of it, is to be held in private, the Tribunal may determine who is entitled to attend the hearing or part of it.

(6) The Tribunal may give a direction excluding from any hearing, or part of it, any person whose conduct the Tribunal considers is disrupting or is likely to disrupt the hearing.

(7) The Tribunal may give a direction excluding a witness from a hearing until that witness gives evidence.

(8) In this rule, "compulsory purchase compensation reference" means a reference of a question to the Tribunal—

(a) under section 1 of the 1961 Act;

(b) under section 11(4) of the Compulsory Purchase (Vesting Declarations) Act 1981; or

(c) to which the provisions of section 4 of the 1961 Act apply, with the exception of references—

(i) under section 16(7) of the City of London (Various Powers) Act 1967;

(ii) under section 307(1) of the Highways Act 1980; and

(iii) under regulation 96(2) of the Conservation (Natural Habitats, &c.) Regulations 1994.

Hearings in a party's absence

49. If a party fails to attend a hearing, the Tribunal may proceed with the hearing if the Tribunal—

(a) is satisfied that the party has been notified of the hearing or that reasonable steps have been taken to notify the party of the hearing; and

(b) considers that it is in the interests of justice to proceed with the hearing.

PART 10

DECISIONS

Consent orders

50.—(1) The Tribunal may, at the request of the parties but only if it considers it appropriate, make a consent order disposing of the proceedings and making such other appropriate provision as the parties have agreed.

(2) Notwithstanding any other provision of these Rules, the Tribunal need not hold a hearing before making an order under paragraph (1).

Decisions

51.—(1) The Tribunal may give a decision orally at a hearing.

(2) The Tribunal must provide to each party as soon as reasonably practicable after making a decision which finally disposes of all issues in the proceedings or a separate or preliminary issue (except a decision under Part 11 (correcting, setting aside, reviewing and appealing decisions of the Tribunal))—

    (a) a decision notice stating the Tribunal's decision; and

    (b) notification of any rights of review or appeal against the decision and the time and manner in which such rights of review or appeal may be exercised.

(3) The Tribunal must provide written reasons for its decision with a decision notice provided under paragraph (2)(a) unless—

    (a) the decision was made with the consent of the parties; or

    (b) the parties have consented to the Tribunal not giving written reasons.

(4) The Tribunal may provide written reasons for any decision to which paragraph (2) does not apply.

PART 11

CORRECTING, SETTING ASIDE, REVIEWING AND APPEALING DECISIONS OF THE TRIBUNAL

Interpretation

52. In this Part—

    "appeal" means the exercise of a right of appeal under section 13 of the 2007 Act; and

    "review" means the review of a decision by the Tribunal under section 10 of the 2007 Act.

Clerical mistakes and accidental slips or omissions

53. The Tribunal may at any time correct any clerical mistake or other accidental slip or omission in a decision or record of a decision by—

(a) sending notification of the amended decision, or a copy of the amended record, to all parties; and

(b) making any necessary amendment to any information published in relation to the decision or record.

Setting aside a decision which disposes of proceedings

54.—(1) The Tribunal may set aside a decision which disposes of proceedings, or part of such a decision, and re-make the decision or the relevant part of it, if—

(a) the Tribunal considers that it is in the interests of justice to do so; and

(b) one or more of the conditions in paragraph (2) are satisfied.

(2) The conditions are—

(a) a document relating to the proceedings was not sent or delivered to, or was not received at an appropriate time by, a party or a party's representative;

(b) a document relating to the proceedings was not sent or delivered to the Tribunal at an appropriate time;

(c) a party, or a party's representative, was not present at a hearing related to the proceedings; or

(d) there has been some other procedural irregularity in the proceedings.

(3) A party applying for a decision or part of a decision to be set aside under paragraph (1) must send a written application to the Tribunal and all other parties so that it is received no later than 1 month after the date on which the Tribunal sent notice of the decision to the party.

Application for permission to appeal

55.—(1) A person seeking permission to appeal from the decision of the Tribunal must make a written application to the Tribunal for permission to appeal.

(2) The application must be sent or delivered to the Tribunal so that it is received within 1 month after the latest of the dates on which the Tribunal sent to the person making the application—

(a) written reasons for the decision;

(b) notification of a decision to award, or refuse to award, costs;

(c) notification of amended reasons for, or correction of, the decision following a review;

(d) notification that an application for the decision to be set aside has been unsuccessful.

(3) The date in paragraph (2)(b) applies only if the application for costs was made within the time stipulated in rule 10(3) (orders for costs).

(4) The date in paragraph (2)(d) applies only if the application for the decision to be set aside was made within the time stipulated in rule 54 (setting aside a decision which disposes of proceedings) or any extension of that time granted by the Tribunal.

(5) If the person seeking permission to appeal provides the application to the Tribunal later than the time required—

    (a) the application must include a request for an extension of time and the reason why the application notice was not provided in time; and

    (b) unless the Tribunal extends time for the application under rule 5(3)(a) (power to extend time) the Tribunal must refuse the application.

(6) The application must—

    (a) identify the decision of the Tribunal to which it relates;

    (b) identify the alleged error or errors of law in the decision; and

    (c) state the result the party making the application is seeking.

Tribunal's consideration of application for permission to appeal

56.—(1) On receiving an application for permission to appeal the Tribunal may review the decision in accordance with rule 57 (review of a decision), but may only do so if—

    (a) when making the decision the Tribunal overlooked a legislative provision or binding authority which could have had a material effect on the decision; or

    (b) since the Tribunal's decision, a court has made a decision which is binding on the Tribunal and which, had it been made before the Tribunal's decision, could have had a material effect on the decision.

(2) If the Tribunal decides not to review the decision, or reviews the decision and decides to take no action in relation to the decision or part of it, the Tribunal must consider whether to give permission to appeal in relation to the decision or that part of it.

(3) The Tribunal must send a record of its decision to the parties as soon as practicable.

(4) If the Tribunal refuses permission to appeal it must send with the record of its decision—

    (a) a statement of its reasons for such refusal; and

    (b) notification of the right to make an application to the relevant appellate court for permission to appeal and the time within which, and the method by which, such application must be made.

(5) The Tribunal may give permission to appeal on limited grounds, but must comply with paragraph (4) in relation to any grounds on which it has refused permission.

Review of a decision

57.—(1) The Tribunal may only undertake a review of a decision pursuant to rule 56(1) (Tribunal's consideration of application for permission to appeal).

(2) The Tribunal must notify the parties in writing of the outcome of any review and of any rights of review or appeal in relation to the outcome.

(3) If the Tribunal decides to take any action in relation to a decision following a review without first giving every party an opportunity to make representations, the notice under paragraph (2) must state that any party that did not have an opportunity to make representations may apply for such action to be set aside and for the decision to be reviewed again.

Power to treat an application as a different type of application

58. The Tribunal may treat an application for a decision to be corrected, set aside or reviewed, or for permission to appeal against the decision, as an application for any other one of those things.

PART 12

REVOCATIONS AND TRANSITIONAL PROVISION

Revocations

59. The Lands Tribunal Rules 1996 are revoked.

Transitional provision

60. In proceedings which were started before 29th November 2010, the Tribunal may give any direction to ensure that the proceedings are dealt with fairly and, in particular, may—

(a) apply any provision of the Lands Tribunal Rules 1996 which applied to the proceedings before 29th November 2010; and
(b) disapply provisions of these Rules.

APPENDIX 2ZA

PRACTICE DIRECTIONS

Lands Chamber of the Upper Tribunal

1228ZA   1. Commencement, application and interpretation

1.1. These Practice Directions—

a) apply to proceedings before the Lands Chamber of the Upper Tribunal;
b) come into force on 29 November 2010;
c) supplement the Rules and must be read in conjunction with them.

1.2. In these Practice Directions—

a) "the Rules" means the Tribunal Procedure (Upper Tribunal) (Lands Chamber) Rules 2010;
b) "rule", followed by a number, means the rule bearing that number in the Rules.

2. Alternative dispute resolution

2.1. Stay of proceedings

1) Parties may apply at any time for a short stay in the proceedings to attempt to resolve their differences, in whole or in part, outside the Tribunal process. No fee is payable. On receipt of a joint or consent application made in accordance with rule 6 the Tribunal will by order stay proceedings for a six week period (or such other period as may be specified in the order) for mediation or other form of alternative dispute resolution, ADR, procedure to be followed.

2) The parties may apply for a second or longer stay in the proceedings for ADR. The fee for an interlocutory application must be paid and the parties must satisfy the Tribunal that an additional or longer stay of proceedings would be appropriate.

2.2. Costs

In exercising its power to order that any or all of the costs of any proceedings incurred by one party be paid by another party or by their legal or other representative the Tribunal may consider whether a party has unreasonably refused to consider ADR when deciding what costs order to make, even when the refusing party is otherwise successful.

3. Case management

3.1. Introduction

1) Every case will be assigned to one of the following four procedures as soon as the Tribunal has sufficient information:

a) the standard procedure;
b) the simplified procedure;
c) the special procedure;

   d) the written representations procedure.

   2) When filing a notice of appeal under rule 24; a respondent's notice under rule 25; a notice of reference under rule 28; or a response to a notice of reference under rule 29, a party should state which procedure it considers should be followed. The Tribunal will take account of the parties' views when assigning the case. At any time a Registrar or the Judge or Member to whom a case has been allocated for casemanagement may direct that it should be assigned to one of the otherprocedures.

3.2. Standard procedure

The standard procedure applies in all cases not assigned to one of the other procedures. For the standard procedure case management will be in the hands of the Registrars who will give such directions as appear to be necessary. Directions given may, as appropriate, use elements of the special procedure (for example, timetabling through to the hearing date) or the simplified procedure. A Registrar will hold a casemanagement hearing should it appear appropriate to do so taking any views expressed by the parties into account. Each party should also consider the matters referred to in paragraph 3.4(2) below.

3.3. Simplified procedure

   1) The simplified procedure provides for the speedy and economical determination of cases in which no substantial issue of law or of evaluation practice or conflict of fact is likely to arise. It is often suitable where the amount at stake is small. It will not normally be appropriate for cases involving more than one expert witness.
   2) The objective is to move to a hearing as quickly as possible and with the minimum of formality and cost. In most cases a date for the hearing, normally about 3 months ahead, will be fixed immediately. Statements of case will be required in accordance with section 6 below. The hearing will be informal and strict rules of evidence will not apply. It will almost always be completed in a single day.
   3) Not later than 1 month before the hearing, the parties must exchange copies of all documents on which they intend to rely. Not later than 14 days before the hearing each party must file and exchange—

   (i) an expert's report, if they intend to rely on expert evidence; and
   (ii) a list of the witnesses they intend to call at the hearing.

   4) In a case to which section 4 of the Land Compensation Act 1961 or section 175(6) or (7) applies any order in relation to the costs of the proceedings will be made in accordance with the applicable statutory provision. In all other cases no costs order will be made unless the Tribunal—

   (i) considers it appropriate to take the making of an offer of settlement by a party into account;
   (ii) regards the circumstances as exceptional; or
   (iii) considers a wasted costs order should be made.

If an award of costs is made, the amount will not exceed the amount that would be allowed in proceedings in a county court.

3.4. Special procedure

   1) A case will be assigned to the special procedure if it requires case management by a Judge or Member in view of its complexity, the amount in issue or its wider importance. Under the special procedure an early case-management hearing will be held for appropriate directions to be given for the fair, expeditious and economical conduct of the

proceedings. Where appropriate a date for the final hearing will be fixed at the case-management hearing and the steps which the parties are required to take, and any further case-management hearings, will be timetabled by reference to this date.

2) Each party should consider whether it is appropriate to make application for the determination of a preliminary issue and for permission to call more than the permitted number of expert witnesses. It should also identify, and where necessary make application for, any other order that it wishes the Tribunal to make at the case-management hearing. The parties must seek to agree the terms of any order that they wish the Tribunal to make.

3) Not less than 7 days before a case-management hearing the parties must file an agreed position statement summarising the subject-matter of the case and, to the extent that it is possible to do so at that stage, the issues. They must also state the areas of expertise of each expert witness that they propose to rely on and the general scope of their evidence.

3.5. Written representation procedure

1) The Tribunal may order that the proceedings be determined without an oral hearing. An order for the written representation procedure to be followed will only be made if the Tribunal, having regard to the issues in the case and the desirability of minimising costs, is of the view that oral evidence and argument can properly be dispensed with. The consent of the parties will usually be required.

2) Directions will be given to the parties relating to the filing of representations and documents and, if necessary, the Judge or Member allocated to the case will seek to carry out a site inspection before giving a written decision.

3) Costs will only be awarded if there has been an unreasonable failure on the part of the claimant to accept an offer to settle, if either party has behaved otherwise unreasonably, or the circumstances are in some other respect exceptional.

4. Appeals for which permission is required

Permission to appeal is required for an appeal from a leasehold valuation tribunal, LVT, or residential property tribunal, RPT. Permission must be sought from the LVT or RPT concerned. Only if the LVT or RPT refuses permission to appeal may an application for permission to appeal be made to the Tribunal. Permission to appeal from a valuation tribunal in a rating case is not required.

4.1. Time limits

1) If permission to appeal is refused by the LVT or RPT, application for permission to appeal may be made to the Tribunal within 14 days of being sent the decision to refuse permission.

2) An urgency direction may be issued, upon application by a party or by the Tribunal acting on its own initiative, to reduce this time limit (see also paragraph 5.3 below).

3) The Tribunal may extend a time limit but no extension will be given unless there is justification for it.

4.2. Applications for permission to appeal

1) Applicants must specify whether their reasons for making the application fall within one or more of the following categories:

  a) The decision shows that the LVT or RPT wrongly interpreted or wrongly applied the relevant law;
  b) The decision shows that the LVT or RPT wrongly applied or misinterpreted or disregarded a relevant principle of valuation or other professional practice;

c) The LVT or RPT took account of irrelevant considerations, or failed to take account of relevant consideration or evidence, or there was a substantial procedural defect; and/or

d) The point or points at issue is or are of potentially wide implication.

2) The application must make clear whether the appellant is seeking:

(i) an appeal by way of review;

(ii) an appeal by way of review, which if successful will involve a consequential re-hearing; or

(iii) an appeal by way of re-hearing.

3) If the application does not specify otherwise, the application will be treated as an application for an appeal by way of review.

4.3. Approach of the Tribunal to applications for permission to appeal

1) The Tribunal will determine an application for permission to appeal without a hearing unless it appears to the Tribunal that a hearing is necessary or desirable. Applicants who want the application to be dealt with at a hearing must explain why a hearing is necessary or desirable.

2) The Tribunal will give permission to appeal only where it appears that there are reasonable grounds for concluding that the LVT or RPT may have been wrong for one or more of the reasons (a) to (c) set out in paragraph 4.2 above. In considering whether to give permission the Tribunal will have regard to the importance of the point to the decision itself and in terms of its wider implications (reason d) and to the proportionality of an appeal.

3) If the Tribunal gives permission to appeal—

a) It may do so on such conditions as it thinks fit;

b) In view of the limitation on the Tribunal's power to award costs in an appeal from an LVT contained in the Rules, it will not be appropriate to impose conditions relating to costs in appeals from the LVT. It would, however, be open to an applicant for permission to undertake to pay all or part of a respondent's costs;

c) It may direct that the appeal is, or any of the issues in the appeal are, to be dealt with by review rather than by rehearing;

d) It may direct that the application for permission to appeal should stand as a notice of appeal.

4) If the Tribunal gives permission to appeal the appeal will proceed unless—

a) permission was given in part only or subject to conditions; and

b) within 14 days of the date that the Tribunal sent notice of the decision to give permission the applicant notifies the Tribunal that the applicant does not wish to proceed with the appeal.

5. Appeals

5.1. Types of appeal

1) When permission to appeal to the Tribunal has been given by another tribunal the notice of appeal must make clear whether the appellant is seeking:

(i) an appeal by way of review;

(ii) an appeal by way of review, which if successful will involve a consequential re-hearing; or

(iii) an appeal by way of re-hearing.

2) If the notice does not specify otherwise, the appeal will be treated as an appeal by way of review.

3) The Tribunal will take into consideration any views the parties have expressed on the type of appeal proceedings but may direct that the appeal or any of the issues in the appeal are to be dealt with by review rather than by rehearing.

5.2. Time limits

1) If the LVT or RPT gives permission to appeal, a notice of appeal must be filed with the Tribunal within 1 month of the date that the decision giving permission to appeal was sent to the appellant.

2) An urgency direction may be issued, upon application by a party or by the Tribunal acting on its own initiative, to reduce this time limit (see also paragraph 5.3 below).

3) The Tribunal may extend a time limit but no extension will be given unless there is justification for it.

5.3. Urgency directions

1) For appeals from the RPT an urgency direction may be issued to shorten the time limits that otherwise apply to the following actions:

a) giving notice to the Tribunal of an appeal when permission to appeal has been given by the RPT

b) filing and serving a respondent's notice;

c) filing and serving a statement of case.

2) Any urgency direction may also permit the application to the RPT for permission to appeal to stand as notice to the Tribunal of an appeal.

3) An urgency direction may be made by the Tribunal acting on its own initiative or on application by a party. An application for an urgency direction must be made in accordance with the Tribunal procedure for applying for directions.

4) In reaching a decision the Tribunal will take all written representations into account. An urgency direction will not be made unless the Tribunal is satisfied that it is in the interests of justice to do so.

6. Statements of case

6.1. General

1) Each party to an appeal under Part 4 of the Rules, a reference under Part 5 of the Rules or an application under Part 6 of the Rules must provide a statement of its case.

2) The purpose of statements of case is to enable the issues to be determined by the Tribunal to be identified. Each statement of case must therefore set out the basis of fact and of law on which the party relies. It must be in summary form but contain particulars that are sufficient to tell the other party the case that is being advanced and to enable the Tribunal to identify the issues.

6.2. Appeals under Part 4 of the Rules

1) A statement of case must be contained in or be provided with the following:

a) A notice of appeal under rule 24;

b) A respondent's notice under rule 25.

2) The following provisions of the Rules and these Practice Directions are to be noted in relation to the above:

a) An application to the Tribunal for permission to appeal must contain the grounds of appeal on which the applicant relies (rule 21(3)(d));

b) A notice of appeal must contain the grounds of appeal on which the appellant relies (rule 24(3) read with rule 21(3)(d)); and, where application to the Tribunal for permission to appeal has been made under rule 21, the application must have stated those grounds (rule 21(3)(d));

c) An application for permission to appeal may stand as a notice of appeal (Practice Direction 4.3(3)(d)); and

d) A respondent's notice must contain the grounds on which the respondent relies in opposing the appeal or in support of a cross-appeal (rule 25(4(c)); and where application to crossappeal has been made under rule 22(2) the application must have stated the grounds on which the application was made.

3) Where any notice of appeal or respondent's notice does not contain or provide a statement of case that complies with the requirements of paragraph 6.1(2), application must be made at the time the notice or respondent's notice is provided for an extension of time for providing the statement of case.

4) Where the Tribunal is of the view that any notice or respondent's notice does not contain or provide a statement of case that complies with the requirements of paragraph 6.1(2) it will order that a statement of case be provided.

5) A party that considers that another party has failed to provide a statement of case that complies with the requirements of paragraph 6.1(2) may apply to the Tribunal for an order that such statement of case be provided, and the Tribunal will decide whether an order should be made.

6.3. References under Part 5 of the Rules

1) A statement of case must be contained in or be provided with the following:

a) A notice of reference under rule 28; and

b) A response to the notice of reference under rule 29;

2) The following provisions of the Rules are to be noted in relation to the above:

a) A notice of reference must contain the matters set out in rule 28(3)(g) and (h);

b) A response to the notice of reference must contain the summary required by rule 29(2)(c) and, where the person making the response is the claimant, the matters set out in rule 29(2)(d);

3) Where any notice or response does not contain or provide a statement of case that complies with the requirements of paragraph 6.1(2) application must be made at the time the notice or response is provided or made for an extension of time for providing the statement of case.

4) Where the Tribunal is of the view that any notice or response does not contain or provide a statement of case that complies with the requirements of paragraph 6.1(2) it will order that a statement of case be provided.

5) A party that considers that another party has failed to provide a statement of case that complies with the requirements of paragraph 6.1(2) may apply to the Tribunal for an order that such statement of case be provided, and the Tribunal will decide whether an order should be made.

6.4. omitted

7. Preliminary issues

1) On the application of any party to proceedings or on its own initiative the Tribunal may order any preliminary issue in the proceedings to be disposed of at a preliminary hearing where such issue is properly severable from other issues in the proceedings and where its determination might effectively dispose of the whole case or reduce the issues in the case, thereby saving costs and avoiding delay.

2) An application by a party for the determination of a preliminary issue should set out with precision the point of law or other issue or issues to be decided. It should where appropriate be accompanied by a statement of agreed facts, and it should state whether in the view of the party making the application the issue can be decided on the basis of the statement of agreed facts or whether evidence will be required. If evidence is said to be needed the application should state what matters that evidence would cover. The application should state why, in the applicant's view, determination of the issue as a preliminary issue would be likely to enable the proceedings to be disposed of more expeditiously and/or at less expense.

3) If the Tribunal decides to order that the issue should be determined as a preliminary issue it will give directions as to the filing in advance of the hearing of any experts' reports, witness statements, documentary evidence and statement of agreed facts that appear to it to be required.

8. Expert evidence

8.1. Agreeing matters of fact

Where more than one party is intending to call expert evidence in the same field, the experts must take steps before preparing or exchanging their reports to agree all matters of fact relevant to their reports, including the facts relating to any comparable transaction on which they propose to rely, any differences of fact, and any plans, documents or photographs on which they intend to rely in their reports.

8.2. Form and content of expert's report

1) An expert's report should be addressed to the Tribunal and not to the party from whom the expert has received instructions. It must:

    (a) give details of the expert's qualifications;
    (b) give details of any literature or other material on which the expert has relied in making the report;
    (c) say who carried out any inspection or investigations which the expert has used for the report and whether or not the investigations have been carried out under the expert's supervision;
    (d) give the qualifications of the person who carried out any such inspection or investigations; and
    (e) where there is a range of opinion on the matters dealt with in the report—
        i) summarise the range of opinion, and
        ii) give reasons for his or her own opinion;
    (f) contain a summary of the conclusions reached;
    (g) contain a statement setting out the substance of all material instructions (whether written or oral). The statement should summarise the facts and instructions given to the expert which are material to the opinions expressed in the report or upon which those opinions are based.

2) The instructions referred to in sub-paragraph 1(g) above will not be privileged against disclosure but the Tribunal will not, in relation to those instructions order

disclosure of any specific document or permit any questioning in the Tribunal, other than by the party who instructed the expert, unless it is satisfied that there are reasonable grounds to consider the statement of instructions given under sub-paragraph 1(g) to be inaccurate or incomplete.

8.3. Written questions to experts

1) Where they think it necessary to do so, a party should put written questions about the report of an expert instructed by another party. Normally such questions should be put once only; should be put within 1 month of service of the expert's report; and should be only for the purposes of clarification of the report. Where a party sends a written question or questions direct to an expert and the other party is represented by solicitors, a copy of the questions should, at the same time, be sent to those solicitors. It is for the party or parties instructing the expert to pay any fees charged by that expert for answering questions put under this procedure. This does not affect any decision of the Tribunal as to which party is ultimately to bear the expert's costs. An expert's answers to questions put in accordance with this paragraph will be treated as part of the expert's report.

2) Where a party has put a written question to an expert instructed by another party in accordance with the above paragraph, unless the Tribunal orders otherwise it should be answered within 3 weeks. The Tribunal or a Registrar may order that the question must be answered and the Tribunal may also make such an order in relation to a question that has not been put in this way. If the question is not answered the Tribunal or a Registrar may make one or both of the following orders in relation to the party who instructed the expert: that the party may not—

    i)   rely on the evidence of that expert; or
    ii) recover the fees and expenses of that expert from any other party.

8.4. Discussions between experts

1) After the exchange of the experts' reports, and again if rebuttal reports are exchanged, the experts of like discipline should usually meet and, where the Tribunal so directs must meet, in order to reach further agreement as to facts; to agree any relevant plans, photographs, etc; to identify the issues in the proceedings; and where possible, to reach agreement on an issue. The Tribunal may specify the issues which the experts must discuss. The Tribunal may also direct that following a discussion between the experts the parties must prepare a statement for the Tribunal showing those facts and issues on which the experts agree and those facts and issues on which they disagree and a summary of their reasons for disagreeing. The Tribunal will usually regard failure to co-operate in reaching agreement as to the facts and issues as incompatible with the expert's duty to the Tribunal and may reflect this in any order on costs that it may make.

2) The contents of the discussions between the experts are not to be referred to at the hearing unless the parties agree. Where experts reach agreement on an issue during their discussions, the agreement will not bind the parties unless the parties expressly agree to be bound by the agreement.

8.5. Computer-based valuations

Where valuers propose to rely on computer-based valuations they must agree to employ a common model which can be made available for use by the Tribunal in the preparation of its decision. Directions should be sought from the Tribunal at an early stage if there is difficulty in reaching agreement.

8.6. Single joint expert

1) A party may apply for an order that expert evidence in the proceedings should be given by a single joint expert jointly instructed by the parties to the proceedings. The

application should include submissions on the matters to be taken into account by the Tribunal set out in paragraph 2 below.

2) When considering whether expert evidence should be from a single joint expert the Tribunal will take into account all the circumstances and in particular, whether:

 (a) it is proportionate to have separate experts for each party on a particular issue with reference to—
  (i) the amount in dispute;
  (ii) the importance to the parties; and
  (iii) the complexity of the issue;
 (b) the instruction of a single joint expert is likely to assist the parties and the Tribunal to resolve the issue more speedily and in a more cost-effective way than separately instructed experts;
 (c) expert evidence is to be given on the issue of liability, causation or quantum;
 (d) the expert evidence falls within a substantially established area of knowledge which is unlikely to be in dispute or there is likely to be a range of expert opinion;
 (e) a party has already instructed an expert on the issue in question;
 (f) questions put in accordance with paragraph 8.3 are likely to remove the need for the other party to instruct an expert if one party has already instructed an expert;
 (g) questions put to a single joint expert may not conclusively deal with all issues that may require testing prior to the final hearing;
 (h) a conference may be required with the legal representatives, experts and other witnesses which may make instruction of a single joint expert impractical; and
 (i) a claim to privilege makes the instruction of any expert as a single joint expert inappropriate.

8.7. Reliance on expert evidence by another party

When a party has disclosed an expert's report any party may use that expert's report as evidence at the hearing.

9. Procedure at the hearing

1) The procedure at a hearing of the Tribunal is within the discretion of the presiding Judge or Member. Except under the simplified procedure, the procedure adopted will generally accord with the practice in the High Court and the county courts. In particular, the claimant, applicant or appellant will begin and will have a right of reply, evidence will be taken on oath, and the rules of evidence will be applied. The Tribunal will throughout seek to adopt a procedure that is proportionate, expeditious and fair in accordance with the overriding objective.

2) Cases assigned to the simplified procedure list will be heard by a single Judge or Member. The procedure at the hearing will be informal and strict rules of evidence will not apply.

10. Site inspections

1) Where appropriate the Tribunal will seek to enter and inspect the land or property that is the subject of the proceedings, and, where practicable, any other land or properties referred to by the parties or their experts.

2) At such inspection, the Tribunal will (unless otherwise agreed) be accompanied by one representative from each side and will not accept any oral or written evidence tendered in the course of the inspection. The Tribunal may make an unaccompanied inspection without entering on private land.

3) The Tribunal may enter land only with the consent of the occupier. If the occupier is a party to the proceedings the Tribunal may take into account the withholding of consent to enter and inspect that party's land when deciding any application for costs.

11. Fees

The fees to be paid in respect of proceedings in the Tribunal are specified in the Upper Tribunal (Lands Chamber) Fees (Amendment) Order 2010. Unless the Tribunal directs otherwise, the appropriate hearing fee is payable by the party initiating proceedings, but without prejudice to any right to recover the fee under an order for costs. A solicitor acting for a party must be on the record, and will be responsible for the fees payable by that party while he or she is on the record.

12. Costs

12.1. Power to award costs

1) Under section 29 of the Tribunals, Courts and Enforcement Act 2007 the Upper Tribunal has power to order that the costs of any proceedings incurred by one party shall be paid by any other party or by their own or the other party's legal or other representative. This power is limited by the Rules in the case of appeals from LVTs (see paragraph 12.6 below).

2) In awarding costs the Tribunal may settle the amount summarily or direct that they be the subject of detailed assessment by a Registrar on a specified basis (see paragraph 12.10 below).

12.2. Exercise of discretion in awarding costs

Costs are in the discretion of the Tribunal, although this discretion is qualified by particular provisions in section 4 of the Land Compensation Act 1961 (see paragraph 12.3(2) below) and where the case is heard under the simplified and written representations procedures (see paragraph 12.8 below). Subject to what is said below the discretion will usually be exercised in accordance with the principles applied in the High Court and county courts. Accordingly, the Tribunal will have regard to all the circumstances, including the conduct of the parties; whether a party has succeeded on part of their case, even if they have not been wholly successful; and admissible offers to settle. The conduct of a party will include conduct during and before the proceedings; whether a party has acted reasonably in pursuing or contesting an issue; the manner in which a party has conducted their case; whether or not they have exaggerated their claim; and the matters stated in paragraphs 2.2, 8.3(2), 8.4 and 10 above.

12.3. The general rule for costs

1) The general rule is that the successful party ought to receive their costs. On a claim for compensation for compulsory acquisition of land, the costs incurred by a claimant in establishing the amount of disputed compensation are properly to be seen as part of the expense that is imposed on the claimant by the acquisition. The Tribunal will, therefore, normally make an order for costs in favour of a claimant who receives an award of compensation unless there are special reasons for not doing so.

2) Particular rules, however, apply by virtue of section 4 of the Land Compensation Act 1961. Under this provision, where an acquiring authority has made an unconditional offer in writing of compensation and the sum awarded does not exceed the sum offered, the Tribunal must, in the absence of special reasons, order the claimant to bear their own costs thereafter and to pay the post-offer costs of the acquiring authority. However, claimants will not be entitled to their costs if they have failed to deliver to the authority, in time to enable the authority to make a proper offer, a notice of claim containing the particulars set out in section 4(2). Where a claimant has delivered a claim containing the required details

and have made an unconditional offer in writing to accept a particular sum, if the Tribunal's award is equal to or exceeds that sum the Tribunal must, in the absence of special reasons, order the authority to bear their costs and to pay the claimant's post-offer costs.

12.4. Standard basis and indemnity basis

The Tribunal will normally award costs on the standard basis. On this basis, costs will only be allowed to the extent that they are reasonable and proportionate to the matters in issue, and any doubt as to whether costs were reasonably incurred or reasonable and proportionate in amount will be resolved in favour of the paying person. Exceptionally the Tribunal may award costs on the indemnity basis. On this basis, the receiving party will receive all their costs, except for those which have been unreasonably incurred or which are unreasonable in amount, and any doubt as to whether the costs were reasonably incurred or are reasonable in amount will be resolved in favour of the receiving party.

12.5. omitted

12.6. Appeals from Leasehold Valuation Tribunals

On an appeal from an LVT the Tribunal may not order a party to the appeal to pay costs incurred by another party unless, in the opinion of the Tribunal, the party ordered to pay costs or its representative has behaved unreasonably in bringing, defending or conducting the proceedings. Where in view of such conduct it does order a party to pay costs the Tribunal may not award more than the LVT could order in such circumstances (currently £500).

12.7. Offers to settle

1) In any proceedings before the Tribunal any party may make an offer to any other party to settle all or part of the proceedings or a particular issue on terms specified in the offer. Neither the offer nor the fact that it has been made may be referred to at the hearing if it is marked with 'without prejudice save as to costs' or similar wording, or if it is said to be a 'Calderbank' offer.

2) Offers to settle part of proceedings or a particular issue must clearly identify which part of the proceedings or the issue that it relates to. Offers should also state whether or not the offer is open for acceptance indefinitely or for a specified period of time. An offer should state whether or not it includes interest (if it has been claimed), at what rate and for what period it covers. It should also state whether or not it includes agreement to pay the other party's costs and either the amount or the basis of those costs.

3) The party making an offer to settle must send a copy of it to the Tribunal within a sealed envelope enclosed with a cover letter. The Judge or Member hearing the case will not see the offer (it will remain in its sealed envelope separate from the Tribunal's case file) or be informed of its existence until after the proceedings have been determined. If requested by a party to do so, the Judge or Member may then consider the offer, when considering the question of the costs of the proceedings.

12.8. Simplified and written representations procedure

Where proceedings are determined in accordance with the simplified procedure or the written representations procedure, costs will only be awarded if there has been an unreasonable failure on the part of the claimant to accept an offer to settle, or if either party has behaved otherwise unreasonably, or the circumstances are in some other respect exceptional.

12.9. Submissions on costs

Where, as is almost invariably the case, the Tribunal issues a written decision determining the substantive issues in the proceedings, this will be sent to the parties with an invitation to make written submissions as to costs. Following consideration of these submissions the Tribunal will issue an addendum to the decision determining the liability for costs. It may be possible, particularly where there are only two possible outcomes of the proceedings, for the Tribunal to invite submissions as to costs at the conclusion of the hearing. This procedure will be followed wherever possible. Where the issue of costs is particularly complicated the Tribunal may hold a costs hearing before making an award.

12.10. Assessment of costs

1) In a simple case or on an interlocutory hearing the Tribunal may make a summary assessment of costs. A party who proposes to apply for a summary assessment must prepare a summary of the costs and serve it in advance on the other party.

2) Costs which cannot be agreed by the parties must be referred by the receiving person to a Registrar to be the subject of a detailed assessment. A party who is dissatisfied with a Registrar's assessment of costs may apply to the Registrar for a review and, if still dissatisfied, may apply to the Chamber President for a further review.

These Practice Directions are made and issued by the Senior President of Tribunals in exercise of powers conferred by the Tribunals, Courts and Enforcement Act 2007 and with the agreement of the Lord Chancellor as required under section 23(4) of the 2007 Act.

LORD JUSTICE CARNWATH

SENIOR PRESIDENT OF TRIBUNALS

29 November 2010

APPENDIX 2ZB

The Upper Tribunal (Lands Chamber) Fees Order 2009

(SI 2009/1114)

(as amended by the Upper Tribunal (Lands Chamber) Fees (Amendment) Order 2010 (SI 2010/2601))

1228ZB **Citation, commencement, extent and interpretation**

1. This Order may be cited as the Upper Tribunal (Lands Chamber) Fees Order 2009 and comes into force on 1st June 2009.

2. This Order extends to England and Wales and applies to proceedings in the Lands Chamber of the Upper Tribunal.

3. "The Rules" means the Upper Tribunal (Lands Chamber) Rules 2010 and any reference in this Order to a rule by number alone means that rule in the Rules.

Fees payable

4. The fees payable in respect of proceedings before the Lands Chamber of the Upper Tribunal are set out in the Schedule to this Order.

5.—(1) A notice, application or other document in respect of which a fee is payable must be accompanied by a cheque or postal order made payable to the Tribunals Service for the amount of the fee.

(2) Otherwise, and unless the Upper Tribunal directs otherwise, a fee shall be payable by the party by whom the proceedings were commenced (without prejudice to that party's right to recover the fee from any other party pursuant to an order for costs) on receipt of notification from the Upper Tribunal.

6. The proceedings referred to in paragraphs 2, 9, 10 and 12 of the Schedule do not include an appeal against a determination by Her Majesty's Revenue and Customs under the under section 222(4A) of the Inheritance Act 1984 or a reference under sections 47(1) or 47A of the Taxes Management Act 1970.

Exceptions

7. Where it appears to the Lord Chancellor that the payment of any fee prescribed by this Order would, owing to the exceptional circumstances of the case, involve undue financial hardship, the Lord Chancellor may reduce or remit the fee.

8.—(1) Subject to paragraph (2), when a fee has been paid where, if the Lord Chancellor had been aware of all of the circumstances, the Lord Chancellor would have reduced or remitted the fee under article 7, the appropriate amount shall be refunded.

(2) No refund shall be made under paragraph (1) unless the party who paid the fee applies for a refund within 6 months of the date of payment.

(3) The Lord Chancellor may extend the period of 6 months referred to in paragraph(2) if the Lord Chancellor considers that there is good reason for an application being made after the end of that period.

SCHEDULE

FEES TO BE TAKEN IN THE LANDS CHAMBER OF THE UPPER TRIBUNAL

Item	Fee £
Lodging an application for permission to appeal	
1. On lodging an application for permission to appeal under rule 21 (application to the Tribunal for permission to appeal)	200
Lodging a reference or an appeal	
2. On lodging a notice of reference under rule 28 (notice of reference) or a notice of appeal under rule 24 (notice of appeal)	250
Interlocutory or consent order application	
6. On lodging an interlocutory application	100
7. On lodging an application for a consent order (rule 50) (consent orders)	150
Hearing a rating appeal	
8. On the hearing of an appeal from the decision of a Tribunal with jurisdiction to hear rating appeals, 5 per cent of rateable value as determined in the final order of the Tribunal, subject to—	
(a) minimum fee	250
(b) maximum fee	15,000
Hearing a reference or other appeal (excluding one where the hearing fee is calculated on the basis of rental value)	
9. On the hearing of a reference or an appeal against a determination or on an application for a certificate of value (excluding one where the hearing fee is calculated on the basis of rental value), 2 per cent of the amount awarded or determined by the Tribunal, agreed by the parties following a hearing, or determined in accordance with rule 46 (decision with or without a hearing), subject to—	
(a) minimum fee	250
(b) maximum fee	15,000
Hearing a reference or other appeal where the hearing fee is calculated on the basis of rental value	
10. On the hearing of a reference or an appeal against a determination where the award is in terms of rent or other annual payment, two per cent of the annual rent or other payment determined by the Tribunal, agreed by the parties following a hearing, or determined in accordance with rule 46 (decision with or without a hearing), subject to—	
(a) minimum fee	250
(b) maximum fee	15,000

Item	*Fee*
	£

Hearing (no amount awarded)

12. On the hearing or preliminary hearing of a reference or appeal (not being the determination of an application under paragraph 11 above) where either the amount determined is nil or the determination is not expressed in terms of an amount   500

Copies of documents

13. For a photocopy or certified copy of a document, or for examining a plain copy and marking as a certified copy   1 (for each page, subject to a minimum total of £10)

14. For supplying published decisions to subscribers   1 (for each page, subject to a minimum total of £10)

Determination of amount of costs

15. For a determination by the Tribunal of the amount of costs under Rule 10(5)(c), for every £1 or part thereof allowed.   0.05

INDEX